Tunxis
Community
College

Education That Works For a Lifetime

Dreamers of the Colorado:

The Mojave Indians

Part 2 – Their Culture and Arts

Edited by Frances L. O'Neil and Paul W. Wittmer

Dreamers of the Colorado: The Mojave Indians
Part 2: Their Culture and Arts

Tunxis Community College Publication

Copyedited by Frances L. O'Neil and Paul W. Wittmer
Cover and book design by Bryan R. Bonina
Project management by Deborah Young
Printed in the United States of America

Please direct comments and inquiries to:
Tunxis Community College Foundation
271 Scott Swamp Road
Farmington, CT 06032
(860) 255-3604
www.tunxisfoundation.org

Sunbelt Publications Inc.
P.O. Box 191126
San Diego, CA 92159-1126
(619) 258-4911; fax: (619) 258-4916
www.sunbeltbooks.com

17 16 15 14 13   5 4 3 2 1

Library of Congress Cataloging-in-Publication Data

Dreamers of the Colorado : the Mojave indians : part 1 their land and religion / edited by Frances L. O'Neil and Paul W. Wittmer. :
pages cm.
Includes bibliographical references and index.
ISBN 978-0-916251-28-4 (softcover : alk. paper) 1. Mohave Indians--History. 2. Mohave Indians--Social life and customs. I. O'Neil, Frances L.
E99.M77D74 2013
979.1004'975722--dc23
2013021537

Cover Photos:
Front cover background photo by Jeffrey J. Garton;
Front cover lower left and back cover photos by Peter Furst.

Copyright Acknowledgments

Every reasonable effort has been made to trace the owners of copyright materials in this book, but in some instances this has proven impossible. The editor and publisher will be glad to receive information leading to more complete acknowledgments in subsequent printings of the book and in the meantime extend their apologies for any omissions.

Table of Contents: Part 2 – Their Culture and Arts

Preface

These articles, some written by present-day Mojave men and women and others by researchers, were selected by the editors because they best represented the culture and magnificent arts of the Mojave people. To this day the tribe remains vibrant and heavily invested in their artistic traditions

Acknowledgments

We should like to express our deep gratitude to the Mojave people. They have paid us the great compliment of treating each of us as one of their own.

Mojave elders, Betty and Lew Barrackman

Many thanks also to the following people for their contributions to this volume:

Cathryn Addy
Paula Baird
Patricia Bode
Bryan Bonina
Susan Christy
Susan Dantino
Colleen Keyes
Patricia Kuzianik
Diana Lewandowski
Rosemary Nevers
Behnaz Perri
Michael Rooke

Chapter One

Psychological Development

Photo by Jeffrey L. Garton

Infancy and Childhood Among The Mohave Indians

by William J. Wallace

Introduction

The Mohave are a Yuman-speaking tribe living along the Colorado River where it forms the boundary between California and Arizona. They share with other river Yuman peoples a distinctive and specialized culture based upon river valley agriculture and dominated by dream revelations and militarism. The data on infancy and childhood presented here were obtained from Mohave living at Needles, California, and on the reservation at Parker, Arizona.

I. Infancy

Pregnancy is revealed to a Mohave woman only by the cessation of the menses, there being no other recognized signs. Immediately, she takes precautions for the benefit of the developing child. She must not look at a dead dog or her child will die or be born a cripple. Other people warn her if a dead dog is lying around so that she will not go near it. To see a snake, or a similar crawling creature, would cause her baby to be born with teeth; to paint her face during pregnancy would result in disfiguring marks upon the child's face. A pregnant woman should not look in a mirror or her offspring will be cross-eyed, nor should she cover her face while sleeping or her baby will be born with a caul. Looking at an aged person, a cripple, or a corpse, however, does not affect the unborn child, nor does staring at a particular person cause the child to resemble him.

An expectant mother continues to eat regular meals, but she adds quantities of boiled corn to her diet "so that she will have plenty of milk." Salt is not forbidden. Her husband observes no food taboos. A husband and wife sleep together during the period of pregnancy but have no intercourse because "that would spoil the baby and be dirty for it." The wife must not lie flat on her back or she will have a hard time of it. She can sleep on either side, but not on her stomach. The husband must lie in the same direction as his wife or the fetus will become crooked.

There is no method of predicting the sex of an unborn child by the condition or actions of the fetus, but the mother "can see what her baby will be three or four months ahead in a dream." If she dreams of feathers or a bow it will be a boy; if she sees a bead necklace, a skirt, or a doll in her dreams, it will be a girl. There is no attempt to influence the sex of the developing child, though the Mohave seem to prefer male children.

Activity is believed desirable for a prospective mother until the very time of labor, so she continues her regular tasks. As her period of pregnancy advances, however, she may be seized with spells of nausea and vomiting, and has short respites from work. She takes things easy for a time and avoids lifting heavy objects. Her female relatives assist her and prepare foods that are easily digested and "give her what she wants to eat." If the attacks of nausea are serious, it is thought that the baby does not want to come out and face the world and is trying to kill the mother. This rarely occurs, but when it does a shaman is called in to blow on the woman's body "to flatten down the child in there." A shaman may also be summoned if the fetus is believed to be in the wrong direction. He "sits and feels the stomach of a woman and straightens it out." Miscarriage may be caused by a malevolent shaman.

The fetus is believed to have a conscious existence of its own and can experience things and express itself. If it becomes displeased or unhappy it may cause trouble for the mother. While still in its mother's womb a child can have a power-giving dream (sumach ahot). Later in life the same dream will be repeated to refresh the individual's memory.

Abortion is rare. An unmarried girl occasionally may induce miscarriage by carrying a heavy load on her back for a long distance or by having someone press her stomach or step on her back. The fetus is then buried immediately. There is no particular stigma attached to illegitimacy, so that a girl usually does not resort to abortion. The Mohave are fond of children and readily take in a bastard child and treat it the same as other children. There is a feeling that abortion is "not right" and a married woman never does it.

Birth

It is known that pregnancy has a duration of nine months. ("We count nine months from the time a woman has her last period.") The exact date on which the birth will occur is not calculated, but a woman knows when it is imminent "because the movements of the child tell her that it wants to come out." The expectant mother eats nothing for four or five hours before parturition, and she drinks no water "because it makes it hard for the child to force its way out of the water bag" if she does.

The woman remains in her own house as the time of childbirth approaches, and she is attended by close female relatives. There is no absolute ban on the presence of the husband, but he usually leaves. At the onset of labor the woman faces north "because the child would be ashamed to come out any other way and would move around inside if the mother faces any other direction". The woman gives birth seated on the ground. She leans back but holds neither rope nor stick. Two midwives assist: one in back "so that she will not fall over backwards;" the other in front who holds her around the abdomen and squeezes gently from time to time. The midwife in front, opens the parturient's legs and takes the child with both palms open. She does it rapidly "so blood will not run in the baby's eyes and mouth." The rear woman presses hard so as to force out the afterbirth which the other midwife receives.

Some women have a short labor of 20-30 minutes; others experience a difficulty and "want to stand up or walk around" and have to be restrained by the midwives. A woman tries not to cry out because "the other women will make fun of her" later if she does. A mother-to-be is not given medicines to hasten delivery or to ease the labor pains. Prolonged and painful parturition is usually believed to be caused by sorcery or through the reluctancy of the child to be born, and a shaman is summoned. A number of women die in childbirth.

The placenta is wrapped up in barkcloth by the midwife, and the husband takes it out to bury it. He places it in a deep hole and covers it up. No one should observe the burial.

One of the midwives cuts the umbilical cord with a sliver of stone. Usually a piece an inch or two long remains and this is folded over and tied about one-half inch from the navel with a piece of bark string. In a few days the stump dries up and falls off. The father then takes it out and buries it. If the remnant fails to drop off when it should, a "clay powder" obtained along the river bank is rubbed on to hasten the drying-up process.

The newborn baby is dipped in warm water and then dried with a piece of soft inner bark of the willow. A chalky powder is applied to its entire body. This is repeated for four days and "then a child gets its real skin." After the fourth day an infant's face may be painted with a mixture of red pigment and deer fat.

Stillbirths occasionally occur and are believed to result from such causes as an expectant mother seeing "snakes, lizards, or anything that crawls, or a dead dog." A stillbirth is immediately buried. An infant born with a caul is thought to have the power of seeing into the future, but is not considered unlucky. There is no explanation for birthmarks other than "the mother painted her face while she was carrying the child." No significance is attached to these blemishes.

If a child is born crippled or deformed, it is left out on the desert to die because "there is no other way to heal it." After death it is immediately cremated. This is the only socially sanctioned form of infanticide. Twins are not destroyed, although they are regarded with awe because "they come from the sky and are in this world merely as visitors." They are credited with knowledge of supernatural things. Two male twins are preferred to any other combination. No physiological reason is given for the birth of twins. Triple births are unknown. The order of birth of children, either in twin or single births, is not considered significant. The first-born, for example, is not regarded as superior to subsequent children.

The new mother pays strict attention to her diet. She eats sparingly for "quite a while" and refrains from using salt for four days. Wheat mush and boiled corn are her principal foods. Fish and mushrooms are also eaten but not the flesh of wood rats because "her child will get a skin disease if she eats wood rats." Rabbit meat is avoided for two years lest her offspring develop an earache and a rash on its body. Cold water is also avoided. The father also abstains from rabbit flesh and does not use salt in his food for four days. He also refrains from smoking. The mother of a new born child must not touch her face or hair with her fingers, so a scratching stick of shredded arrowweed is provided.

Infant Care

A child is not put to the breast for the first four days. In the meantime "sweet stuff" (mesquite beans in warm water) is allowed to drip into the infant's mouth "so it will not starve." Sometimes little drops of wheat mush in warm water are substituted. The colostrum is considered to be harmful and care is taken to squeeze it all out. The mother cannot touch her own breast except with a cloth for one month ("or she will lose her milk"), so another woman presses out the fluid on to hot rocks each morning and evening for four days. This is also believed to increase lactation.

After the fourth day the child is fed whenever it cries or shows signs of hunger. Usually one breast serves for an entire meal, the other being saved for the next feeding. The mother holds her offspring, either in or out of its cradle, up to her breast, or lies down beside it. She also may nurse her baby as she walks along, holding the child on one side within reach of her breast. An infant is always permitted to eat as much as it desires. Usually a baby falls asleep after feeding and it is permitted to sleep as long as it wishes.

When a mother lacks milk or if the supply is scanty, a female relative kneads her breasts and steams them over hot rocks. This is done twice each day "until the milk flows easily." If this treatment fails to stimulate lactation, a relative who is nursing a child of her own acts as wet nurse. A substitute is also employed to suckle a child if the mother dies in childbirth or soon after. If no nursing woman is available an attempt is made to keep the infant alive by feeding it gruel of wheat or corn in warm water. When a mother is away during the day, an infant's grandmother offers it her breast or feeds it a little wheat mush in warm water.

A baby is not weaned until it is two years of age or older and "begins to stop of its own accord." Other foods are gradually introduced, however, and breast feeding is lessened as the child gets older. Wheat or corn mush is given to a three- or four-month-old child along with its mother's milk. Solid foods, such as meat, are not. fed to a child "until it has teeth." A two- or three-year-old "is hard on its mother because it bites her breasts" and adults "start making fun of it so it will stop nursing."

Four days after birth an infant is placed on a cradle board. This is a narrow arch of willow or mesquite wood with long parallel sides to which transverse rods are lashed. Materials for the cradle are prepared in advance but actual construction of it does not start until after the baby is born. The father makes the frame and his female relatives prepare the other parts. The shape of a cradle and its decoration denote the sex of the infant. A boy's cradle is not as broad as a girl's so the boy will have "narrow hips and nice straight legs." Feathers decorate a boy's cradle; blue and white beads a girl's. A mattress of shredded willow bark lines the cradle.

An infant, swathed in cloth, is tied into the cradle with two bands of woven bark. The bands for a boy are black and white, those for a girl "red or any other color." The infant's legs are tied down "so it will not get bow-legged," and the hands are also confined. The baby soon learns to lie quietly in the cradle and here it stays except when taken out for cleaning or to crawl about. Each time it is removed its anus and legs are rubbed up and down "to make them straight." When an infant wets or soils itself, it is taken out and wiped, and the mattress is removed and hung up to dry, or if soiled, soaked in water and then dried. Mattresses are used over and over again, and two or three are always kept on hand. A baby is confined to the cradle for most of the day until it is able to walk. If the first cradle is outgrown, a larger one is substituted.

At night the cradle board is placed beside the mother, either flat on the floor or slightly tilted, and the straps confining the infant's hands are loosened. Occasionally it is propped up so that the baby can look around. If the child is fretful the mother or father hums a little tune and jiggles the cradle up and down by holding it on the lap and lifting the knees alternately. A baby is carried in its cradle, either balanced on the mother's head with a bark ring, or under one arm supported on the hip. It is never transported on the back.

An infant is bathed "when it is dirty—not very often." During the summer months a mother occasionally takes her offspring to a shallow lagoon to bathe, but usually she lays the child across her lap and rubs warm water over its body with the palm of her hand. Care is taken to keep the child free from skin irritations. If it develops a rash, a powder of white clay is sprinkled on the affected parts. A pot of this is always at hand and it is tasted before being applied "to make sure it is not salty." Each time the mother takes her child out of the cradle to bathe it, she pinches its nose "to make it long and narrow." When a baby is young its fingernails are peeled off so that it will not scratch itself. Later they are trimmed with a sliver of stone.

No clothing other than the swaddling cloth of the cradle is worn by a child. While crawling about it is completely naked. When an infant is four days old, its hair is singed with hot coals so that it "will have thick hair." Also on the fourth day the father or another male relative pierces its ear lobes. "Boys will be mean and rough unless their ears are pierced" but "girls' ears are pierced just so they can wear earrings." When a female child is able to sit up, beads or bangles are put in its ears.

Children seldom cry. When a baby cries, it is thought to be hungry and is suckled or the mother dips her finger in water and gives the child her finger to suck. If crying continues, the mother jiggles the cradle and hums a lullaby. Constant or continued squalling is construed as a sign of illness, and the child's head is felt to see if it is feverish. If it is, a doctor is called in to diagnose the cause of illness.

Amusements for an infant are few. No playthings are given to it while in its cradle and finger and hand sucking are impossible because its hands and arms are bound. The mother usually keeps her child nearby while she works so that it does not feel alone. Sometimes she improvises and sings little songs describing the beauty and good behavior of her offspring. Adults are fond of children and often stop to tickle them saying, "kach a kach," or make grimaces or figures with the hands and fingers. A baby is occasionally taken out of its cradle and permitted to crawl around the house. Pebbles and other small objects are provided as playthings. If the infant shows a tendency toward left-handedness while playing, it is encouraged to use its right hand because "left-handed people are not liked" and "people make fun of them." A child seldom sucks on its hands or fingers while out of the cradle. Such actions are regarded as a sign of hunger and the child is offered food.

As a youngster gets older its periods of freedom from the cradle increase until it spends most of the day crawling about. Gradually it learns to stand "by pulling itself up against things." Adults encourage it to walk by holding out their hands. Usually "a child learns to walk when it is about a year old," but a sickly or weak child "takes much longer."

Toilet training begins when a youngster starts to walk about with some sureness. If the child urinates or defecates on the floor, the mother wipes it up and shows her displeasure by saying, "a:k". In this manner, the child gradually learns not to relieve itself in the house, but instead to go outside. A two-year-old is taken by its mother into the brush close by the house. Adults tease youngsters who are slow in learning bladder and bowel control.

When about six months old a child begins to call its mother "tata;" sometimes also the father. Parents encourage talking and "try to teach children words" and are "very proud" if their offspring learns to speak at an early age. As a youngster grows older instruction in correct speech is increased and "the mother or father keeps saying a word until the child catches it." Stuttering and lisping seem to be unknown.

The health of a youngster is carefully guarded. Its bowel movements are watched to see that it does not get constipated. Listlessness and a "hot head" are diagnostic of illness and a shaman who is a specialist on children's diseases is called in. No aids are given to an infant in teething, however, nor are there any first tooth observances. When a youngster loses his first deciduous tooth a male relative stands some distance away facing the child and flips the tooth toward it. This is done to insure good teeth. Baby teeth are allowed to fall out by themselves. There is no special attitude toward a child whose teeth erupt in an unusual manner or order.

A girl receives the family name of her father at birth and is also given an individual personal name by her grandmother or other kinswoman. A male child is called "humar" (child), or "humar ikinja" (child male), or by an affectionate term until he begins to walk. Then "any relation" gives him a name describing a physical or personality trait (e. g., "Mean Boy," "Tall and Light"). A boy may change his name a number of times, but a girl keeps the same one throughout life. Like a boy, she is often called simply "Kumar," or "humar hachinja" (child female). There is no naming ceremony for either sex.

Affection and regard mark the parent-child relationship. Parents fondle and sometimes kiss a child but never rub noses with it. The entire care of a baby devolves upon the mother, though a kinswoman now and then relieves her of some duties. The father takes an affectionate interest in his progeny, but has little to do with the actual upbringing beyond occasionally rocking the cradle or carrying his infant son or daughter on a long trip.

II. Childhood

Daily Life

Both boys and girls go about naked during early childhood, but when they are about ten years old "they become ashamed and want to wear clothes." A boy then begins to wear a breech-clout of shredded willow-bark, and a girl dons a two-pieced skirt of the same material. If it is cold, a rabbit skin blanket may he thrown about the shoulders. Bare footedness is habitual, even for adults. Young boys wear the hair straight and short, girls long and loose.

Mothers bathe their offspring either in the morning or evening in a warm shallow lagoon or lake created by the overflowing of the Colorado River. Some mothers bathe their children daily, whereas others bathe them infrequently. After a child is older, little attention is paid to its cleanliness and there are no regular baths. Youngsters, however, spend a great deal of time swimming, so that they are usually clean.

Children eat with their parents; often they are served first. Meals are prepared either once or twice a day, but a pot of food is continuously kept simmering on the fire so that a hungry youngster can help itself to food any time during the day. A young child is fed by its mother or father, but a youngster soon learns to feed itself and is provided with a separate pottery bowl. Dried foods are scooped up with two fingers, stews and mushes with three. The right hand is always used in eating because "it is bad to be left-handed" and because "the left hand is used in going to the toilet." Parents discourage a child from using its left hand by slapping the fingers. Children are permitted to eat as much as they wish if there is sufficient food, but are cautioned "not to eat too much or they might get sick" and not to waste food. Left-overs are poured back into the cooking pot. Adults advise youngsters not to eat too much fish because "it is too fattening and they will have big bellies when they grow up." A child is usually not persuaded or coerced to eat. Lack of appetite is usually construed as symptomatic of illness.

A young child sleeps between its parents "where it is warm" until it is seven or eight years old. Then it begins to sleep alone. Usually the soft, sandy floor of the house serves as a bed with the fire for warmth. Sometimes straw or shredded bark or, if it is cold, an old rabbitskin blanket is used for a mattress. In summer children and adults sleep out under the flat-topped sunshade or ramada. Youngsters are allowed to stay up as late as they desire, but after a hard day's play they are ready for bed soon after dusk. An old man tells tales until all the children are asleep. Stories about Coyote (Hukthare), the sly Trickster, and a man-eating giant (Fiu—"Big Man Pack") are favored. Children are usually up with the first morning sun, although if a child wishes to stay in bed late it is permitted to do so.

Toilet training, already begun in infancy, is continued, though it is not unduly stressed. A mother continues to take her off-spring out into the brush with her until the child is old enough to go alone. A youngster is instructed to "go behind a bush," "out of sight," and "to wipe with leaves or grass, using only the left hand." Boys are less modest than girls in their excretory habits, and often urinate near the houses. If a little girl should do this, she is told "to go away" because "it does not look nice for girls to do that."

Concern for a child's health does not diminish as it becomes older. The physical condition of a youngster is carefully watched and if signs of illness are observed, treatment is given immediately. A number of medicines and home cures, most of which are standard remedies for adults as well, are administered. Greasewood boiled in water is gargled to relieve a toothache. Burns are treated with a salve made from a ground-up vine ("like a cantaloupe"). A warmed hand is placed on an aching head and slight cuts are swabbed with "an oil made of roots." A shaman is called in to treat serious illnesses and severe wounds.

Recreation

Children find ample time for play and their pastimes are numerous and varied. Many amusements are in imitation of the life of adults and thus serve an educative as well as a recreative function. Little girls play with dolls made by themselves or by their mothers from arrowweed, unbaked clay, or, occasionally, rags. Miniature shelters are constructed for the dolls and imaginary conversations are carried on between them. "Cooking" with grasses and mud in little, crudely-formed clay pots is a game enjoyed by most girls. Girls also play tag, run races, and climb trees. Both girls and boys play cat's cradle and ring-and-pin.

The pastimes of boys are more active. They soon learn all the games played by the men, and teams of boys compete in shinny, kickball, and in hoop and pole games. Shooting with bows and arrows at bundles of grass or arrowweed tossed into the air leads to proficiency in the use of the bow. Running after a wind-blown hoop of willow is a favorite sport which develops physical endurance. Many of the diversions for boys are in reality mock battles or individual contests and are a definite part of the training process for the life of a warrior. Opposing lines of boys put small clay balls on the end of sticks and sling them at one another. Wrestling matches, which often result in rough and tumble free-for-alls, also harden boys for military service. Normally, the boys themselves arrange these games, but sometimes adults encourage them to engage in rough sports. The older people get boys up early in the morning and "the boys all run together and try to see who runs the fastest and farthest." Boys who cannot run long distances are "joked about by the other boys and the women." Those who excel are "all praised when they get back."

Swimming and playing in the water are the favorite sports of both boys and girls, and during the hot summer months, youngsters spend most of their time in the water. Both sexes learn to swim while still quite young, first, in a shallow lagoon, later in the river itself. Older children instruct the younger ones. Children and adults normally swim with an overhand stroke with the hands open and the feet going alternately up and down. They also swim on their backs with a back arm stroke and tread water. Before entering the water, an individual wets his hair with a handful of water "to avoid the shock." Usually youngsters dive in head first or feet first, but the more timid immerse themselves gradually by wading into the water. Floating logs serve as boats, and games of water tag are played. Boys and girls play together in the water when they are young, but as they grow older, separate play groups are formed. Both sexes cover the genital with mud while drying or sunning themselves on the river bank. If the sun is hot, mud is also plastered on the hair.

Boys and girls do not play together regularly after they are six or seven years old. Girls tend to play more sedentary games in small groups of three or four individuals, whereas boys are more active and rove about in gangs. Playmates are usually relatives or children from neighboring houses. If a boy plays with dolls or seems to prefer the company and pastimes of girls "his parents dress him in a little girl's skirt and tease him." "When a child is a boy, his parents want him to be like a boy and act like other boys."

Disputes often arise during play and children fight hard and savagely. Sometimes adults have to come out and "tell them that it is just a game and they should have a good time and not fight over it." Beyond settling serious quarrels, adults seldom interfere in the games of children, though if youngsters are noisy in their play, a crotchety old man may tell them to be quieter or to go some place else to play. If they pay no heed, he may scold them and chase them with a stick.

Children like pets and often have puppies of their own to care for. These are given descriptive names (e. g., "Spotted," "Little One"). Fledglings of doves, quail, and other birds are also kept as pets. Cages of willow sticks are made for them and grass seeds are gathered for their food. The young of small mammals are captured and raised. When a boy sees a ground squirrel with young he pours water down the hole until the young squirrels come out. The pets belong solely to the youngsters and are not disposed of or disturbed by adults. The property rights of children are respected.

Youngsters enjoy chewing milkweed gum. Boys gather the plants in the summer and drain the milk into a hollow pumpkin stem. This is then placed in hot sand until the liquid congeals into a rubbery mass. Arrowweed root gum is also chewed. The "red stuff from the roots is melted out in a pot and then dropped in water": a kind of "black stuff" results which is used as chewing gum. Children are also fond of "sugar" (honey dew) from aphid secretions on willow leaves. The leaves are sucked or the excrescences are picked or washed off the leaves and then boiled in water. The resulting liquid is sipped or it is allowed to evaporate until bits of solid sugar remain.

Education and Discipline

As soon as instruction and advice are likely to be effective, parents and other relatives initiate a process of training and correction. A boy is given a small bow by his father and is instructed in its use. When he is old enough to be useful, he accompanies the men on hunting trips and fishing expeditions, staying close by them and observing their actions. Gentle chidings await the boy who fails to come home with game or fish. Gradually a boy learns to use the weapons and equipment of men, and later he is instructed in their manufacture by his father and grandfather. All of this training is casual and sporadic and no effort is made to compel a boy to learn.

Every effort is made by a mother to interest her little daughter in the domestic duties she will be called upon to perform as an adult. A young girl first plays at cooking; later she receives instruction, and finally is allowed to prepare the family meal. Other skills, such as pottery making, and the weaving of rabbit-skin blankets are all taught to her by her mother, or other kinswoman. A girl accompanies the women when they set out to collect wild vegetable foods, and she is told where to look for the best mesquite or screw beans and how to gather them. When the women return the little girl carries home some of the gathered foods in a small carrying cloth. The gathering of firewood and fetching of water are also tasks in which a young girl assists her mother.

Older boys and girls occasionally aid in the planting and harvesting of crops, thus learning the techniques necessary for successful farming. There is no compulsion to make them work in the fields and, if they do not wish to, they simply run off. Young children are kept out of the agricultural plots because "they step on things" and because "it is too hot for them to work out in the sun."

Along with the learning of practical skills, goes instruction in tribal lore. The grandfather acts as chief instructor, sitting by the fire each night and lecturing to the children as they lie in bed. He also tells them stories, many of which are didactic, in pointing out correct behavior. Children also absorb a great deal of traditional lore informally by listening to the conversations of adults. From infancy on, they are taken to all ceremonials by their parents and they "sit around and watch, or just play around and stay awake as long as they can." Young boys and girls are occasionally invited to join in the dances. Children also attend all funerals and soon become acquainted with the phenomenon of death and the observances connected with it.

There are some items of knowledge which, it is believed, cannot be learned. Myths and song cycles, curing and bewitching techniques, and other abilities and information can only be obtained through dreaming. Consequently no effort is made to educate youngsters in these matters. Actually, many of these items are gradually absorbed from the cultural environment although they may later be described as supernatural gifts obtained in a "sumach ahot" or power-bestowing dream.

Parents are much concerned over the conduct of their children and are ashamed if their behavior falls below the expected standard. Exhortations on correct deportment are given by parents, or, more often, by the grandfather. Boys and girls are told to "live well" and "to try and get along with other children and people throughout life." They are advised "not to be mean" and "not to say mean things" and to "always be honest." Generosity is stressed as a desirable characteristic. Some families stress correct behavior much more than others.

Children are constantly cautioned against dangers, both real and supernatural. Youngsters "are told to be careful of fire or they might burn things up" and to look out for rattlesnakes which are particularly fearsome to the Mohave. Both boys and girls are warned "never to go far away" and "always to say where they are going." A girl is advised to avoid "strange boys."

Sexual knowledge is acquired early and easily. Adults are free in their sexual relations and most children observe their parents or other adults engaging in intercourse. Older people also converse freely about sexual matters and frequently use obscene expressions and gestures. This does not necessarily imply promiscuity or great sexual looseness, but it does indicate frankness in sexual matters foreign to many other tribes. Sexual play among children is mildly discouraged. Masturbation and other manipulation of the genitals is frowned upon. "If a boy begins to play with his private parts, it looks like he is going after a girl and an older man has to have a talk with him." Boys and girls are not supposed to fraternize after early childhood because "people think badly of them if they do." If a number of boys and girls are seen together, the girls receive most of the public disapproval because "they should stay at home and behave." A girl who prefers the company of boys is called a "kumalo" ("bad girl").

Disciplinary methods are mild. Parents usually do not spank a misbehaving child, but instead "they talk to the child when he does wrong and tell him not to do it again." If the misdeed is repeated, "they tell him the same thing." Parents are indulgent and much given to fondling and joking with younger children. Parental affection and a protective attitude toward children are demonstrated in a number of ways. Despite this benevolent attitude, parents expect and usually receive respect and obedience. Children are, on the whole, docile and well-behaved. If an older boy "gets to be real bad and mean," his mother or father "tells the other boys to beat him up." All the boys then get together and give him a sound thrashing. A child sometimes runs off and hides in order to escape a scolding or punishment. and returns only when he thinks that his misdeed has been forgotten. If a youngster has a temper tantrum, his mother "talks to him and tries to make him stop," but if the fit of ill temper continues, it is ignored. Continued outbursts of temper and misbehavior are diagnosed as indicative of future shamanistic tendencies.

A bugaboo, in the form of a ghost (nijevithi), is often employed to intimidate an unruly youngster. ("If you do not behave, a nijevithi will come and take you away.") Sometimes a child is told "to go away and never come back," and "it usually goes off for an hour or two and then returns and no one says anything." Rewards for good behavior or accomplishment, beyond an occasional word of praise, are few. Rarely, a child is taken visiting "if he does something nice."

Conclusion

Infancy is an agreeable period of life. A baby receives care and affection from its parents and other adults. It is fed when hungry and permitted to sleep at will. Confinement in the cradle inhibits its actions and amusements are few, but a parent or other adult is always close by so that it never feels lonely. Little emphasis is placed upon the development of basic habits, and there is no attempt to force training upon a young child. Mohave infancy is characterized by great indulgence—indulgence of a kind that seemingly encourages a secure, unconfused personality in the infant.

Childhood, like infancy, is pleasant for Mohave boys and girls. They lead a free and easy life with few restrictions upon their behavior. It is, however, the time when the meanings of Mohave culture are acquired. Part of this is brought about by stimulated learning or conscious instruction by adults, but a great deal is simply absorbed through exposure to the domestic and community environment. Children perceive what goes on around them, and in their conversation, actions, and play, imitate what they see and hear. Much of a child's education comes from members of his own age-group who share their knowledge with him. Children are given good, if somewhat casual, care and are allowed ample freedom with time for play and opportunity for self-expression. From an early age, parents and other adults regard them benevolently as rational beings important in perpetuating tribal and cultural continuity. Indulgence continues to mark the parent child relationship and disciplines are weak. Again, a sound, balanced personality is fostered by the methods of child care.

Mojave Pottery, Mojave People

by Jill Leslie Furst

According to Bourke in the 1880s, the Mojaves did not perform public puberty feasts for a daughter, but at first menstruation she stayed quietly in a corner of the house for four days. She also observed food taboos and could not eat watermelon, meat, or salt or drink coffee. She was allowed to consume beans, grass seeds, and cantaloupe, and she ate lightly at this time, probably to be sure that she would be abstemious and healthy for the rest of her life. Her family placed her over hot sand and stones; afterwards, they believed, she would grow rapidly to womanhood.

Some Mojaves said that a girl received little discipline or instruction at puberty because she would dream what she needed to know. Nevertheless, her mother would already have instructed her in women's work, and a teenage girl was ready to assume the role of wife and mother. Her family paid close attention to her dreams at menarche, because these reveries would provide information about the course of her future life.

Boys' coming-of-age rites were not as consistent. Devereux noted that the ceremonies did not occur at a specific age and did not necessarily mark puberty, although the youths were generally between ten and fifteen. The ceremonies were not compulsory, nor were they required before a boy could go to war. Instead, they overlapped with the time when he began to stray from home. The rituals promoted a young man's health and welfare and were supposed to give him endurance in the future.

Male initiation included piercing a boy's nose. The man who performed this service was not necessarily a shaman. Nose piercing was not a hereditary office, nor did the piercer obtain any special power in his dreams. He did not require the aid of assistants, and his function had no special name. Nonetheless, a mythological precedent validated the ritual. According to one story recounted by Devereux, in ancient times, when only birds existed, they had no nostrils. They held a council near Spirit Mountain to gain endurance, and they decided to have their noses pierced. They predicted that later the Mojaves, as well as their Quechan and Cocopah neighbors, would also do this. Mastamho advised the birds to sleep on their stomachs and to put their heads on their arms to prevent their heads from rolling and their noses from flattening on one or both sides. The duck did not listen and slept face up, which is why its bill is flat.

Some fifty years earlier, Bourke's informants located the nose-piercing event at a flat-topped, rocky mesa known as Mat-ho-ko-sabbi, or "place of the land of holes in the nose." This landmark sat about a hundred yards from a pile of stones close to an iron column that, in the 1880s, marked the boundary between California and Nevada. This was probably the place where the birds and animals raced at Mastamho's behest to determine how and where they would live. Bourke's informants said that all the animals met to engage in games at this place. They ran, jumped, and swam, and then the birds had holes bored in their beaks. The duck was last, and Mastamho argued that the bird's nose was too flat to be perforated. Duck insisted that he could not help it, and wanted his nose bored anyway. Mastamho complied, and when the birds raced in a circle, duck and dove won. Their bored beaks enabled them to race even with their mouths shut. Mojave runners emulated the birds by having their noses pierced, and if a young man dreamed of ducks and doves, he was destined to become a good, strong runner.

Devereux recorded memories in the 1940s that, at the time of initiation, a skilled piercer announced that he would perforate the nose of any boy who appeared at a certain place at a specified time. The rite always occurred in the summer. Boys wishing to participate first spent four days at home, abstaining from sex, salt, and mesquite beans (which were believed to cause cramps during footraces). They drank water and ate only thin gruels. Violation of food taboos was a serious offense; the Mojaves believed that it led to laziness during the rest of the young man's life. If a boy dreamed during the four days, his family paid attention to the visions, but these dreams had no more significance than did his others.

Families brought their sons to the appointed place, and the nose piercer perforated their nasal septums with a stick. He pierced only the lower, fleshy part, so that later the nose would not collapse or flatten, as would happen if the cartilage were bored. Then he inserted a small willow or arrowweed stick. The youth was not to cry out, and anyone who did was ridiculed. The piercer instructed the boys not to touch their noses but to sleep on their stomachs with their heads on their arms, so that their noses would not flatten. The boys then went home, where their parents watched them to be sure that they slept in the right position.

Four days later, the boys rose early and ran from the Fort Mohave area to what is now Ehrenberg, Arizona (across the state line from Blythe, California), returning before noon. The total distance was more than sixty miles. Sometimes an experienced runner accompanied them to set the pace and push them along. After the race, they removed their nose sticks, and the ritual ended. The youths were expected to run well and to eat lightly for the rest of their lives, because large meals made people drowsy and lazy.

Poor boys wore sticks or twisted bark in their pierced noses, but the wealthier ones inserted strings of blue and white beads or shells.

Walapai men, by Heinrich Mollhausen. The Walapais lived in harsher terrain than the Mojaves, who traded their agricultural products for Walapai game and red face and body paint. The two people spoke related Yuman languages and were often allies. (Ives 1861, Indian Portraits, plate V.)

The richest sported ornaments of triangular haliotis shell, obtained from the Quechans and Cocopahs, who traded for shell on expeditions to the Pacific coast.

Nose piercing gave a boy endurance, but he also needed to dream in order to be successful at running. Youths who had visions of water birds that migrated long distances were fated to be runners. The Mojaves were known for covering great stretches along the Colorado River and even across the desert. A trained, well-seasoned runner sometimes loped as much as one hundred miles a day at a steady pace and could outlast and outdistance a horse. In the late nineteenth century, Captain Bourke wrote of hiring a runner for two dollars and sending him ahead to Fort Mohave to inform the commandant of his arrival. The man trotted the twenty-one miles over a heavy sandy road between 10:00 AM and 1:30 PM, and the achievement was regarded as merely commonplace. Bourke also reported that a runner could start from Fort Mohave, cover the two hundred miles to the Mojave reservation, rest a while, and start back for the Needles Peaks in less than twenty-five hours. Astonishingly, runners did not drink any water while they ran.

As a psychological anthropologist, George Devereux was interested in personality. He observed that the Mojave shared their food, shelter, troubles, and joy with relatives and friends. They laughed often, because laughter was a sign of friendship and a good disposition, but they also expressed grief publicly. Men cried when they were sad or unhappy, and narrations of troubles often unleashed sympathetic tears from listeners. The Mojaves considered undemonstrative people to lack normal human feelings, and they resented any friend who would not disclose difficulties. Friendship entailed trading confidence for confidence.

Devereux found the Mojaves to be loyal people who did not gossip behind friends' backs. They often praised others, and the highest tribute was that a person was a "real Mojave." Men and women who misbehaved were avoided and criticized, as were those who associated with worthless or despicable people.

Adults married, farmed, hunted, fished, gathered and prepared food, and still found time to adorn themselves on a regular basis. Fathauer and Stewart provided solid information about

Mojave housing and food procurement, storage, and preparation in the 1930s and 1940s. At the same time, Castetter and Bell explored recent Yuman agriculture. Taylor and Wallace wrote about Mojave face painting and tattooing in the same decades. Much of our knowledge thus is based on the memories of older Mojaves, especially as retold to Fathauer and Stewart, and reaches back to the early decades of the twentieth century.

Marriage and Courtship

Teasing was a sign of affection among the Mojaves. If a young woman said terrible things about a man and committed the breach of etiquette of mentioning his dead relatives (something that was expressly prohibited), he knew that she loved him. Young couples usually arranged their own unions, always observing the rules against marriage within the clan or to close relatives on the mother's side. They agreed to live together, usually in the vicinity of one family or the other. Many marriages were successful, and incompatible people separated and found other spouses.

Stories from the ancient First Times explained why some people were lucky in love and others were not. Mockingbird, for instance, won the woman he wanted, despite an unattractive appearance. If a man dreamed of this bird, he would be successful with women, even if he were ugly. A few similar mythic patterns also existed for women, usually of a more cautionary nature. If a woman dreamed of a curve-bill thrasher, for example, she would be promiscuous.

Anthropologist Alfred Kroeber noted that Mojave women enjoyed a higher status than did the women of most Native peoples, and that they spoke freely and ate and worked alongside men. Although expected to be modest and deferential in their behavior, they were among the more influential and liberated women in nineteenth and early-twentieth-century Native America. The first chairperson of the Tribal Council was, in fact, a woman: Frances Wilbur Stillman.

Clan structure was strong, but on a day-to-day basis the family was the most important unit. People worked within their nuclear families most of the time. They undertook the majority of their activities with parents, spouses, siblings, and offspring, or in cooperation with members of their extended families. Land ownership was vested in a family, and cultivation of the land, was a family matter.

Photo by Jeffrey L. Garton

Jolene

From *The Dancing Healers* by Carl A. Hammerschlag

The Mohave graveyard was a flat, stone-strewn field with few gravestones. In the old days there had been no grave markers at all. The human ashes, following cremation, were simply covered with dirt and left unmarked.

The end was the end; there was no engraved immortality. One returned to the earth, the eternal source, to become a part of it, to nurture those coming after. Previous lives, like the land, were a gift for unborn generations. Connections to the people who ended there and to the place itself could help avert disasters.

The Mohaves, a small tribe living around Parker, Arizona, are reluctant to talk to me of death and rebirth, not because I am unsympathetic, but because I am not Mohave. The few rituals that remain to them are carefully handed down to other Mohaves as an oral tradition.

In general terms, the Mohaves see dying as just another aspect of the life cycle. As in the creation myths of most religions, death and rebirth are part of an unending circle that connects all Mohaves with those who came before and, ultimately, to their supernatural ancestors, Matavilya and Mastamho, who created the Colorado River, produced light, shaped the land, and separated the Mohave people into clans.

I have also come to interpret death as the final adaptation to life. Death is when the body parts no longer communicate with one another in the old language. Death is an expression of what we once knew as life, but in another form. The task of healing, as I see it, is to maintain communication within the body as long as it is sensible to do so.

The Mohaves believe that when one dies the spirit is freed and goes on a voyage to the spirit world to be reunited with all its ancestors, a passage the living are not to interfere with. The body is only a container for the spirit, a reminder of this earthly life. If the body is not cremated, it becomes a burdensome connection to the earthworld and makes the spirit voyage more difficult.

Thus, when someone dies, friends and relatives return all of his or her possessions or attachments to earth. Toys, photographs, special gifts, clothing—all are burned. The deceased's name is not mentioned anymore. After the Mohave cryhouse ritual, tears are no longer shed for the lost loved one. Tears weigh the spirit down and make the voyage difficult.

I first met Jolene when she was ten. Her mother, Gail, a light-complexioned Anglo, and her father, Gabe, a full-blooded Mohave, were friends of mine. Jolene was a tall, bright child, an honor student who attended college on a scholarship. She was elected one of sixteen official representatives (the youngest of them) of the state of Oregon to the National Women's Conference in Houston, Texas, in 1977.

Jolene was usually active and striving, but while away at school she became depressed. She wrote to her father, who in turn explained in a letter that the forces of evil could sometimes capture one's energies. Jolene said that she wanted to take a break from all work and school and no play. She wanted to reevaluate and rededicate herself. She told her father that she wished to come home at semester break. She felt burdened, and she had dreams of dying.

Gabe knew of the unconscious, of self-doubt, uncertainty, guilt, and pain. He agreed that his daughter should return to recharge her personal energy.

At semester break, however, Jolene decided not to come home. Gabe told her to go and sweat—he would send her the sage and herbs to do it in the traditional way.

Ritual cleansing has been a part of almost all cultures. Christians have baptism and sprinkling; Jews ritually immerse themselves before Yom Kippur, the Day of Atonement. Indians go to the sweat lodge to cleanse the body and the soul before ceremonial occasions. To speak and listen to the Creative Source in the sacred grounds, you must get yourself in the appropriate frame of mind and be as cleansed and new as possible.

Cleansing is another ritual that has lost its sacramental quality for us. Now we go to a health spa and sit in the sauna or steam room as a social event or a beautification scheme. The native tradition, however, teaches that the steam is the breath of our grandparents and that the rocks producing the steam are invested with the spirits of all the people who have gone before. Sweating, with your ancestors breathing on you, has a healing influence.

We need to learn to separate the ordinary from the sacred, to learn to appreciate the mystery in small things whose origins we forget. Steam, incense, and smoke and ritual paraphernalia like candles and fire remind us of those mysteries.

Gabe wanted Jolene to go into a steam room and see it in a cleansing way. Then she would be prepared to receive the spirit.

She could receive her message by dreaming, her father advised her, and she should use the dream message to overcome the dark influences and help restore her balance. She had to do it now, while she was vulnerable to the forces of darkness. To let it go longer would only make it harder to shake later. He compared the dilemma to a hardening jello mold: you could not ignore the forces of darkness, or they would harden you. They had to be exorcised—met and conquered. (I think it not a bad definition of neurosis: the forces of darkness capturing and holding you until your "jello" hardens.)

He told Jolene that he and other friends would pray for her. My friend believed that prayers in any form, songs, and silence were acceptable to God as long as they were sincere. And he told Jolene that she must pray too. Her healing must ultimately come through her own being.

Jolene took the herbs to a steam room and cleansed herself as her father had suggested. She did better in school and was no longer worried; she became more involved in campus activities. The dreams of death dissipated, but she later wrote to her father asking that she be cremated in the Mohave way if she died.

Before the school year was over, Jolene was riding in a small car with some friends. The car collided head-on with another and Jolene sustained a massive head injury. The doctor initially said that she would not survive. My friend went to the Midwestern medical center to be with his daughter.

Jolene was in a neurology intensive-care unit, a fantasyland of life-sustaining mechanical wonders that overwhelmed Gabe. She was unresponsive, but he sat at her bedside and spoke to her.

There was no way to explain why the accident had occurred to his daughter, no way to determine why it should be Jolene lying there in a comatose state. As we had often said to one another, "shit happens."

Gabe was a father maintaining a connection with his daughter even though she was unconscious. He was speaking with her as she existed between worlds and helping her to make a choice between those worlds.

In the old way, he perceived Jolene as existing in another dimension of life. She could see and hear things that he could not, but he could remind her of life in this dimension by telling her of his thoughts and visions. He spoke to Jolene of their home and his wish to take her back with him. He described the desert sage and ocotillo, the river and the sacred mountains of the reservations on which they had lived. He talked about Tempe, the house they lived in while he attended graduate school. He talked about her sisters, her mother, himself. He told her that in the place where she now existed she could still hear him and that he would stay with her.

Six weeks after the accident, Jolene was medically stabilized and, still unconscious, was transferred to Phoenix. When I saw her, she did not appear to hear me. Gabe assured me that she did hear, for he had seen her move her eyes. By the seventh week, Jolene opened her eyes. Gradually she improved, at first responding to words by blinking her eyes. Later she pointed to printed cards to indicate when she wanted the television channels changed and other simple requests. She still could not speak or move.

One evening I asked Jolene if she remembered the events following the accident. By pointing to the cards, she picked out her recollections. She did not recall the intensive care unit at all—she remembered hearing, seeing, and smelling her Arizona home.

Some weeks later, Jolene developed respiratory problems, and she was placed on a positive pressure breathing machine and fed through a tube threaded into her stomach. She occasionally appeared in respiratory distress, but her spirits were good.

Eleven weeks following the accident, she could sit up strapped in a chair. Jolene remembered more and more of the time before and after the accident, but not of the accident itself. She recalled visions of her family, her favorite haunts, the swimming holes.

During this time she developed a complication from the tracheotomy tube in her neck. A stricture had developed at the place where the tube ended in her trachea, but it was not seen as a serious problem. Periodically Jolene became racked with fever. She developed pressure sores on her buttocks. Her lungs became clogged with infection, but she was alert.

One evening Jolene tapped her head and pointed toward the wall at her feet. Her father changed the direction in which she was lying, moving her so that her head pointed to the north. The Mohave cremate their dead with the head pointed south. Jolene was not yet ready to die.

One day, Jolene was found in bed with the tracheotomy tube expelled. The doctors manually held open the hole in her neck as they attempted to insert another tube, but it could not get beyond the narrowed opening. A smaller tracheal tube was tried. Jolene did not complain, but she winced in pain at the manipulation.

While the doctors prepared the operating room for surgical reinsertion of the tube, Jolene suffered cardiac arrest. Three hours after the tube had been found expelled, all resuscitation efforts had failed and Jolene was pronounced dead.

She was taken back to Parker, where her family would translate her body the old way—after an elaborate ceremony. Jolene would be cremated. Her spirit journey had begun, and the magical intaglios that had been carved centuries ago at the bases of sacred mountains in the Colorado River Valley would show her the way.

After the cremation, I sat with Gabe and Gail for a while at their house. Gabe said, simply, that Jolene had completed her circle here. Hers had been only a moment in an unending spiral. All Indian life symbols are circular, without beginning or end. Gail said that her daughter was now released to choose again what to be.

All rituals, all sacraments, are ways of preparing us for the inevitable truth that disasters occur, that "shit happens." Most of them are small when compared to dying, but one day we too will make our journey into another space.

If I, as a physician, cure someone and aid him or her to become less vulnerable to that disease again, then I am a good doctor. But if I, as a doctor, cure someone, aid him or her to become less vulnerable to that disease, and help him or her to understand his/her place in the universe, then I am a healer.

All the great dancing healers I have met have enabled their people to build bridges over the unknowable gaps, the mysteries, of our existence. They deal directly with the transition of death, and they participate in ritualized mourning. Then they get back to the business of living.

An Account of The Mohave Mourning Ceremony

by Kenneth Stewart

Reprinted with permission of Wiley-Blackwell Publishing Company.

The Mohave Indians of the Colorado River valley, like other Yuman and Shoshonean tribes of southern California and western Arizona, customarily conduct a commemorative mourning ceremony. The Mohave rite is not a mourning "anniversary," since it is not held annually; rather; two or three years ordinarily elapse between commemorations. Not all deaths are signalized, the ceremony being held only in memory of the recent death of a chief or distinguished warrior.[1] The Mohave ceremony lasts for a single day and night only, and is thus abbreviated in contrast to the four-day Yuma ceremony and the six-day functions of the Cocopa, Diegueno, and southern California Shoshoneans.

The Mohave ceremony (nyimichivauk) is held in the fall, in September or later, after the harvest.[2] The date is set by a certain shaman (ahwhe kochkwar), who also notifies the relatives of the eminent dead in whose honor the ceremony is to be held. Invitations are sent to the Mohaves living down river at Parker, Arizona, and to neighboring tribes, the Walapai and Chemehuevi. As many as four or five hundred people may attend.

A large, rectangular, flat-topped, open shade or ramada, measuring approximately sixty feet by thirty feet, is erected to shelter the spectators. From the rafters are hung as decorations bunches of feathers and ceremonial weapons fashioned on the days immediately preceding the ceremony.[3] Extending south from the ramada is the ceremony ground, about fifty yards in length.

The central feature of the ceremony is a sham battle, in which the chief participants are young men, ranging in age from twenty to thirty. They are in war regalia, with black paint on their foreheads and red paint on their hair. Early in the morning ten "warriors" line up on the starting line in front of the shade, facing south. Two of the men, who represent war leaders, wear feather headdresses and carry "potato-masher" clubs, gourd canteens, and bows wrapped in red-painted fiber. The war leaders stand slightly in advance of the other men. The other eight warriors carry no clubs or bows but bear the feathered pikes (okwil), which function as the equivalents of standards in Mohave warfare.

To begin the activity, each of the two leaders selects four pike-bearers and marches them fifty yards south on the ceremonial ground, then back to ramada. They circle the shade, one group passing clockwise, the other counter-clockwise. The ceremonial ground and ramada are thus encompassed four times, whereupon the men walk to the north end of the ground, turn around, and stand there, the leaders in front of the others.

Each leader now picks a man from among the warriors, and one of the pairs thus constituted walks into the crowd of Indians under the shade, the men moving cautiously, furtively, as if among the enemy. Meanwhile, on opposite ends of the starting line in front of the ramada stand two women "making a noise."

It is now about nine or ten a.m., and the two leaders begin a symbolic reconnaissance of enemy territory. Four upright arrows have been placed at intervals of twelve yards on the ceremonial ground between the ramada and the north line. These represent water holes. The leaders go out from the north line to the nearest water hole, inspect it, and report back to the other men, saying that they have seen enemy footmarks, which apparently are about three days old. They then run to the second water hole, investigate, and report two-day-old tracks. The procedure is repeated at the third water hole, and the tracks are described as one day old. The scouts tell the men that they think they were seen at the third water hole by the enemy and, after the gourd canteen has been passed around, they say that, although it is extremely dangerous and the enemy may discover them and kill them, they are going on to the fourth water hole. In the event that they do not return, the remaining men are to advance and attack.

However, no tracks are found at the fourth water hole, nor is the enemy in the vicinity. The leaders run back to the main body of warriors, report, and decide to start out en masse for the enemy camp. They walk single file until they come to the ramada, and once more the two squads diverge, one circling to the left, the other to the right.

Again they return to the north end and stand there, feathered pikes planted in the ground. What resembles a rifle drill follows; with one of the leaders giving such orders as "Take your okwil and put it on your right shoulder," the warriors obeying in unison. When the men have shouldered pikes, one of the leaders yells for about thirty seconds, and before he ceases the other leader commands all the other men to yell. They do so, and then all run south, circle the shade, and stand in front of it on the starting line. The men remain motionless for a minute, then shout again and run north. Sixteen circuits in all are made in this fashion, the warriors making full speed every fourth run, loping the balance of the time. After the sixteenth run they stand on the starting line in front of the ramada, their okwils planted in a row, and they rest for a short while.

While the warriors are resting, a shaman (ahwhe kwajakwar kusuman) sings four songs, telling of the origins of the war paraphernalia. Running is resumed after the rest period and follows a pattern identical with the prior performance. The series of sixteen runs is repeated eight times. Upon completion of this phase of the ceremony, the ten man dash to the river and dive in with their eyes wide open. They sit in the water for thirty seconds and then come out. These ablutions are in imitation of the purification of warriors returning from the enemy, and the men must dive in the water four times in all. Bathing is repeated each morning for four days, and food restrictions are also enjoined during this period, with meat and salt taboo to the participants. The relatives of the dead for whom the ceremony is held likewise bathe and observe food restrictions for four days.

Ten fresh men run in the afternoon, following a procedure identical with that executed by the morning runners. In the evening the "night shift," as my interpreter expressed it, begins its run. The "night shift" must perform throughout the night, and consequently the men run less strenuously than the day shift. They complete the eight series of runs, rest for an hour and a half or two hours while the shaman sings of the ways of the weapons, and then they resume their running.

Near sun-up the shaman sings his last songs and informs the runners that only four more runs remain. These runs are all at full speed. The spectators are awakened, and at the conclusion of the running the ramada is evacuated and set afire, while the people stand about wailing as at a funeral. Food and clothing are thrown into the flames. When the fire begins to blaze the runners again divide into two squads of five men each, and they run in a circle around the conflagration, clockwise and counter-clockwise respectively. Finally, meeting halfway, they break their feathered pikes and throw them into the fire, and then speed to the river and dive in.

[1] The account was obtained from Chief Pete Lambert, 80, at Needles California, incidentally to a study of Mohave warfare made under the auspices of the Department of Anthropology of the University of California in March, 1946. Emett van Fleet and Clinton Hogan assisted as interpreters.

[2] The mourning ceremony is more than a memory to the Mohave, since a rite was held at Needles for two Mohave soldiers killed in Europe in World War II. The ancient custom of destroying the property of the dead was adhered to by burning the shirts and other garments of the two soldiers.

[3] The feathered pikes of the runners are made on the morning of the ceremony.

Chapter Two

Political Structure/ Relations with Others/ Economic Development

Photo by Jeffrey L. Garton

Mohave Chieftainship in Action:

A Narrative of the First Contacts of the Mohave Indians with the United States

by George Devereux

The demand for effective leadership is especially strong in times of crisis. Even democratic societies, which ordinarily have elaborate systems of checks and balances, tend to develop in times of crisis centralized leadership, which, in principle, is of limited duration.

It is proposed to record in the following pages the history of the leadership which Yarate:va, the last independent Mohave chief, provided for his tribe in a time of crisis and readjustment. His leadership, as will be seen, was democratic in the strictest sense of the term. This is rather significant since, on the whole, White officials —if only for the purpose of having someone "responsible" for the actions of the tribe—tended to act on the assumption that Indian chiefs exercised absolute authority, and, therefore, often encouraged cooperative chiefs to increase the scope of their traditionally limited authority. Since Yarate:va's leadership remained within the traditional scope of Mohave chieftainship, one is led to suppose that this was due primarily not to some special component of his personality make-up, but to what Talcott Parsons would call the "structurally generalized goals" of Mohave society. It is, therefore, desirable to preface an account of Yarate:va's leadership with a sketch of Mohave chieftainship.

One of the least understood segments of Mohave culture is government. In the field of political institutions the most salient difference between the Mohave and their non-Yuman neighbors was the relatively negligible institutionalization of Mohave government and chieftain-ship. This state of affairs was probably partly determined by the fundamentally anti-formalistic and uncompulsive orientation of the Mohave. At the same time, and again in contrast with their Yuman neighbors, the Mohave had an intense national consciousness and, thus, despite the informality of their government, were capable of acting as a unit, in peace as well as in wartime. It may even be legitimate to suggest that the unusual laxity of Mohave political institutions was made possible precisely by the automatic cohesiveness which was determined by the intensity of Mohave nationalism.

The Mohave chief was, primarily, a servant of the tribe, with little personal power and many cares and duties. This was so typical of Mohave chieftainship, that every informant, when asked whether he knew anyone who suffered from obsessive ruminations, misunderstood the question and cited the chief's constant preoccupation with public welfare as an example. The lack of personal power also encouraged personal maturity, and safeguarded the chief against the danger of being "infantilized" by the possession of power.

It might also be added that an account of primitive leadership in action may be of more than academic interest to thoughtful leaders in all fields of endeavor, especially at a time when many people seem inclined to assume that one's choice lies solely between authoritarian leadership and parochialistic anarchy

It is therefore felt that an account of the leadership which a typical and great Mohave chief provided during a critical period of Mohave history may serve to exemplify the manner in which mature and constructive leadership may be exercised in a democratic society, even in times of national distress and defeat.

The following account of the first contact between the Mohave and Americans was obtained during my fourth field trip, in 1938, from Tcatc, an octogenarian woman belonging to a prominent Mohave family. Since she was the granddaughter of the first Mohave chief to treat with Americans, and appears to have witnessed several of the events mentioned in her narrative, it is probable that, unlike many oral traditions her account is likely to be reliable in most respects, especially since she was extremely eager to have me record this story (cf. below). Her statements were translated by two expert interpreters.

The following narrative is pieced together from three separate accounts labeled respectively (A), (B), and (C). In order to make it obvious that these different versions supplement, rather than correct each other, I have carefully shown from which version each of the following paragraphs was drawn. The close concordance between these three versions clearly reinforces the impression that the narrative is, on the whole, an adequate presentation of events, as they were seen through Mohave eyes.

It is also worth pointing out that all three versions were obtained under circumstances which justify the assumption that nothing had either been added or omitted.

Narrative (A) was obtained spontaneously. Tcatc was simply asked to discuss whatever seemed to interest her most at that moment. In reply to this invitation, Tcatc begged me to record the deeds of her grandfather, lest they should be forgotten.

Narrative (B) was not merely a spontaneous offering, but was given in disregard of my instructions. I had asked Tcatc to dictate a brief story of her life, but had to abandon the project when, after a few lines concerning her own life, she consistently spoke only of her grandfather's deeds.

Narrative (C) was elicited by mentioning the cannibalistic practices of the Yavapai, as recorded by Gifford.

Nothing can convey in a more convincing manner Tcatc's eagerness to save these events from oblivion than the fact that, in telling her story, she utterly disregarded the very stringent taboo on the names of the dead, although, as a rule, she was very careful not to violate this prohibition.

The closing paragraphs of Tcatc's narrative make it evident that she dictated this narrative primarily because she realized that her own relatives were no longer interested in the Mohave past. Since Tcatc had repeatedly told me that she considered me as a "favorite grandson," she simply entrusted me with the task of perpetuating the Mohave past. In publishing this narrative I therefore seek not only to make a contribution to ethnology, but also to discharge a personal obligation toward a deceased friend.

Tcatc wanted to safeguard against oblivion not merely Yarate:va's deeds, but also her own memory. Before she died, she spontaneously broke her lifelong rule of complying with the taboo on being photographed, and asked a. young Mohave to take her picture, and send it to me so that I would not forget her. I hope that in publishing the account of her grandfather's deeds, by whose code, and according to whose example she had tried to live, I am also, in some small measure, perpetuating the memory of one of the kindest human beings it has been my privilege to know.

Summing up, available evidence indicates that the following account is as accurate as Tcatc's memory could make it.

TCATC'S ACCOUNT

(The notation (A), (B) and (C) indicate from which version of Tcatc's narrative a given paragraph is taken).

I still have lots of things to tell you that I have never told yet. When the people were still living there, at Newberry Mountain (Avi: kwame:), my folks—I was not living then—lived at a place called Aha kwaai:y (water wood). There was also a small lake, filled with driftwood from the overflow of the Colorado River, and a road which came down through a place called Akwak' heyo:v (deer seen). That was the only road they had at that time.(A)

I was born at the Intake, just this side of La Paz, during the last war between the Mohave and the Chemehuevi (Paiute?). That was after the Maricopa-Mohave war, I was born after the Mohave took possession of this region (Parker, Arizona). Before that the Maricopa and the Pima owned it.(B)

The Maricopa and the Kohuana were living at Parker, Arizona, at that time.(A)

The Mohave-Chemehuevi war took place after that. It was fought near La Paz, and I was born just this side of La Paz, on the eastern shore of the Colorado River. Before they moved down here, the Mohave used to live around Needles (California). Before that, there was nothing down here except mesquite and screw-beans. Then the Mohave came down here and began to plant. (B)

I am an only child. I remember when I was around five years old. It seems that my parents were originally from East of Needles. When I was about five years old, they decided to go back there. No, I was only about one and a half years old when they left here. There is a boundary cone east of Needles—do you know where that is?—Anyway, it is east of Needles. That is where my parents were from, originally,—just below that place. That is where they went back to when I was about one and a half years old. They stayed there for about five years. Then they decided to leave that place for good, and came down here. They came here in a boat, down the Colorado River. (Interpreter A. remarked "It was not a real boat. It was a raft made out of something that grows in water, something similar to tule, but round.") It was tied into three bundles and they put their belongings, and the small children inside, and the older ones waded or swam with the raft, depending on whether the water was deep, or not. I have been here ever since, and never returned to live in Needles. Now I am still here, and the others all left (i.e. died), so that I am all alone. Now I don't have the things I had then; the food stuff they had then, the things they had planted, the beans and whatever else they used to raise. (B)

When the first White man came, he came in a wagon down the road I spoke of before, which extended to the end of their village. An ipa: kunami:yh (person brave, a kind of tribal hero) whose only desire was to kill foes, killed this White man. Every now and then, when a White man came there, they did the same thing. (See Appendix I)(A)

My mother's father Yarate:va, of the Nyoltc gens, was chief at that time. The Whites pronounced his name Arateva. At that time soldiers were passing back and forth there, and the Mohave killed some of them.(B)

When the news of this event became known among the Whites, they sent a regiment of soldiers to that place. The Mohave had a war with the Whites at Akwak' heyo:v. The Whites were using firearms and killed off nearly half of the Mohave men who were in that battle.(A)

Thereupon the soldiers started killing the Mohave right and left, regardless of whether they were guilty or not, until so many old folks were lying around dead and uncremated that my maternal grandfather felt that it was wrong.(B)

It was two or three days before they were able to take care of the dead, and to cremate them properly. Some of the corpses. that were left unguarded had been eaten by wild beasts, and all that was left of them were the bones. These bones were buried. My grandfather grieved over this situation. Then the Mohave went on the warpath again. They came to Parker, had a war with the Maricopa and the Kohuana, and beat them out of the country. They then returned home (to Needles) and in a year some of the Mohave came down to Parker to live. There were quantities of mesquite beans, screw-beans, hamose: atalyk and wild game here, but the Mohave did not seem to want to eat these, and, as a result, they actually starved. The land was good, but they didn't seem to want to cultivate beans, pumpkins and watermelons.(A)

There was a White man living at La Paz, who had plenty of (American) food which the Indians had never tasted. Since they were not friendly with the White man at that time, they kept on going hungry. When my grandfather saw this situation he was even more grieved, and worried about what could be done. He made a trip on foot to La Paz and talked with the White man. He told the White man that he was hungry and this White man gave him flour, sugar, coffee, bacon and beef and told him to eat. My grandfather had no idea of how to prepare this food. Yet, when he received these goods, he turned them over to a group of hungry Indians who were with him. The White man showed them how to prepare the food and they ate. This was the first friendly meeting between Whites and Indians. In time these Indians became well acquainted with these White folk, and the White man employed some of the young Indians to work for him. Then my grandfather made a trip back home, but he was still worried about the situation here, because, even though they remained here, they made no use of the land. So, in a year, he returned here with some other Indians, and gave the Indians here some land and told them to cultivate it, but they must have been lazy. They would rob the nest of the muskrat of the screw-beans and mesquite beans which the rat had stored there. Then too, they were working for this White man, for what he would give them (i.e., food). He had some horses, for which the young men cut some of the so-called hu:tce grass. They sold this grass for 10c a bundle, and bought food with their wages. When my grandfather returned to his home, he told the Indians again that individual plots of land had been given to all those who first made the trip here (Parker). The

Yuma too had helped us in this war to chase the Maricopa and the Kohuana out of this country, but they were not given any land and were told to move out.(A)

My grandfather was living at Needles, and went to La Paz. Then they started to give rations, and he went back to Needles once more.(B)

After he told the Indians back there, at his home, about the situation at Parker, he decided to take a trip. No one knew where, or how, or for what purpose this trip was taken. But he was going to take a trip. He left his home, and went West. Maybe he went to Riverside, or perhaps to Los Angeles. Later he made a report of his visit there. He said that the Whites were very wealthy, and farmed on a large scale: two or three hundred acres. He said that should the White man come to the land of the Mohave, he would not take just a small plot of land but would probably take the whole valley of Parker to make his living. That was not the thing that my grandfather wanted.(A)

He decided to visit (consult) several people before going to Washington to talk to the President.(A)

After that, he went to Washington with a White man. It took him two years. The real name of the White man is forgotten, but the Mohave called him Tam Leera.(B)

It took him a long time to get there, and on his way he saw so many White men that he decided that it was hopeless to do anything against them, because the Mohave would just be killed off. They saw the Indians being pushed back and the land taken. The White men taught him that that was the way to get land—to push people out by force. The Mohave had done that same thing to the "Pima" Indians. My grandfather felt that even though this land (the Needles area), had been formerly his, the soldiers had taken it away from him,—just as he had taken the land around Parker from the "Pima". He therefore asked (the President) that the Mohave should be settled here (Parker).(B)

Interpreter spontaneously asked Tcatc who the President was whom her grandfather had visited. Tcatc replied that she did not know his name, but that he was a good man—"not like some we had had since, or like the present one".(B)

When he went before the President at Washington, he told him of the battle with the white soldiers at Akwak' heyo:v. He said that what he had come to Washington for was to preserve the land here, at Parker, for the future use of his tribe, but that the Whites must first make a peace treaty with the Indians.(A)

Anyway, he told whomever he spoke to at Washington that he would be just like a brother to the Whites, and would lay aside his bows and arrows, and be a brother to everyone who came to his valley.(B)

However, the Whites must send some good White man to this country, to look after the Indians and the affairs of the Indians, and the dealings of the White man. He added that from that day on the Indian would not again draw a bow and shoot an arrow at the White man. He also said that they must point out (present) the White man as a brother and as a friend. He asked the President to give him in writing the reasons which he (Yarate:va) had set forth to the President, on the occasion of this trip.(A)

He then returned to Parker and settled there.(B)

He returned to his home and told the Indians there that because they had been beaten in the war with the White soldiers, the land, which they had (originally) occupied, was no longer theirs. He therefore made them move to Parker, and from there he went down to La Paz, to the White settlement. There he told the Whites of this peace-treaty with the President of the United States. Then he moved back up to within six miles of the town of Parker, to a place known as Matatcke:tceve. Since this same treaty was also known at Phoenix, and at Prescott, in a few years there was a superintendent at Fort Mohave.(A)

My grandfather had a lot of troubles, however, because of Pascual, the chief of the Yuma, and because of the other Mohave chief, Homose: kohot, who was Pete Lambert's paternal grandfather. Those two did not agree with my grandfather. They did not like leaving the land, up at Needles, that had given them birth and (supernatural or dream) power, the land that had given them everything they ever had.(B)

At that time they were digging the canal up there. These two did not agree with him, but my grandfather argued that the Mohave were so greatly outnumbered that the only way they could exist and keep on living was to live like the Whites, and be at peace with the Whites; only thus could they increase. But the other two did not agree with him and felt kind of bitter against him. My maternal grandfather said: "It is not as though you could always live the way you used to. Some day you will have to live like the Whites, and come in contact with them, and it is better that you should live in peace with them. What I have decided may seem cowardly to you, but in the end it is going to be the better way".(B)

My grandfather also made other trips to Washington.(B)

The same year that the superintendent was appointed, the digging of the old Dent canal was also begun. It was started at a place known as Avi ahmo: (stone mortar). At that time very little was known about American coins and bills. When the order came through to begin digging this canal, they were paid fifty cents a day to dig it. The food that the White man at La Paz taught the Indians to eat was not much use. The Indians cultivated their crops near what is now known as the "Twelve Mile Slough", and the Indian women supplied their working men with food from these gardens. Then, while this canal was being dug, my grandfather also asked for money, so that they might pay the workers a few more dollars or even a few more cents. Then word came to Phoenix from Washington to ship money to Parker. It was then that Lehigh (?), a White man from La Paz, made a trip to Phoenix, and started back with a chest full of coin, and currency. Then, near what is known now as Vicksburg, the Yavapai massacred the convoy and that money never reached the Indians here. I already told you about that massacre once before.(A)

I heard that a Mohave named Tcikuhava anyay (taken in light), of the Tcatc gens, left Parker and went to Phoenix. He was coming back with a White man, when, in the mountains to the East of here, the Yavapai killed both the White man and the Mohave. This White man, Lehigh (?), was taking a wagon of money to (from?) the East somewhere, and, while they were on their way, the Yavapai killed him. They cut open the White man's stomach, to look at his intestines. Then they just threw his innards on the wagon, and burned the wagon. They left the White man behind, but took the Mohave, whom they had captured alive, to their country, and then killed and ate him. They said that if they let him live, he would tell the Indians precisely who had done this deed. They did not want that to happen, and so they ate him. Then a group of Yavapai went down to the Pima country, and they had the scalp of this Mohave with them. The Pima asked them whose scalp it was, and the Yavapai replied "It is a Mohave scalp, and we have eaten him". This happened long ago, at a time when they had peaceful feelings (toward the Mohave) among the Pima and the Maricopa, and said that it was all right for the Mohave to go and visit them. That is how two Mohave happened to see the remains. They were Musetara (group of stars), of the Vaha:th gens, who was my uncle, and Sukiyet (picked). These Mohave then went to Prescott and told some people about it, and they got a regiment of soldiers who began to comb the mountains for these Yavapai .Eventually they found a party of Yavapai, who said that they had been in the massacre, and they put them in jail at San Carlos.(C)

There was a man known as Salt. That is what the Americans called him, and the Indians remember him only by that English name. He had a store near the old Agency, and I was right back of the store. I was then about 10 years old. One day the Government told the Indians of the raid on the money that had been sent. This Salt was therefore watching for that money, in case it should be passed in his store. One day, when I was riding a dog near the store, two Yavapai men came to the store and bought some food. Then they left the store, and went off toward the east. They did not do anything to these two men, and so they left. The digging of the old canal still went on and my grandfather moved his place (house) along with the progress of the digging. In three years he moved to the side of the old Agency and there he died. While the canal was being dug, a group of soldiers was living where the pumping plant is now. (See Appendix III) These soldiers threatened the Indians, saying that they would kill them all off if they did not complete the canal. They also threatened to cut off the ears, nose and lips of all the Indians.—That is what made them dig! When they made these threats my grandfather went to the superintendent, whose name the Mohave pronounced as Tauktatana, and who was the second Superintendent the Mohave had had. He told him that, according to the President, his friend, there was to be no violence between the Mohave and the White. He also told the Superintendent that if they wanted to talk that way to the Mohave, they (the tribe) could go to the President about this matter.(A)

After the canal was put in use, and they could use it and raise crops, melon, pumpkin, corn, wheat, they realized that the old man had been right, and that in the end it was better this way.(B)

This irrigation system was put in before the boundaries of the reservation were known to the Indians.(A)

Later on they set the reservation aside, and marked its boundary line. In the meantime I had gotten married, and I was living in my own home when they fixed up the boundary line.(B)

After the death of my maternal grandfather, his sister's son Kul-ho Kwira:u (or Korau) (boat fast), of the Vi:mak gens, became chief.(B)

He took up what was left of his (the chief's) authority.(A)

He realized that the old man had been right in what he had said, and therefore he took up his ideas, and tried to teach his people the way the old man had taught them.(B)

Two years later word was sent from Washington, asking the new chief to go to Washington. They also sent $100.00, for transportation. He made the trip and made a report of the affairs with the Indians. He was also given a medal, and his name was inserted in place of the name of my grandfather on all the papers. The year he returned from his trip to Washington, the old Dent canal was also completed. The Government supplied a handpump, and turned the water into the canal for the irrigation of cultivated gardens. However, in a short time the mouth of the canal was stopped up with sand.(A)

When my grandfather went to Washington, he brought back this paper and a medal they gave him. All the Indians were told that what my grandfather had said to the President constituted an invitation for the Indians to follow the White man's way of living, and that this was to be a part of the program of the future Indians.(A)

At present the authorities never say anything about these papers and medals. Today the White man is taking more money, as well as land, from the Indians, because later on these papers were turned over to Harold Wade Aholy tcuva:u (ashes placed) of the Mu:th gens), when he was very young,—too young to understand such matters, and these original papers seem to have been lost by Wade, when he was young, and played with liquor, and got himself jailed at Riverside and suchlike. Because of this, we now have to pay for irrigation water, and the one who makes money is the White man who is growing cotton and raising cattle. What my grandfather had said was that whatever money came to the Indians from his crops or cattle was to be his, and his alone. What has happened today is precisely what my grandfather was afraid of: to be in debt to the white man.(A)

When, about eight years ago (1930?), Harold Wade died, the Reverend Randall Booth, the Indian Missionary, offered the papers and the medal to Sam Jones. Of course he had only substitute papers. When Sam Jones refused to take them, he gave them to Thomas Stevens (Suri:p—to bother or to annoy—of the Mu:th gens). Booth did this despite the fact that these papers, and the full authority that these papers give the bearer, should have been given to one of my relatives, to Kearney Miller, Ralph Miller, Charles Scott, Norman Scott, Abraham Scott, Theodore Patch or Willis Wade. There was some talking about these papers and medals before Harold Wade died, and the Reverend Randall Booth, the Indian missionary, got hold of them. Of course, they were just substitute ones, the originals having been lost. At Harold Wade's funeral I told people about my grandfather. I reported that while my grandfather's brother was still living, my grandfather had said that if his brother managed to raise sons, these papers and the medal should go to them. According to my grandfather's words, one of the seven whom I have just named should have the papers and the medal now. Actually, the Reverend Booth has them now. My grandfather also said that if there were no children in his brother's family, the tribe should pick a man, who is interested in tribal affairs and in the progress and welfare of the Indians; a man who would see the needs of the Indians and would try to do something about them. That man, my grandfather said, should have the papers and the medal. Two of the seven eligible men, Willis Wade and Abraham Scott, have no children. The others do have children, but they cannot inherit these papers, because they do not have them (the actual objects) in their possession.(A)

I am more or less the only surviving member

of that family, who actually saw and heard these things. And what I am telling here is a true record of this thing,—as told by me. It has never been written down. I am the only one left to tell this, as I saw and understood it. I want you to write down and publish this, so that it will not be lost. What I am telling is a thing I never told before and which has never been written down. I have young relatives in my family, who should know these things, but they have never had it written either.(A)

APPENDIXES

The following narratives illustrate various incidents of the first contact between the Mohave and Americans.

I. Hivsu: Tupo:ma's Account: During the Goldrush to California the Mohave attacked some covered wagons passing through Needles. The Whites were killed and their mules were butchered and eaten. When this raid became known, some soldiers were sent against the Mohave from the west. They came along the Salt Sea (or Salton Sink?) near the Colorado River, and went upstream in a boat, until they reached Needles. Four of the headmen of our tribe: Kamitokuat, Coctah and Hukram—I forget the name of the fourth,—then decided to hold a council with the soldiers and take the punishment on themselves, so that the tribe might be left in peace. They held the council, and as soon as the soldiers made peace with the tribe, they took the four chiefs to Yuma on the soldiers' boat. The chiefs were then jailed at once, However, their doors were not locked, so that, toward mid-night, the soldiers sneaked in on the prisoners and shot (lynched?) two of them. The other two escaped somehow, and traveled upstream on the California side of the River until they reached Needles, having had nothing to eat nor drink during the whole journey. When they arrived, they were only skin and bones, and dropped in a dead faint. During this campaign one of the soldiers belonging to the Western corps, while passing through La Paz, cohabited with a Mohave woman and paid her $1.00 cash. Then he left her, and nothing further was ever heard of him. The woman became pregnant and gave birth to D. W.

II. Ahma Huma:re's Account: The arrival of American troops was caused by the murder of a White foreman, who had shot a Mojave boy for teasing his child.

III. Dr. M. A. I. Nettle's Account: During this period a Negro cavalry regiment was stationed in Mohave territory. This explains why some Mohave Indians have Negroid features. (The Mohave denied any general admixture of Negro "blood"; it is certainly not obvious to the naked eye of the anthropologist, unaided by anthropometric instruments.)

The Persistent Identity of the Mohave Indians 1859-1965

by Frederick J. E. Gorman

In order to trace the efforts of the Mohave Indians to retain their collective identity in contrasting cultural environments over the past three hundred years, I have adopted the analytic framework developed by Spicer (1971) to study persistent cultural systems.

The Mohave are assigned membership in an ethnohistoric culture complex that has been labeled both "Lower Colorado" (Kroeber 1939: 42) and "River Yuman" (Castetter and Bell 1951:40; Forbes: 1965:15). They shared this distinction on linguistic and ecological grounds with neighboring tribes, such as the Quechan ("Yuma"), Maricopa, Halchidhoma, Kohuana, Kamia, Kohima, Halikwami, and Cocopa, who also lived on or near the lower Colorado River. It is difficult to determine precisely the spatial boundaries of the River Yuman complex, because, like others, it existed in the face of an overlapping of different cultural characteristics. For example, all of these member tribes exhibited aspects of theology and social organization of kindred that linked the River Yumans to southern California groups rather than with those to the east (Forbes 1965:42). The River Yumans also shared elements of cosmogony, tribal organization of occupational status, and aspects of material culture with certain cultures in the Southwest and Mexico (Forbes 1965:42). The Mohave, Quechan, and Maricopa are held to be the archetypal representatives of the River Yuman complex, for the specialized aboriginal way of life that developed along the Colorado River is thought to have been manifest earliest among these three tribes (Forbes 1965:35).

Mohave Identity as a Product of The Oppositional Process

Persistent identity systems are the product of continuous conflict between a "people" and the "controllers of surrounding state apparatus" over "issues of incorporation and assimilation" into the large entity (Spacer 1971:797). The implication is that this "oppositional process" is necessary for the formation and maintenance of persistent identity groups, and that several "conditions of opposition" are involved (Spacer 1971:797).

Spanish and Mexican Attempts to Incorporate the Mohave

The Mohave are known to have been located in the northern region of the lower Colorado River for at least three hundred years (Castetter and Bell 1951:44; Stewart 1969x:259), and. the tribe has outlived two state organizations. Like the Navajo (Spacer 1971:797), the Mohave were never actually incorporated into either the Spanish Empire or nineteenth-century Mexico. The Mohave allegedly participated in the successful Quechan Revolt of 1781 against the Spanish (Forbes 1965:200), but they were too remote from settlements of the latter to have been affected directly (Stewart 1969x:259).

Later, the Mohave were "technically incorporated" by Mexico, although the Lower Colorado region was ineffectively controlled during the early nineteenth century (Stewart 196941:259). This tribe, together with the Quechans, thwarted Mexican attempts to maintain land routes to California (Forbes 1965:241; Forbes 1973:22; Stewart 1965:188). In SLIM, the Mohave maintained their independence throughout the hispanic period (Stewart 1969x:259) largely because of their peripheral location and their formidable military reputation.

During the following years, 1820-1859, the Mohave harassed Anglo-American pioneers and U.S. military expeditions even though they were preoccupied with intertribal warfare (Stewart 1969x:262). Anthropologists (Castetter and Bell 1951:72; Stewart 1965:187) have defined Mohave warfare in this period as a semi-religious, identity-promoting activity (Devereux 1961:492) that has persisted into this century in the form of contentious, pantribal sentiments of militant nationalism. The Quechan and the Mohave are each thought to have maintained a distinct group of part-time professional warriors (Forbes 1965:16, 42, 75; Fathauer 1954:102-11; Stewart

1947:260-67) to engage in organized combat with their occasional allies (the Yavapai and Cocopa) against other River Yumans, principally the Kohana, Maricopa, Halchidhoma, and Cocopa. They are also known to have fought non-Yumans, such as the Northern Chermehuevi, Ute, Apache, Southern Paiute, Diegueno, Pima, and Papago (Castetter and Bell 1951:44; Stewart 1968:10). The Mohave in particular exhibited military spirit to the point where they functioned as a unit (including women when necessary) in offensive and defensive operations, and they were venturesome to the extent that they raided and traded from the Hopi mesas to Los Angeles (Castetter and Bell 1951:44 4; Devereux 1961:428; Forbes 1965:61; Forde 1931:138; Stewart 1947a:261).

Mohave relations with other River Yumans during this period exhibit another aspect of Spicer's (1971:797) oppositional process. There is some evidence that the Mohave attempted to dominate the Kohuana by forcing this tribe to reside with them for five years after expelling Kohuana allies, the Halchidhoma, from the Colorado River Valley around 1829 (Stewart I969a:265).

Incorporation of the Mohave began after the tribe was soundly defeated by a sizeable contingent of the United States Army in 1859 (Forbes 1965:338; 1973:22; Stewart 1965:188), and a military post (later named Fort Mohave) was established immediately thereafter in the Mohave Valley. The outcome of this confrontation might have been different and incorporation delayed had the Mohave not lost a substantial number of their infantry two years earlier in a disastrous battle with the Pima and Maricopa near Tempe, Arizona (Devereux 1961:427; Stewart 1969a:261).

US Incorporation Pressures and Mohave Responses, 1859-1890

The Mohave experienced three historical phases of economic and political pressure for cultural assimilation into the United States between 1859 and 1965. Less is known about the pressures that were exerted upon the Mohave during the first phase of their incorporation, 1859-1890, than about those which occurred during later periods (cf. Stewart 1969b). The tribe does seem to have experienced nondirected changes (Spicer 961b:521) in its aboriginal subsistence economy from 1859 to 1890 which were of no particular interest to United States military and civil authorities. Like other River Yumans, the Mohave traditionally practice a transhumant subsistence strategy in which scattered rancherias were moved from the lower Colorado River flood banks to the mesas and back according to a seasonal schedule of riverine farming and fishing alternating with upland hunting and gathering (Castetter and Bell 1951:71 Forbes 1965:100; Forde 1931:140; Kirchoff 1954:530). Agricultural production among the Yuman tribes began to decline between 1852 and 1877 as transportation wage labor (Castetter and Bell 1951:73; 84) grew in response to the establishment of US military posts along the Colorado River. These installations were supplied by naval transport vessels, and numerous individuals from several River Yuman tribes (notably Cocopa, Quechan, and Mohave) were engaged as riverboat pilots, crew men, and woodcutters (Dobyns, Stoffle, and Jones 1975:163; Shen 1965:1-12). Many of those who were committed to a cash economy by 1877 shifted to farm wage labor in commercial irrigation agriculture projects that were being organized in the Yuma and Imperial valleys after the Southern Pacific Railroad replaced naval transportation of militia supplies in that year (Dobyns, Stoffle, and Jones 1975:163). Others chose intermittent work as railroad hands, saloon porters, or small cash farmers (Bee 1963:210; Devereux 1961:66).

The political pressure to change was direct, however, for US military sanction was immediately applied to curtail Mohave warfare (Stewart 1973:32.3). This military action contributed to the formation of a permanent split in the tribe between 1862 and 1865, which occurred where a peaceful faction (Fathauer 1954:117) moved from the Mohave Valley to Parker, Arizona, on the newly established Colorado River Reservation to take advantage of agricultural opportunities there (Stewart 1969a:26). The less pacific segment of the tribe remaining in the Mohave Valley was probably responsible in 1865 for the two-year expulsion of Chemehuevi from the Chemehuevi Valley which separated both Mohave factions (Stewart I969a:265).

Both groups of Mohave thereafter maintained their common idea through interaction over the eighty-mile distance between them by means of intermarriage, shifts of residence, visitation for ceremonial purposes: for shamanistic curing, or hospitalization and schooling (Devereux(1961:84, 111, 143, 191, 199; Fathauer 1951a:91; Stewart 1969a:263).

Between 1870 and 1890 the Mohave were exposed to disease and poverty (Stewart 1969a: 263; 1973:323), but they did not resist incorporation through participation in the nativistic cults that were popular elsewhere during these decades. The most common themes of such vitalization movements—restoration of ancestors and their property—were anathematical to Mohave values (Devereux 1961:319). Rather, they intensified native patterns that were incompatible with Anglo-American values, as did the Navajo (Vogt 1961:326). The Mohave appear to have increased their preoccupation with the statuses of warrior and shaman, the ceremonial practice of funeral cremation, and perhaps mythology. After the curtailment of warfare, warriors began to gratify their ambitions through sexual conquest and shaman-killing actions which represented an exaggeration of basic, traditional themes (Devereux 1961:327, 519). Shamans were frequently assassinated for allegedly causing epidemics of unfamiliar diseases or crop failures, but these killings were no longer the tribally organized, public events they once had been (Devereux 1961:399, 1(16, 521). Mohave belief in malevolent witchcraft and the practice of shamanism may have increased in these decades (cf. Stewart 1973:323). The Mohave also developed a "contempt" for the "all-absorbing" Anglo-American interest in property which they consciously expressed through funeral immolation of a deceased individual and all of his property, including the residence (Devereux 1961:317). This ritual destruction prevented the accumulation of capital, and a mythology was developed initially to rationalize the contrast with funeral practices of Anglo-Americans (Devereux 1961:190) and later to exclude them from the ceremony itself.

Mohave Adjustment to the Reservation System of Incorporation, 1890-1930

Incorporation pressures intensified during the second phase, 1890-1930, when the reservation system was designed to produce homestead communities (cf. Spicer 1961h:528), and the Mohave experienced cultural disorganization that was manifested primarily in terms of "declining family cohesion" and "chaotic sexuality" (Devereux 1961:477). The Mohave retained their collective identity, however, by shifting emphases on membership in Mohave clans and on the statuses of warrior versus shaman while further intensifying their funeral practices. A systematic American attempt was made to alter Mohave identity by redefining native education, naming, and settlement practices. In 1890 Fort Mohave was converted to an industrial boarding school which functioned as a mechanism of forced acculturation (Sherer 1965:10) through compulsory attendance of Mohave children. The Indian Agency School established on the Colorado River Reservation (Devereux 1961:482) served a similar function.

In 1905 all Fort Mohave Indians (Sherer 1965:49), together with those on the Colorado River Reservation (Devereux 1961:131), were required to take English surnames (according to their membership in a lineage and not a clan) in order to provide the basis for land allotments. The Mohave resorted to compartmental usage of English names; that is, they continued to use clan names among themselves (Sherer 1965:49). Several ethnographers (Bee 1963:225; Fathauer 1951x:131; Kroeber 1925:732; Sherer 1965:16; Spicer 1952:324), noting the lack of ritual and visible symbolism that characterized membership in Mohave and Quechan clans, have been led to think of these as relatively unimportant. Clan membership is thought to have regulated exogamous marriage within most of the River Yuman tribes (Bee 1963:222; Devereux 193'):53, Fathauer, 1951x:129; Forbes 1965:36; Forde 1931:145; Spier 1953:325), and it is systematically related to the custom of addressing females by their clan names (Devereux 1961:130, Forbes 1965:38, Kroeber 1925:732; Sherer 1965:65). The Mohave were unable to relinquish clan naming because it was an important internal characteristic of the process by which they maintained their collective identity, as will be shown later.

In 1911 the Fort Mohave Reservation was established for the Mohave Valley group (Stewart 1969x:263). The land allotment system was employed by the Department of the Interior to partition extended families on Mohave rancherias into nuclear families; these were to become the new units of autonomous land use (cf. Devereux

1961:68). This transition may have been accepted by the Mohave with a minimum of adjustment since few of their rancherias had been local corporate groups in the past (Spier 1953:325), and perhaps because their wage-based economy in nonagricultural pursuits at this time might have made it easier to maintain the nuclear family without continuous cooperation of relatives, as Bee (1963:214) has observed among modern Quechans. Those agricultural Mohave on both reservations who later found that farming by nuclear families was unprofitable compared to land-lease arrangements with outside farmers may have leased their lands and regrouped into extended family households as did the Quechans (Bee 1963:212). Retention of the warrior status in this period is evident in the eagerness of middle-aged males to serve in the First World War (Devereux 1961:520). The assassination of shamans by warriors began to decline around 1890 on the Colorado River Reservation and after 1905 on the Fort Mohave Reservation (Devereux 1961:407). Witch-killings were reported up to 1925, but the trend may reflect a decline in the incidence of epidemics attributed to them and Devereux's (1961:521) assertion that it no longer provided the "morale-building aggression of warfare." Legal sanctions were instituted in an attempt to end witch-killing on both reservations by the end of this period (Stewart 1973:320). Shamanism may have become an important symbol of opposition on the Colorado River Reservation after 1910. It became common practice for shamans to treat Mohave patients before or after hospitalization on the reservation despite the fact that adequate native health care was provided from this date onward (Devereux 1961:174, 478).

Tribesmen intensified their "ceremonial transfer of Mohave property to the land of the dead" as early as 1903, when they reportedly began to purchase American manufactured goods expressly to destroy at funerals as an expression of "antagonistic acculturation" (Devereux 1961:317, 349, 521). Funereal destruction was no longer restricted to the property of the deceased alone.

Redefinition of Mohave identity, 1930-1965

During the third and final phase under consideration, 1930 to 1965, the Mohave experienced both directed and nondirected changes. The latter affected not only the political and economic status of the tribe but their settlement as well, and these changes seem to have been readily absorbed. In 1931 the boarding school was closed and a substantial number of families moved from the Fort Mohave Reservation across the river to the public school area of Needles, California (Sherer 1965:10). Public education of the Mohave Valley faction thereafter was apparently effective, because all but the aged possessed an elementary education and could speak, read, and write English by 1965 (Sherer 1965:12). This goal may have been attained by the Indian Agency School one or two decades earlier on the Colorado River Reservation (cf. Devereux 1961:232).

Completion of the Parker Dam in 1938 caused Lake Havasu to flood the farms of those who remained on the Fort Mohave Reservation, and they too moved to Needles or to the Colorado River Reservation (Stewart 1969a:263). By 1965 about 70 percent of the Fort Mohave Indians had regrouped at Mohave Village in the Mohave Valley (Sherer 1965:12). The Chernehuevi were forced to abandon their Chemehuevi Valley Reservation that was also inundated by the flood of 1938, and this tribe moved south to reside permanently with the other Mohave faction on the Colorado River Reservation (Stewart 1969a:262). The availability of work on the Parker Dam project coupled with wage and agricultural price inflation during these years made manufactured goods more accessible to the Mohave, who were regarded as "acculturated in most external ways" (Devereux 1961:111, 222, 506; italics mine). At the end of this phase the Mohave and Chemehuevi began to profit from leases of reservation land to outside commercial farming interests and later from the tourist development of their Bluewater Marine Park (Stewart 1969a:263).

The trend toward material acquisition was accelerated by an economic sanction that was directly applied to compel the Mohave to accumulate capital. In the 1930s families continued to impoverish themselves periodically through massive destruction of personal property at funerals, despite their awareness of property inheritance among whites (Devereux 1961:449, 450 453). The government began to interfere with this process by withholding house-construction loans from the Mohave, but any residence owned outright by them was still burned at the death of its adult inhabitant during this decade (Devereux 1961:453). Property destruction gradually became limited to the personal effects of the deceased (Fathauer 1951a:124), as was the case with the Quechans (Bee 1963:221), but among the Mohave some of it still had considerable value (Devereux 1961:453).

Continuation of the law against shaman-killing had an uncertain impact on the incidence of Mohave witchcraft during the third phase. Many natives believed that witchcraft had increased to the extent that "the tribe was threatened with extinction" (Devereux 1961:197), although Devereux (1961:316) thought the law had the opposite effect of reducing its incidence. Mohave belief in witchcraft and the practice of shamanism is still very much alive in the late twentieth century, particularly among older adults, although the young and the highly acculturated participate to a lesser degree (Devereux 1961:234, 320; Stewart 1973:322).

The status of warrior appears to have been retained by the tribe during this period. Braves believed to be potential shaman-killers were identified on the Fort Mohave Reservation in the late 1930s (Devereux 1961:149). Some of these may have dispatched their victims by more subtle means than previously or induced their suicide through severe physical punishment; at least one outright killing is known to have occurred during these years (Devereux 1961:398-99, 402, 412). Many middle-aged males attempted to enlist in the armed services during the Second World War as they had in the First (Devereux 1961:520).

Mohave Resistance to an Aspect of Political Incorporation

I am unable to present information on the oppositional aspect of Mohave political incorporation in terms of the conditions mentioned by Spicer (1971:97), because the extent to which the reservation system of political organization contributed to the oppositional formation of Mohave identity remains unstudied. The Mohave are known to have exercised control over ethnic membership in their polity, however, despite attempts by the Department of the Interior to redefine this membership. The Mohave allegedly resented wartime internment of Japanese-Americans on the Colorado River Reservation, because these Nisci had come against their will (Devereux 1961:319). This resentment was expressed again in 1952 to successfully end the postwar transplantation of landless Hopi and Navajo to that reservation (Stewart 1969x:263). In sum, the Mohave developed reasonably well defined symbols of identity—funereal cremation, warrior and shaman statuses, and clan naming and affiliation—that differentiated the tribe from the Anglo-Americans who sponsored or endorsed the reservation programs that the Mohave opposed.

The Mohave Identity System

Mohave Symbols of Collective Identity

The first component of two that define the Mohave identity system consists of a set of collective identity symbols of the oppositional type that everybody commonly believes when displayed alone or in association with other symbols. These collective identity symbols are meaningful in that the Mohave persistently identify themselves by reference to them, and they assume these were also held by their ancestors (cf. Spices 1971:796). The Mohave remain highly conscious of their tribal identity and their unity (Devereux 1961:521), unlike a number of other River Yuman groups in the late twentieth century (Kroeber 1920:482; Dobyns, Ezell, and Ezell 1963; Kelly 1972). Two of the three Mohave collective identity symbols are not materially visible nor are they often ritually or liturgically displayed (Devereux 1961:319; Fathauer 1951x:72).

Mohave clan affiliation and naming is the first collective identity symbol because it constitutes the basis of their marriage system, the institutional means by which they maintain their identity (cf. Spices 1971:799). In order to understand the extreme importance of clan affiliation in Mohave thought about marriage (Fathauer 1951x:131; Spier 1953:324), it is necessary to define the different marriage patterns that are recognized by them. The most persistent entity uses a marriage system that is partly, rather than completely, closed. This condition implies that there are two marriage patterns in these societies: marriage within the group and marriage outside of it. To understand how marriage embodies common belief about Mohave identity, the variety of rules that characterize their marriages must be accounted for, rather than simply assigning one marriage pattern to the tribe (Adams and Kasakoff 1975:168). A description of marriage within the tribe requires that clan exogamy be distinguished from clan endogamy. Marriage outside of it entails a difference between two alternative forms that depends on the sex of the Mohave spouse involved. In effect, the tribe employs rules for making four kinds of marriage (ef. Devereux 1961:142).

Clan exogamy is the preferred form of marriage among the Mohave themselves, for it is considered to be an expression of "nationalism" (Devereux 1939:510). This practice systematically perpetuates their collective identity in a way that will be discussed later. Descent among the Mohave is the basis for clan exogamy, because patrilineal membership in a clan provides the orientation for initiating this first type of marriage; that is, the clan itself is the exogamous unit (Devereux 1939: 513; Kroeber 1925:732). This observation was contradicted later by Fathauer (1951x:138), who inferred that lineages within clans were the exogamous units.. This discrepancy will be examined later. The Mohave do not mention the fact that clan exogamy is and has been a highly informal union that is practically devoid of ritual. For the most part, this kind of marriage simply involves the establishment of a common residence by the couple after a casual affair, regardless of the previous marital status of either spouse (Devereux 1961:358). Despite the rigor with which they reckon partners, each Mohave marries, on the average, three times and has numerous sexual relationships with various partners who are permitted to do so from puberty to maturity (cf. Fathauer 1951 u). Females usually take the initiative in forming or dissolving both marriages and extramarital relationships. Both spouses retain the right to divorce, and the union can be dissolved at will by either partner. I do not know if this form of serial monogamy has been discouraged among the Mohave through the increased marriage license and divorce fees that have made temporary marriage among the Quechans (Bee 1963:225) costly. The offspring of clan-exogamous unions are called "real. Mohave," and all adult statuses later become available to them (Fathauer 1951x:124).

Clan endogamy is considered to be a form of "incest," that is "antinationalistic" (Devereux 1939:529). This practice entails the "social death" (Devereux 1961:357) of the bride through forfeiture of her membership in her lineage and her clan. Thereafter she is regarded by her kinsmen as "no longer one of them" and simply as "the wife of her husband" (Fathauer 1951x:137). Endogamy imposes an additional punishment, for each spouse loses the right to divorce, and permanent union is expected in contrast to casual exogamous marriage (Devereux 1961:360; Fathauer 1951x:137). The offspring's access to all of the varieties of adult status is not restricted in principle, but it seems to have been in practice, for the children of endogamous marriage were regarded by the Mohave as likely to practice shamanism by adulthood (see the case studies in Devereux 1961). It seems possible (although unlikely) for the Mohave to engage in this type of marriage outside of the tribe with spouses who are affiliated with specific Quechan, Cocopa and Yavapai clans that the Mohave consider to be equivalent to certain of their own (Devereux 1961:131, 144, 207).

The third and fourth types of marriage were made outside of the tribe, unlike the first and second which occurred among the Mohave themselves. For the most part, the Mohave regard tribal exogamy as miscegenation which threatens the tribal marriage cycle (Fathauer 1954:108) and erodes their collective identity (Devereux 1961:443). Although both forms of marriage within the tribe are mythologically foreordained (Devereux 1961:363), Mohave marriage with aliens is not. This suggests that tribal exogamy is of comparatively recent origin and reflects cultural adjustment to historical factors, such as warfare, which may have been stimulated by the Spanish colonial slave trade (Stewart 1965:188), and acculturation, which characterized Mohave relations with Americans after 1850 (Stewart 1973:263).

The Mohave distinguish two types of tribal exogamy according to the cultural identity of the male spouse. Marriage between a Mohave male and an alien female appears to be the more tolerable form, because it extends patrilineal membership in the clan to offspring and access to all adult statuses (Fathauer 1951x:88). Prior to 1850 this type of union involved concubinage in which female war captives were given to aged, single Mohave males. The reluctance of young and middle-aged Mohave males to engage in war-captive concubinage largely negated the possibility of divorce from this type of union (Fathauer 1954:100). The reason for this will be given later. The less tolerable type of tribal exogamy involves alien males and Mohave females. While the right to make a union of this kind is not formally recognized by the tribe, the right of the Mohave female to divorce is emphasized by her kinsmen. Lack of patrilineal membership in a Mohave clan formerly marked the offspring of these marriages as victims of infanticide (except in the rare instance in which the father happened to be a member of a Quechan, Cocopa, or Yavapai clan that has its counterpart among the Mohave, as previously mentioned). Since the tribe does not possess a mechanism of adopting the offspring of unions with alien males into the Mohave mother's clan, the children were called "not real Mohave" (Devereux 1941:578; 1961:131; Fathauer 1951 u:88). This situation has been summarized succinctly:

> In brief, both adults and children are asked to think of the child first and foremost as a link in tribal continuity. By contrast, children whose fathers refuse to recognize them belong to no gens and therefore do not qualify as individuals capable of ensuring social and tribal continuity. Hence, such children can be destroyed without a biological loss to the tribe .... By contrast, the full-blood defective, whose paternity was not in dispute was, at least in principle, viewed as a bonafide link in tribal continuity ... who could not be killed without violating a major value of Mohave culture (Devereux 1961:258-59).

These marriage patterns suggest that the persistence of Mohave identity depends to some extent on the biological continuity of the tribe; note that Spicer (1971:796) does not consider this to be an essential characteristic of identity maintenance.

Mohave shaman and warrior statuses constitute the second collective identity symbol because the activities of each either promoted the tribe's sense of well-being or disrupted it. In addition to their self-appointed task of defending the tribe in aboriginal times, warriors benefited the Mohave by killing malevolent witches; certain shamans performed this latter task as well (Devereux 145-46, 246, 265). The shamans' ability to cure unfamiliar disorder than those which they cause is also recognized as a common benefit (Devereux 1961:179, 339). On the other hand, both shaman-killing warriors and shamans are believed to practice malevolent, disruptive witchcraft (Devereux 1961:45). Shaman-killing warriors and shamans are also similar in that both are believed to practice clan endogamy and vicarious suicide (Devereux 1961:46, 285, 472).

The third identity symbol is the funeral rite; both its configuration and its meaning have been studied from the perspective of ethnopsychiatry by Devereux. This ritual expression of collective identity among the tribe embodies a mythologically foreordained set of common beliefs about relations between living and dead Mohave. For example, mythological precedent is invoked to contrast their funeral behavior—emotional intensity that is followed by forgetting the dead—to that of the Anglo-Americans, emotional control and remembrance of their deceased (Devereux 1961:190).

The Mohave attempt to sever all connections with their dead in three ways. First, mention of the names of all deceased relatives and ancestors is prohibited. This practice is rigid to the extent that its violation is regarded as the cultural expression of insanity among them (Devereux 1961:190).

Second, the Mohave believe that those who predecease them pass through a sequence of metamorphoses which make them elusive to mourners who wish to join them unless they too die shortly thereafter. This provides the mandate for the ritual attempt at suicide by close relatives of the deceased on his funeral pyre (Devereux 1961:432, 435; Stewart 19476:147). Devereux (1961:363) noted that the only other type of ritual suicide in Mohave culture occurred at the celebration of clan endogamy. This was the only formal marriage ceremony among the Mohave, who occasionally celebrated it as a mock funeral with a pyre during the nineteenth century. Its purpose was to convert the consanguineal tic between the couples' families to an affinal linkage. This involved the observance of the mourning ritual (including the destruction of the groom's property) by both sides as an expression of the social death of each spouse prior to their assumption of their new married status (Devereux 1961:309, 358, 363-64, 369; Fathauer 1951a:137).

Third, the Mohave are strongly linked to their dead through property that had been loosely shared, such that the "difference between ownership and use... is minimal" (Devereux 1961:446-

47). Severance of this material connection has been discussed earlier as an aspect of the oppositional process. Belief in the necessity of property destruction by the principals involved and also of appropriate behavior by funerary officials and observers is enforced by fear of a particular type of insanity that is said to result from noncompliance (Devereux 1961:179, 190; Stewart 1947b:148).

Spheres of Participation in the Mohave Identity System

The second component of the Mohave identity system is more complex than the first. The Mohave maintain their collective identity by participating in two and perhaps three of the spheres of common understanding that have been isolated by Spicer (1971:799).

The Mohave participate in the language sphere through their use of a "terminology of opposition" (Spicer 1971:799) by which they maintain a boundary between themselves and the dominant group. Their common modes of reference have changed, however, during each historical phase of their incorporation. From 1859 to 1890, for example, the Mohave appear to have verbally distinguished themselves from Anglo-Americans, whom they labeled apen kutcthamy ("beaver eater"), which probably identified these "most foreign and dangerous of aliens" as the source of "foreign disease" (Devereux 1961:45, 135).

During the subsequent phase, 1890 to 1930, the Mohave expanded their terminology of opposition by referring to both whites and blacks as hi:ko (a term of unknown meaning). Inclusion of the latter group probably resulted from exposure of the tribe to a black regiment of federal cavalry that was stationed on the edge of the Colorado River Reservation at the turn of the century. In contrast to their attitude toward whites during the period, the Mohave were not thought to be prejudiced toward blacks, although this label may possibly have identified them (and whites) as sources of venereal disease (Devereux 1961:135, 456).

The Mohave again expanded their oppositional terminology during the most recent phase, 1930 to 1965. The younger and more acculturated tribesmen adopted into their native language the labels by which the dominant group referred to itself, namely, "American" or "white." Continuing opposition is evident, however, in the fact that these Mohave readily accepted friendly whites but expected them to conform to Mohave standards of behavior. The highest praise bestowed on a conforming individual occurred when he was considered to be "really a Mohave and not a white man at all" (Devereux 1961:135, 137, 523).

Participation in the moral sphere may be the most important means by which the tribe maintains its identity. Mohave dreaming, stereotypy, and xenophobia express three respective sets of values that pertain to ideal behavior among themselves versus that which they attribute to others. The Mohave believe that every human activity has a mythological precedent (Devereux 1961:53). Their culture hero Mastamho established this precedent by teaching the Mohave how to dream of power that is necessary to successfully conduct all daily activities, especially those of reproduction and survival (Devereux 1961:47, 161). Dream power does not change in the form in which it is given to Mohave who seek it from one generation to the next, a fact which reflects the essentially static nature of their cosmology (Devereux 1961:12; Fathauer 1954:98). Myths also remind the Mohave that their acquisition of power by means other than dreaming is a cause of insanity among them, and also that insanity will result from an individual's refusal to use dream power once it has been acquired (Devereux 1961:53, 57). The degree to which an individual is able to modify Mohave "dream culture" depends on his ability to convince fellow tribesmen that his dream power is genuine, and also upon the extent to which his dream is congruent with the traditional patterns (Devereux 1961:141).

The Mohave have a stereotypic view of ideal behavior among themselves. During one historical phase, however, the values that underlay this stereotype appear to have been transferred from association with one collective identity symbol to another; this will be discussed later.

Xenophobia or fear of strangers is a major moral theme that conditions Mohave relations with all other ethnic groups including their former allies, the Quechans. Intimate physical contact with non-Mohave that involved combat, sexual intercourse, food-sharing, or handling of material possessions was perceived by the Mohave to cause their most basic psycho-physiological disorder, which they termed either "enemy" or "foreign disease" (Devereux 1961:129, 132; Fathauer 1951a:90). Foreign disease is mythologically foreordained as the prototype of all disorders among the Mohave, who also believe that foreign disease and witchcraft have been the two most prevalent forms of disorder among them (Devereux 1961:32, 135). A third type of contamination, that resulting from Mohave dream interaction with deceased relatives, is termed "ghost disease" (Devereux 1961:21-24; Fathauer 1951c:607; 1954:104). This internally directed form of xenophobia structures another dimension of ideal behavior among the Mohave themselves.

The political sphere of identity maintenance among the Mohave is less well known. Its aboriginal form has been partially reconstructed in relation to Mohave social organization (Fathauer 1951 u), clan affiliation and naming (Sherer 1965), and the reservation system of incorporation (Stewart 1969b). The fragmentary and inferential nature of this information suggests that Mohave participation has been a less important means of identity persistence than the development of common understanding in the areas of language and morals. This imbalanced emphasis is a plausible and effective way to maintain collective identity, according to Spicer (1971:799).

Maintenance of Mohave Identity

Spicer (1971:799) defined the maintenance process in terms of "varying participation [in the language, moral, and political spheres]" and as "fluctuations in the intensity of [participatory] sentiments that are associated with the [collective identity] symbols." His definitions can be made operational to understand Mohave identity maintenance during an incorporation phase by specifying the way that each sphere of participation articulated with each collective identity symbol. Although the Mohave share knowledge of these articulations, not all of them take the form of sentiments that they express as codified statements (cf. Kasakoff 1974:156).

The Reconstructed Maintenance Process, 1859 -1890

Mohave sentiments that articulated participation spheres with collective identity symbols during the initial incorporation phase of 1859 to 1890 are largely inferential in the sense that they were remembered by aged informants during the subsequent phases (Devereux 1961:5, Fathauer 1951a: 127, and Sherer 1965:3 provide examples).

Mohave participation in all three spheres appears to have been linked by the symbol of clan affiliation and naming. Articulation is evident in the moral sphere through the practice of dreaming, for the tribe perceived its common welfare to depend on reservoirs of dream power that were possessed by each clan and which its members gained by dreams of a totemic nature (Devereux 1961:90). Clan exogamy among the Mohave is thought to increase the access of the offspring to clan reservoirs of dream power through bilateral filiation (Fathauer 1951a:90). Fathauer (1951a:90) identified this desire to "perpetuate biological bonds with the ancestors" as the sentiment of "biological and mystical continuity" in Mohave culture. These two threads of continuity were regarded by the Mohave as being intertwined, since there was a tendency to regard certain clans as likely to produce certain offspring who would have certain power dreams (Fathauer 1951a:90). Clan exogamy is thought to have been the predominant form of marriage among the Mohave during this period (Kroeber 1925:732).

Mystical continuity was threatened by the alternative form of marriage within the tribe. Clan endogamy was perceived not only to limit access to dreams (Fathauer 1951 b:274), but also to invert dreampower, and the consequence of this inversion was the practice of malevolent shamanism by either spouse or by their offspring (Devereux 1939:529; 1961:65, 87, 96). These individuals prepared for shamanism by deliberately contracting an endogamous marriage, according to some Mohave informants. Other Mohave believed that the permanence of endogamous marriage, inadvertently prompted one spouse to resent the other. This animosity was manifest when the dissatisfied partner became a shaman in order to bewitch and murder his or her spouse and children (Devereux 1961:59, 87, 199, 285, 373). Clan endogamy is implied to have been rare during this period (Devereux 1961:411, 509).

Mohave stereotypes of behavior among themselves or Anglo-Americans are not known from this period. Xenophobia was strongly articulated with clan affiliation and marriage in terms of moral sentiments about disease. Clan endogamy was said to invoke ghost (?) disease upon all members of two clans which permitted marriage between cross-cousins, for example, or on the lineages within one clan that allowed parallel cousins to marry (Devereux 1961:17, 87, 140, 149:358, 366; Fathauer 1951a:137). Tribal exogamy was associated with foreign disease (Devereux 1961:21, 24, 136; Fathauer 1951c:607, 1954:104), and for this reason it threatened the persistence of Mohave mystical identity because it was said to "weaken the blood" and "disturb continuity with the ancestors" (Fathauer 1951a:90). Marriage outside of the tribe that involved Mohave males and alien females exposed the former to foreign disease that was not inevitably debilitating or fatal (Devereux 1961:137). Nevertheless, this type of union appears to have been restricted to old males, who (being unafraid of the malignant influence because it developed slowly) received female war captives, since young and middle-aged Mohave males were reluctant to contract foreign disease by this means (Devereux 1961:129 Fathauer 1954:100, Stewart 1947a:271). Although the children of aged Mohave fathers and alien mothers possessed membership in Mohave clans they inherited foreign disease from their mothers (Fathauer 1951 a:90) The incidence of these marriages is unknown. Tribal exogamy between Mohave females and alien males exposed the women and her clanless offspring to foreign disease that was implied to have been debilitative or fatal. From 1859 to 1890 halfbreed children of this sort were usually hurled at birth to conceal the evidence from the reservation authorities Devereux 1961:139, 142, 143, 262, 519, 578; Fathauer 1951x:88). The implication is that this type of union was fairly common, perhaps more so than among the Quechans (cf. Bee 1963:224).

The common mode of reference to "real Mohave" children of clan-exogamous unions versus "not real Mohave" halfbreeds, who were unacceptable clanless offspring of Mohave females and alien males, expressed sentiments that articulated the language sphere with clan affiliation. This terminology of social separation probably helped to maintain the internal solidarity of the tribe (cf. Spider 1971:799).

There is weak evidence for clan-affiliated participation in the Mohave political sphere during this phase. As among the Quechans, there seems to have been a prestige-ranking of clans that may have been related to hereditary political positions (cf. Bee 1963:218). Among the Fort Mohave faction, the hereditary great chieftainship is said to have been in possession of the Malika clan, while the Neolge supplied tribal orators, Oach and Gottah provided tribal singers, and so on (Sherer 1965:51). An all-male tribal council is implied to have been in existence on the Colorado River Reservation toward the end of this period (Devereux 1961:189), but whether participation in it was also structured by clan affiliation is unknown. This sphere clearly warrants more study before confident inference can be made.

There is some evidence that the statuses of warrior and shaman were articulated with the moral sphere of participation during this phase, particularly in terms of sentiments that pertained to dreaming and xenophobia. The constructive and destructive potential of both these social types was derived from power dreams (Devereux 1961:304; Fathauer 1951x:102; 19516:274; Stewart 1947x:257). Not only was dream power requisite for the possession of either status (Fathauer 1954:99), but the variety of all available statuses was predetermined in Mohave cosmology; thus "in each generation certain individuals automatically occupied statuses that comprised the social system, but the system itself remained unchanged" (Fathauer 1951!:274). The allegedly high incidence of malevolent witchcraft coupled with the rarity of clan endogamy luring this phase suggests that the latter was not the predominant source of inverted dream power necessary for shamanism. Two other possibilities are likely. One native theory ascribed shamanism to a child's dreams during its fetal stage. These dreams and the consequent power which they engendered were not remembered until its adolescence (Devereux 19(1:60; Stewart 1973:317). During the maturation period, both parents observed the child's behavior to detect clues about his or her future status. The effect of this parental monitoring process was thought to guide tire child toward shamanism (Fathauer 195 la:274, Stewart 1973:316). A competitive native theory of shamanism held that individuals simply acquired certain dream powers which eventually deteriorated and turned against their owners, making them embark behaviorally and psychologically on a course which caused them to be murdered (Devereux 1961:56). In this view, individuals drifted toward shamanism by singing semi-shamanistic songs through which they became healers and eventually witches (Fathauer 1951c:605). The Mohave noted that a shaman often brought about his own death by inciting his victim's relatives to kill him. During the phase in question, these avenging relatives were usually members of the elite group of suicidal mallet-club warriors (Fathauer 1954:104; Stewart 1973:319). It should be recalled that these shaman-killers also tended to practice endogamous marriage and malevolent witchcraft.

The xenophobic sentiment expressed as enemy disease may have intensified between 1870 and 1890 among the warrior segment of the tribe. Combat, the source of enemy disease, was now forbidden to the Mohave until 1917, when they would enlist in the armed forces to serve in France during the First World War. In the absence of violent physical contact with aliens, the Mohave apparently became susceptible to enemy disease by merely dreaming about such encounters (Devereaux 1961:43).

The funeral rite was strongly articulated with all three dimensions of participation in the moral sphere. With regard to dreaming, the Mohave believed that they could interact fearlessly with the ghosts of their deceased relatives until the funereal destruction of property, which occurred five days after death. After this day, ghost-dreaming became dangerous (Devereux 1961:139, 177, 186, 192, 452). The stereotype of postmortem behavior among the Mohave dead was (and is) directly related to the funereal destruction of property. The Mohave altered their image of the deceased from a previously beloved and generous relative to that of a dangerous and acquisitive ghost. The destruction of the material possessions of the dead was believed to satisfy the desire of the deceased to accumulate property, and it prevented the ghost from returning to claim what belonged to it (Devereux 1961:187-88, 445-46). The material possessiveness of the dead was regarded as aggression against the living, and the intense hostility felt toward the dead was manifest in this phase by the tendency to mourn an individual (including placement of his body on the funeral pyre) before death actually occurred (Devereux 1961:446, 452).

Failure to sever all relations with their dead exposed the living to any one of the three kinds of ghost disease that were potentially fatal manifestations of their xenophobia. Contamination resulted from the efforts of their deceased spouses or relatives to lure the living through dreams to the Mohave afterlife (Devereux 1961:21-22, 128, 137-39, 180-83, 4 40, 446).

These were, and continue to be, the basic elements and relationships that compose the Mohave identity system. Subtle but important adjustments occurred during the succeeding historical phases of incorporation that affected the efficiency of the maintenance process, however, and these warrant examination.

Fluctuations in the Intensity of Moral Sentiments, 1890-1930

The reservation system of incorporation may have altered Mohave moral participation in the marriage system of clan affiliation and the funeral rite. The intensity of sentiments about dream power through clan exogamy seems to have declined to the extent that the increasing incidence of clan endogamy among the Mohave was becoming known to other River Yuman tribes by the end of this phase. Simplification and eventual obsolescence of the destructive clan-endogamous wedding ceremony during the period may have progressively weakened the sanction against this type of marriage (Devereux 1961:322, 366, 370). Clan exogamy however, remained the predominant practice (Devereux 1961:411; Kroeber 1925:732). The intensity of xenophobic sentiments about the clanless halfbreed offspring of Mohave females and alien males began to decline; this tendency was reflected in isolated instances in which such children were informally permitted to use (but not adopt) their mother's Mohave clan name (Devereux 1961:131, 143). The fear of foreign disease from this course remained strong, and infanticide was "still an effective barrier to miscegenation, since as late as the 1920s, the reports of the commissioner of Indian Affairs listed fewer halfbreeds among the Mohave and the Yuma [Quechans] than among many other tribes" (Devereux 1961:135). The weakening of this sentiment in regard to clan affiliation may have originated around the turn of the century when the Mohave began to neutralize their fear of foreign disease by pretending that certain likeable whites and other aliens were "really . . . Mohave" (Devereux 1961:134). This practice however, does not seem to have been frequent.

The statuses of shaman and warrior continued to be articulated with the moral sphere in terms of xenophobic sentiments during the second phase. As carriers of foreign disease, those clanless halfbreed offspring who were spared from infanticide were still considered dangerous, and their adult status was usually restricted to the practice of shamanism (Fathauer 1951:a90). As for warriors, Mohave servicemen who returned to the reservations after the First World War were still considered to have been exposed to enemy disease (Devereux 1961:43).

The moral sphere of Mohave participation in the funeral ritual may have involved a stereotypic equivalence of aliens with the ghosts of their kinsmen in that the same kind of behavior was ascribed to each during this phase (Fathauer 1951c:607). For example. the Mohave viewed themselves as "warm" and "generous" to each other with native and white foods and money, although they did not represent themselves this way to Anglo-Americans, whom they viewed as "cold, unethical and grasping"; these violations of their value system were also attributed by the Mohave to their ghosts (Devereux 1961 '79-81, 188, 312).

The intensification of property destruction at funerals during this phase may have been a symbol of Mohave opposition to incorporation, but it also has been linked by Devereux (1961:439, 446, 452) to a simultaneous decline in the incidence of suicide at funerals. Devereux thought that immolation of additional purchased property represented a "compensation to the dead for the mourner's failure to follow him into death." Since the Mohave believe that ghosts are sent to earth to obtain additional property when it is scarce in the "land of the dead" (Devereux 1961:442), it seems equally possible that intensification represented an attempt by the tribe to compensate for the previous scarcity of property available for immolation during the last decades of the preceding phase (1870-1890) when they were poverty-stricken.

In overview, the maintenance process in the moral sphere of participation in the Mohave identity system seems to have involved dynamic equilibrium. Although the symbolic aspects of clan affiliation probably played a lesser role in identity maintenance than before, this trend may. have been offset by the intensification of the funeral rite.

Redefinition of Moral and Political Participation in the Mohave Identity System, 1930-1965

The Mohave increasingly committed themselves to the American cash economy during the third phase of their incorporation. Wage labor reduced the amount of leisure time that was previously available for participation in pantribal ceremonies, such its "Harvest" or "Memorial," which were important occasions for the ritual expression of their collective identity (Devereux 1939:529; 1961:317; Fathauer 1951a:134). These things were accompanied by others of a less visible nature in the moral and political areas of common understanding among the Mohave. Pronounced fluctuations in the intensity of moral and political sentiments that were associated with clan affiliation and the statuses of warrior and shaman lead me to believe that the Mohave probably redefined two spheres of participation in their identity system during this third phase.

Sentiments about the acquisition of dream power that articulate the moral sphere with clan affiliation seem to have been altered. Kroeber reported in 1951 that the "dream core of Mohave culture" remained relatively intact despite "overwhelming acculturation pressures" (Devereux 1961:320). Apparently dream power did not fare as well among the Quechans under later, similar circumstances (Bc: personal communication). Also, Mohave clans appear to have continued their function as reservoirs of dream power that could be acquired or transmitted to offspring by means of marriage within the tribe (Devereux 1961:222). The Mohave were a highly homogeneous population as recently as 1950, and Fathauer (1951x:91) noted that individuals were called "Mohave," and who were therefore unmixed with other groups, were approximately 95 percent fullblood. Which seems to have changed are the kinship criteria that distinguished clan exogamy from endogamy. The traditional definition of clan exogamy given below was operative in 1939:

> Both father's and mother's kin are held to be blood relations, and sexual intercourse, including homosexual relations and sexual

games among children, is prohibited between any ego and his ascendants, descendants, and cousins, including second cousins. Even if no blood relationship can be traced, a person should not have sexual relations with any other belonging to the same gene (Devereux, 1939:5 3).

Fathauer (1950:130) could not confirm this practice by 1946, for some Mohave informants insisted that marriage of spouses having the same name was permissible, provided the relationship was more distant than third cousins on either side, a definition which approximates Quechan exogamy (Bee 1963:22 I). It would seem that clan affiliation was no longer a jural criterion of exogamy versus endogamy among the Mohave, but rather it simply became a de facto criterion that was likely to remain in effect due to the small size of the marriage pool.*

This alteration may have caused some confusion among the Mohave about how clan endogamy was to be defined, however, for "incestuous" marriage was rumored to have been frequent during the late 1930s on the Colorado River Reservation. Clan endogamy was not often recognized by the Mohave during this decade when it involved second cousins at least (Devereux 1961:136, 357, 509). The rise of clan endogamy can also be attributed to two other factors. After 1930 the groom's property was no longer destroyed at clan-endogamous weddings, a change which probably relaxed the sanction against this marriage practice (Devereux 1961:.322). By 1946 most younger and more acculturated Mohave exhibited only partial understanding of their kinship system, and many middle-aged adults were unable to agree on kinship terminology. Moreover, some of the aged did not remember the nomenclature of distant kinship (Fathauer 1951a:127). The same trend was manifest among the Quechans during this phase (Bee 1963:216, 218).

Changes in the intensity and form of foreign-disease psychoses among the Mohave suggest that a relaxation of their xenophobic sentiments about tribal exogamy occurred during this time. Although marriage to non-Mohave continued to be discouraged as late as 1950 (Fathauer 1951 u:87), tribal exogamy increased on the Colorado River Reservation during the 1930s and 1940s, while the incidence of foreign disease did not. This trend may reflect the receptiveness of the younger Mohave there to the newly arrived Chemehuevi in 1938 (Devereux 1961:136, 141, 355). It may also reflect the fact that tribal exogamy now also involved halfbreed Mohave who were believed to lessen the impact of foreign disease upon their fullblood spouses. This modification of sentiment was complemented by a continuation of the traditional belief that clan-affiliated halfbreed offspring of marriages between Mohave males and alien females exposed fullblood tribesmen to foreign disease was not inevitably debilitating or fatal (Devereux 7961:131, 138). Diminished fear of foreign disease was especially evident in the successful effort of an internal reform movement to stop the infanticide of the clanless halfbreed offspring of Mohave females and alien males (Devereux 1948:136; 1961:131). While the Mohave began to de-emphasize their susceptibility to foreign disease through physical contact with aliens, they may well have intensified their belief in contagion by merely dreaming about it (cf. Devereux 1961:137). This same dynamic balance also characterized the shifting intensity of enemy disease sentiment during the first phase of incorporation (1859-1890). The new dream emphasis on foreign disease may explain why it began to be manifested in association with the ghost disease: no longer did it appear as an isolated psychosis. By 1938 no Mohave shaman was known to have been able to cure foreign disease (Devereux 1961:128, 136, 141, 179; Fathauer 1951c:607).

There is some evidence that continuation of clan-affiliated membership in the tribal council on the Fort Mohave Reservation may have involved a redefinition of political participation around 1951. Specifically, women were now able to hold the hereditary offices of their clans (including the council chairmanship) if they were the sole surviving adults (Sherer 1965 provides examples). Women were also mentioned in an undefined but possibly similar political context on the Colorado River Reservation in 1933 (Devereux 1961:157).

The Mohave may have redefined a sentiment about dream power and also a stereotype that altered their moral sphere of participation in the statuses of shaman and warrior. The incidence of shamanism was alleged by the Mohave to have increased after 1945, and the status continued to be generally accepted through the 1950s (Devereux 1961:320). Yet in 1946 Fathauer (1951x:102) found that the average Mohave did not have power dreams of the sort necessary to become a shaman (or a warrior); instead, he dreamed of personal matters that were not tribal in scope. This discrepancy strongly suggests that traditional clan-based concepts of dream power were no longer relevant to the practice of witchcraft (cf. Devereux 1961:68, 287). In fact, Wallace (1947:256) observed that the acculturation of Mohave children in schools and hospitals interfered with their interest in shamanistic dreaming to such an extent that few members of the younger generation experienced power dreams of this sort by 1947. During these years, some of the shamans were likely to have been the clanless halfbreed offspring of Mohave mothers and alien fathers mentioned earlier. This may account for McNichols's (1944:170) contemporary observation that Mohave mothers frequently conditioned the kinds of adolescent dreams that characterized future shamans through their own expectations and by reactions to their children's behavior. In other words, these shamans probably based their practice upon dreams of a personal sort. If shamanistic dream power was involved at all, it was likely to have been derived exclusively from matrilateral clan reservoirs.

The Mohave also redefined other moral sentiments that were associated with the status of warrior. During the previous phase (1890-1930), the set of values about ideal behavior among Mohave males involved sentiments of warmth, generosity, strength, and silence. After 1930, however, males apparently began to view themselves as "sober," "stoical," and "stolid," qualities which they considered to be military virtues and which they ascribed to their nineteenth-century ancestors (Devereux 1961:299, 427, 514). Devereux (1961:299-300) has convincingly argued that this new stereotype was absorbed by the Mohave from popular Western literature and film as an expression of their "antagonistic acculturation." He postulated that these newly constituted ideals were used by the Mohave not only to judge conformity among themselves, but also to successfully deceive whites into viewing the Mohave as unemotional after the tribesmen began to suppress the affective content of their communication with them . The new self-image was a symbol of Mohave opposition to incorporation. Xenophobic sentiments associated with the status of warrior seem to have been relaxed insofar as no Mohave shaman was known to be able to cure enemy disease, even though tribesmen returning to the Colorado River Reservation from the Second World War were considered to have been exposed to it. This psychosis was treated in the reservation hospital or cured by a Quechan shaman (Devereux 1961:43).

The xenophobic sentiments of ghost disease that structured part of the moral sphere of Mohave participation in their funeral rites were similarly relaxed. As was the case with foreign and enemy diseases, no shaman was able to cure any of the ghost psychoses by 1934; victims had recourse to the reservation hospital alone (Devereux 1961: 136, 142).

In sum, the dream-oriented framework of tribal identity persisted into the third historical phase, but the critical maintenance mechanism of dream power seems to have been activated less frequently. This is inferred from a decline in the practice of clan exogamy, which had programmatically enhanced the acquisition of dream power. Sentiments that promoted this pattern of marriage and discouraged the other forms were probably relaxed as the result of acculturation, as were Mohave sentiments against inter-ethnic relationships. Although they remained susceptible to all of their xenophobic psychoses, the Mohave were no longer able to cure these themselves; instead they relied upon Anglo-American medical services or those of a Quechan shaman.

The clan-affiliated structure of political participation is known to have persisted on one Mohave reservation through redefinition of membership in its tribal council. Mohave belief in shamanism may also have persisted through redefinition of membership among practitioners of witchcraft. Finally, Mohave males altered their self-image to oppose further incorporation efforts. The persistence of this moral aspect of Mohave identity also involved a redefinition of membership because military ideals were applied to the behavior of all tribesmen, and not only to those who thought of themselves as warriors.

STRATEGIES FOR PERSISTENCE OF IDENTITY

The historical continuity of tribal identity among the Mohave is reasonably well-documented, and for this reason reflection upon it may yield insight into a typology of persistent cultural systems. I suggest that the Mohave possess a type of identity persistence that has diagnostic features. These are simply described below; no attempt has been made to compare or contrast them with criteria aspects of other types of identity persistence.

There are two outstanding external characteristics of the Mohave identity system. After their military defeat, the Mohave chose to resist initial American attempts at forced partial incorporation by exaggerating traditional behaviors associated with certain collective identity symbols instead of' initiating a revitalization movement. According to Spicer's (1971:799) model, nativistic movements restore the political sphere of participation (in an identity system) which has disintegrated as the result of military defeat or repressive incorporation. Prior to such revitalization, however, Spicer believes that collective identity may persist through compensatory participation in the moral or language spheres. Intensification seems to be an alternative to revitalization when the moral sphere consists of values that are antithetical to the concepts of ancestral restoration found in revitalization movements. Intensification movements deserve more study (cf. Vogt 1961:326,).

The second external characteristic of Mohave identity is the compartmental display and manipulation of the tribe's most important symbol of its collective identity—clan affiliation and naming. These practices were retained in opposition to the comprehensive program of forced, directed change that was instituted on both Mohave reservations during the second phase of their incorporation. The tribe's strategy of identity persistence has certain elements in common with the compartmentalization of collective identity symbols in the Eastern Pueblos (cf. Dozier 1961:175-78; Spicer 1961 h:532-33).

The Mohave identity system also has several internal characteristics that may be diagnostic of its type. For the most part, Mohave collective identity symbols are not ritually or liturgically displayed. The least visible of these symbols—clan affiliation and naming—masked the institutional means of social relations (specifically marriage) by which the Mohave maintained participation in their system of meanings. Spicer (1971:799) noted that the institutional mechanism is a poorly known component of identity systems; I suggest that this is so because it is part of a collective identity symbol that is deeply embedded in one or more areas of common understanding. In the case of the Mohave, the relationship between marriage patterns and clan affiliation becomes clear only when the moral sentiments of dreaming and xenophobia are elucidated. It is possible that persistent identity systems of the Mohave type depend on biological continuity more than is realized; if this is so, then it would seem to be a critical weakness of the maintenance process. Tribal exogamy was no less responsible for the erosion of Mohave identity than the incorporation efforts of the reservation authorities.

Xenophobia may also be an integral aspect of moral participation in this type of persistent cultural system. Among the Mohave this mechanism remained unchanged longer than any other because of self-stabilizing fluctuations of dynamic equilibrium in the intensity of its various sentiments. That this insularity mechanism was the only focus of deliberate internal reform among the Mohave nay be symptomatic of normal but extensive adjustments in other areas of this type of persistent cultural system. It is possible that super-stable mechanisms of this sort arc likely to become dysfunctional; Mohave xenophobia, for example, ultimately increased the dependency of the tribe on the medical services of the incorporative group.

*For example, approximately 63 males and 76 females between the ages of 18 and 40 made up the marriage pool of Mohave on the Colorado River Reservation circa 1945 (Fathauer 1951x:18). Every individual was affiliated with any one of perhaps twenty-two Mohave clans, a fact which implies that the number of potential marriage partners in each was small. For this reason, the likelihood of carrying a third or fourth patrilateral cousin who was also a member of the same clan seems low; that is, endogamous marriages were more likely to involve matrilateral cousins. The situation is less clear in the Fort Mohave Reservation during this phase. It is known that seven clans became extinct between 1925 and 1961, leaving only two-thirds (15/22) of them to partition the marriage pool there (Sherer 1965 provides the list of clans). The effect of this diminishment upon a small, closed group of potential sixruses would perhaps also bias endogamy toward the practice of marrying matrilateral cousins. My assumption may he untenable in both cases, because the tribal marriage pool on each reservation was not closed due to intermarriage between them. Frequent intermarriage might have offset these biases such that endogamy was equally likely to involve isobilateral relatives.

Certain facets of identity maintenance among the Mohave probably characterize other types of persistent cultural systems as well. For example, the two nuclear Mohave statuses of warrior and shaman were shown to have complementary and interdependent functions. From a systemic perspective, it seems inevitable that redefinition of membership in one would lead to a similar iteration of the other. Other examples of Mohave resistance to incorporation in the language and moral spheres of participation in their identity system might characterize other types. For example, when the Mohave adopted the language modes of reference that Anglo-Americans used to distinguish themselves from other groups, the tribe encoded these terms with ethnic stereotypes in their moral sphere that were not readily decipherable to whites unless they were already familiar with moral aspects of common understanding among the Mohave.

Certain aspects of Mohave stereotypy might also characterize other persistent identity systems. Specially noteworthy is the fact that the Mohave stereotype of the incorporating group differed according to the identity system context in which they projected it. In the linguistic context of common understanding, Anglo-Americans were implicitly identified as sources of disease. By contrast the material acquisitiveness of Anglo-Americans was equated by the Mohave with the behavior of their deceased relatives in the context of the funeral ceremony. Finally, the Mohave seized upon a white stereotype of themselves when it could be used to maintain their psychological insularity. The dominant group had successfully altered technological, linguistic, and political aspects of Mohave life, but it had not yet deciphered Mohave personality. The tribe used this means to to prevent it from doing so, and I suspect that this strategy is also to be found in other persistent identity systems.

Photo by Jeffrey L. Garton

Ah-Ve-Koov-o-Tut, Ancient Home of the Mojave

by Charles F. Thomas, Jr.

Reprinted with permission of *Desert Magazine.*

When the white man moved into the Southwest and took over much of the hunting range of the Mojave Indians and confined the tribesmen to reservations, the promise was made that adequate water would be furnished for irrigation. Seventy-five years passed before that promise was completely fulfilled for the Indians on the Colorado River Indian reservation at Parker. But just before the war a great dam and diversion works were completed—and today the lands in this fertile valley of the Colorado hold the promise of a secure and comfortable future not only for the Mojave and Chemehuevi, but for thousands of other Indians in the Southwest.

Otasha and I stood on the bluff overlooking the newest of the white man's five dams in the lower Colorado river—the Headgate Rock dam two miles north of Parker, Arizona.

For more than 100 years Otasha had lived by the Colorado, first named Rio del Tizon, the Firebrand River, by Melchior Diaz a year after its discovery by Alarcon in 1540. The aged Mojave had seen the river in all its moods—a mad raging torrent at one season, a sluggish stream that threatened to dry up at others.

I was rather proud of the dam and diversion works Uncle Sam's engineers had built here for the benefit of the Colorado River Indians. But Otasha was non-committal. He had seen too many failures in the government's efforts to irrigate the Indian lands in the great fertile valley that comprises the Colorado River Indian reservation.

"Yes, Mebbeso, this time white man do pretty good job. We see!"

Always, until Boulder dam was completed, the Colorado had been a muddy stream, oftentimes described as "too thick to drink but too thin to plow."

Good fishing and hunting and a mild winter climate had provided here an ideal home for desert Indians. Thousands of acres along its shores, densely wooded with cottonwood, willow and mesquite furnished shade, shelter and game through the seasons, with wood for their crudely constructed houses and fuel for their fires. For countless centuries his tribesmen had farmed, in their fashion, the lowlands of this American Nile, planting crops in areas which had been previously inundated and in dry seasons laboriously carrying water in ollas for irrigation.

"Otasha, how long have you lived here?" Otasha gazed away across the valley, pondering an answer to my question. I could imagine him looking back in memory through the vista of years, in much the same manner as he looked over his home-land, gauging the span of time from important events occurring in Indian life.

"I do not know. All my life. What does a year mean to Indians? Our people come to this land. We live a while. Then we go away. We fish, we hunt, we grind nuts or corn or wheat for meal. We eat. We are happy. We do not measure a year. For a long, long time my people have lived here."

It was difficult to believe the wiry, erect Mojave had seen the passing of a hundred or more years. I asked him regarding his early recollections of the Colorado.

"Yes," he declared, "I was just a boy but I

Two Mojave Indians. He-re-in-ye and his wife Oach, photographed at the starting of Headgate Rock dam construction as one of the engineers was telling them about the project. He-re-in-ye is believed to be over 100 years in age. Photo by William Fox of the Metropolitan Water District.

remember when many white soldiers first come to this country. Old soldiers from Mexico leave and new soldiers come. My father told me of soldiers who come long time ago always looking for gold. Soldiers with axes and spears. They make slaves of Indian men and women. My people do not like to fight. My people have not cared for gold." He pointed to the south. "I saw white men bring camellia. They do not like to swim the river. Some camels drown in the river. Our people did not know animals like that live. Many strange things the white man bring. I see the first steam-boat on the river. Indians run away and say The devil is coming! He blows fire and smoke from his face and kicks water with his feet!'"

Thus he definitely set the date of his birth as prior to the time of acquisition of the territory by the United States or the first journeys of the camels through the desert and the coming of the early day steamboats to the Colorado in the 'fifties. Stories of the camels are legend to us today but the steamers are remembered by many.

An act of congress passed in March, 1865, established the Colorado River Indian reservation from a part of the domain of Arizona and California. It was composed of about 75,000 acres and extended up-stream from Halfway Bend near Ehrenberg to a rocky river point then known as Corner Rock, including within its bounds all land lying between that line and the river, together with certain portions west of the Colorado. This promontory has later come to be known as

Portal of the old tunnel bored through Head gate rock in 1868; first diversion of water from the lower Colorado for irrigation purposes. The tunnel was in use only a short time. Otasha, left, and Frank Homer of the Mojave tribe, both were living when this tunnel was bored.

Headgate Rock.

President U. S. Grant, in 1873, increased the reservation to 210,000 acres, of which about 150,000 acres were bottom lands. Monument peak, the outstanding land-mark of the entire region was chosen as the northern boundary point of the reservation. (See story of first scaling of Monument Peak in April, 1940, issue of Desert Magazine.) In 1915 the reservation was reduced by 16,000 acres by order of President Wilson while more recently it has been increased 19,000 acres.

With its establishment Col. Charles Poston, Superintendent of Indian Affairs in Arizona, hoped to bring about a grouping thereon of the tribes of Yuma, Yavapais, Hualpais, Chemehuevi and Mojave Indians who inhabited the western part of Arizona and southern Nevada. Col. Poston had as his assistant George W. Leihy, of La Paz, who later became superintendent but was killed during a quarrel in 1866 by a small band of Hualpais and Yavapais. George Dent was the appointed superintendent. Herman Ehrenberg, pioneer of Ehrenberg, was selected as the first agent of the Mojaves.

But centralizing and controlling tribes who had been free to wander as they wished presented serious problems. These tribes had been normally peaceful, warring only against roving bands of Apaches or Yaquis who occasionally came up from the southeast on raiding expeditions. Against the mistreatment of the Spaniards they had been slow to anger or attempt to avenge their oppressions. Even with the later inconsiderations of the Americans they seldom became resentful. Most of the promises of the government were accepted with childlike faith.

The restricting of these Indians to a limited reservation called for more productive farming methods than in the former period when the Indian could range far and wide and fend for himself.

A. F. Waldemar, a civil engineer employed by the United States, suggested a canal be constructed from which the Indians could irrigate their crops. Surveys and estimates were made and sent to Washington and early in the year 1867 congress appropriated $50,000 to construct an irrigating system for the reservation. This was the first money to be appropriated by the government for any irrigation project. Late in that same year work was begun and continued until June, 1868.

"Did you work on the canal?" I asked Otasha.

"No. Not then. My father sometimes worked. The white men promised to pay Indians 50 cents a day and feed them. But Indians never got money. Just got little pieces of meat and Indians have to grind meal for flour. Young men not like to work that way. But we fish and hunt game to eat. The soldiers have horses to ride but the Indians do all the work digging ditch with shovels."

Curiously I checked up on the amount of canal excavated that first year and from old records found five miles had been constructed. It was stated that at times more than 300 Indians were engaged in the work.

In 1868 an additional $50,000 was appropriated and the work continued. A headgate was constructed, the canal enlarged and in July, 1870, water was diverted to the canal. "White man's job then not good like this," reminiscently said Otasha. "They build big box from trees but river washed it out and much water run into canal. Many farms flooded. Much canal washed away and water go back to the river. Many times Indians and white men try to get water for land. The river is like a wild animal. It does not like to be put in a cage!"

In 1870, Lt. Col. Andrews, new Superintendent of Indian Affairs, examined the project and recommended tunneling through Corner Rock and constructing a headgate at its upper portal. Work was commenced, with moneys provided in 1872, and four tunnels were driven, totaling 4152 feet in length. The tunnel through Corner Rock was the shortest, being only 430 feet long, but cut through solid rock.

"White men come from mines to do much of the work in the tunnels," Otasha replied in answer to a query regarding that part of the work. ""They get money. Agents want Indians to work for board and ask for soldiers to make them work. Indians do not like this way of white men but help make the tunnels. At last everything is finished. White men and Indians have great feast and powwow. Many men get drunk on whiskey. The Great One (chieftain) of the Mojaves opened the gate. The water goes into the tunnel. Indians and white men run to other end of tunnel to watch water come out. For many hours the water run into canal and go toward farms. Then tunnels fall in and water stops! Indians do not have water again. Next season white men fix tunnels. Tunnels fall in again. Lots of water in river. No water on farms."

The difficulties caused by the washing out of the unprotected timber supports and resultant cave-ins of the tunnels caused the abandonment of the tunnel plan in 1876. Several wells had been dug on the farms and plenty of water encountered but no means existed for pumping or raising water to the little farms except with crude ropes and buckets.

A large water wheel was constructed in 1879 and mounted upon two barges on the river but one of the barges sank and the wheel was destroyed. Again in 1880 a larger wheel was built but a sudden rise of the river wrecked it soon after it was placed in operation. No further attempts were made to irrigate until 1883 when a shallow trench was cut through to the river and a generous flow of water entered the canal.

Installation of a steam boiler and pump for use of the school farm was the high-light of the year 1884. This pump was used only for the farm and the succeeding years from 1885 to 1891 were marked by serious water shortages, crop failures and hunger.

I asked Frank Homer, a Mojave friend who had migrated from Needles many years ago, regarding a strange story I had heard regarding the eating of mesquite beans. "'Yes," he said, ""two kinds of mesquite beans grow on our lands. One bean is good and makes a good meal. The other bean is very bitter. When crops do not grow the Indians eat the bitter bean ; it makes the stomach small and they do not need to eat as much to live." To test it I later chewed one of the beans and the effect was far more pronounced than eating a green persimmon and I could appreciate better the result the Indians wished to obtain.

Two new pumps and. a boiler were shipped to the reservation by boat from Needles in 1892 and installed below the headgate. The plant operated successfully for three years, furnishing water to crops planted on 100 acres of land. Then badly needed repairs necessitated its abandonment.

By 1898 many of the Indians had become disgusted and discouraged with the various attempts to provide and maintain an irrigating system and moved north to the Needles region where they began farming along the bottom lands near old Fort Mojave. Only about 300 Mojaves remained at or near the headquarters of the Colorado River reservation.

New equipment was again brought down the river from Needles in 1899 and installed and the Indians soon had 850 acres of land planted to crops. The pumping plant was placed in care of an Indian who was paid $240 per year. The chap deserved great commendation for he kept the pumps operating successfully until 1904 before many repairs were required. New machinery was installed in 1905 and 200 acres continued under cultivation.

The Indian Service, in 1911, commenced construction of a new pumping plant. After successful trial runs the system was placed in operation in March, 1913, a little over half a century after the establishment of the reservation. Allotments of ten acres of land were made to each of 500 Mojaves and a few Chemehuevis. Through the following years the area has been slowly improved and the pumping system kept up-to-date with the changes in mechanical methods. A change was made from steam to diesel power and in 1941, with the coming of power generated at Boulder dam, one motor was installed and the larger of two pumps operated with electricity.

In the meantime, the Indian service under the administration of John Collier had been laying plans for a great diversion dam that would bring stable and permanent improvement in the economic conditions of the Indians. Here was a great river valley, similar in character and larger than the Palo Verde or Yuma valleys, with fertile soil and a 12-month growing season. Boulder dam had solved the problem of flood control. A diversion dam at Headgate Rock would provide a generous livelihood not only for the Colorado river Indians, but for tens of thousands of other desert tribesmen if they could be induced to come here.

To R. H. Rupkey, project engineer for the Indian service, was given the task of installing the dam. He brought an able corps of assistants, several of them Indians from various other tribes in the nation. The Colorado river was turned from its age-old channel by a complete diversion type, earth filled, rock faced dam. The south abutment rests against Headgate or Corner Rock, a monument more fitting than a marble statue to the patience, dreams, ambitions and hopes of those who have builded and lived their lives in this little valley of the Southwest.

Spillway at Headgate Rock dam, constructed by the Indian Irrigation service. It diverts water sufficient for 90,000 acres of bottom land along the Colorado river.

The old tunnel was plugged with several hundred yards of concrete. Into the body of the dam was placed 800,000 cubic yards of earth and rock; material which was removed and selected from more than 4,000,000 cubic yards excavated from the site of the newly completed spillway and headgate structure.

Large radial gates control the level of the impounded waters and regulate the flow into the canal. The control structure and spillway contains 11,293,000 pounds of reinforcing steel, embedded in 127,000 cubic yards of concrete.

Cost of the new project to date has been approximately $5,000,000. Through a main canal 40 miles in length and in many miles of smaller laterals, a maximum of 2100 cubic feet of water per second can be delivered to over 90,000 acres of river lands made rich by hundreds of years of sedimentation from the spreading waters of the Colorado. Until the Japanese were moved here and established in the relocation camp at Poston in 1942, less than 5000 acres were under cultivation. The Japanese added 2500 more. Crops raised here are cotton, maize, barley, wheat, melons, vegetables and alfalfa.

The reservation now has an Indian population of about 900. Near Parker, where so much of the effort of the past years has been expended in establishing an irrigation system, lies the headquarters of the reservation. There are located the administration offices, schools, hospital and homes of many of those engaged in the service. Across a wide paved road from the older buildings lie the new, modern office building, dormitories and homes of the employees. Surrounded by green lawns and brightly blooming flowers "Silver City," the headquarters community, demonstrates what can be done in a desert area where water is available. At the Fort Mojave reservation near

Needles about 300 more Mojaves reside and it is hoped these may be persuaded to move to the south. Certain government grants and large amounts of money placed in escrow by the Metropolitan Water District of Southern California as compensation for lands acquired or flooded by Lake Havasu above Parker dam, have created a feeling of independence.

Most of the Mojaves with whom I have visited are appreciative of the efforts of the government to aid them, yet, as with many other tribes of the West, they often question the motives of the white man. One expressed himself thus: "White man say he want to help us. We help white man fix good farm. We build good houses. Then white man wants it. White man take it. Mojaves move and start over again where land is no good. Indians like sheep. White men drive them where he wishes."

The Mojaves are an interesting people. Most of them are good workers and are imbued with a keen sense of humor as well as the patience that is a common trait among the Indians of the West. They have a religious belief deeply rooted in antiquity, of which they tell little. Cremation after death is followed by funeral rites far more impressive and beautiful than the usual customs of their white brothers. The young men are industrious. They performed nearly all the work on the new canal and tunnel and the new road developments of the project.

Otasha preserves at his farm home a few miles southwest from the agency headquarters, a testimonial of which he has genuine right to be proud. "For patriotic services voluntarily rendered" as a nursing assistant during the influenza epidemic of 1918, Otasha was given a Special Service citation by Surgeon General Rupert Blue for the United States. For weeks, it is said, Otasha worked day and night and traveled hundreds of miles about the reservation assisting the doctor and nurse in caring for the ill among his people. "Many times I never sleep for days," he stated. "Many times four days with no sleep. I never get sick. Many of our people die. Many times I sleep walking!

"Young men among the Mojaves laugh at me today when I tell them of old Mojaves. In early days Mojave men great runners. They carry messages for agents and soldiers. Sun come up in the morning, we run from our agency to Needles and come back when sun goes down at night. My friend, John Grant, who died a few weeks ago do that many times. I do it. Other Mojave and Yuma men run the same way. Many times run to Yuma and back in two or three days. Young men today too fat. Not run enough. Many times Mojaves swim from Needles to my home or down the river to Yuma. Women ride on logs."

By airline old Fort Mojave near Needles is a long 50 miles from the Parker headquarters while Yuma is 100 miles away. Today signs are still found on the California side of the river of an old trail said to have been traveled by the early Mojaves. Along its route have been found metates and broken pottery and it passes close to Monument Peak, which I learned was a sacred rock to the Mojaves. I had previously heard a story regarding its importance to the Mojaves and asked Otasha concerning the significance of the rock.

"Many ages ago the Mojave God drove a great wooden stake into the earth. He told Mojaves this marked their land. Today that stake has turned to stone but Mojaves still here. This is our homeland. We never want to leave it," explained Otasha. "The Mojaves lived here before the first soldiers come. My fathers lived here before the first white men come. Always to the Mojave that great rock means home, We call it 'Ah-Ve-Koov-o-Tut.'"

Left to right: Pete Homer, Mojave in the employ of the Indian service, Otasha, and Charles F. Thomas, Jr. writer.

This is River Country

by Bill Brennan

That energetic man of early Arizona, Colonel Charles D. Poston, was busy here, too. Poston was appointed Superintendent of Indian Affairs for Arizona Territory in 1863. He wasted no time in holding a conference at the mining town of La Paz early in 1864. Chiefs and important men of many river tribes were present, including representatives of the dominant resident tribe, the Mojaves. Poston recommended that a reservation be established on the river. He was soon selected as a congressional delegate from Arizona Territory. On March 3, 1865, shortly before his April 14th assassination, President Abraham Lincoln signed an Act of Congress establishing the reservation. The boundaries were changed a number of times before 1916 when President Woodrow Wilson signed an executive order establishing the present 264,245 acre reservation.

The reservation straddles the Colorado River from a point five miles north of Parker to a point several miles above Ehrenberg, fifty miles south. By far the greatest acreage is in Arizona—260,000 acres. Parker Valley, the agricultural heart of the reservation, is in Arizona river lowlands and stretches from Parker to the southern boundary.

On March 2 1867, Congress appropriated $50,000 for the Indian's irrigation system here, the first such federal project, and the Grant-Dent Canal was dug from 1867-71. The early history of irrigated farming here is a dismal one. Banks washed away, tunnels caved in, wells served up alkali water, and water wheels were torn up by the mighty river. Windmills and horsepower rigs on wells and small steam-powered pumps were the next experiments. Undiscouraged by early failures, federal planners had visions of a great agricultural empire here. Parker, a 973 acre townsite, was carved out in the northern end of the reservation in 1909. Lots were sold at auction and a trading center and shipping point was assured.

But by 1914 only 600 acres of land were irrigated by Indian farmers. Inadequate drainage was waterlogging those acres they could pump water to. By 1936, 5,000 acres were being irrigated. In 1941 Headgate Rock Dam was built near Parker and gravity water for the canal system made available by the guaranteed water-level provided by the dam. There were now 10,500 acres of developed land.

The year 1948 saw an accelerated program of land development begin. By 1955, 38,000 acres had been cleared of desert brush and prepared for farming. Yet thousands of these acres were not usable due to a high water table and excessive salts. The next seven years were spent in planning and executing a proper drainage system. Waterlogged acres were reclaimed and salt leached out. (Today, careful daily laboratory measurements insure that drainage waters leaving this valley are saltier than irrigation waters coming in.) By 1963, 34,000 acres were under cultivation. Cotton was the big money crop and alfalfa a profitable one. Wheat,

Parker Dam

barley, maize, melons and lettuce were also grown.

In the meantime the tribal council had been stymied by seemingly insurmountable problems. Pete Homer, Sr., was chairman and most of those now serving on the council were members then, including the present chairman, Herman Laffoon, Sr.

The situation was adequately and dramatically summed up by U. S. Commissioner of Indian Affairs Philleo Nash in March, 1963. Speaking at the annual fair here, he told the tribe that—at the present rate of progress—it would be another 200 years before they would see their agricultural lands completely developed. He promised to do his best to speed up the process.

For a number of years the federal government had refused to spend funds to develop land here. The tribe had no money to do so. Large agricultural firms were eager to develop and farm the rich land but they needed long-term leases to make the venture profitable. Non- agricultural developers of residential, commercial and industrial sites would need still longer leases. The federal authority to make long leases could not be secured. So, the Indians couldn't develop, the government wouldn't, and would not allow private capital to do so on profitable terms for the interested parties.

But a determined Indian Commissioner Nash, Arizona Congressional members Hayden, Goldwater, and Morris Udall, and forces as yet unsuspected were toiling behind the scenes. When good news happened it came in bunches. The first windfall was the September, 1962, authorization to grant 99-year non-agricultural development leases. In the following spring came the much desired 25 year agricultural development leasing authority. The tribe had not recovered from this celebration when the U. S. Supreme Court gave them the biggest boost of all—water for 107,000 agricultural acres—on June 3, 1963. It was almost anticlimactic on April 30, 1964, when President Lyndon Johnson signed the bill giving the Colorado River Tribes title to their reservation.

The tribe has been using these tools well. Within two years 13,000 acres of new land had been leased to farmer-developers. The reservation canal system is being steadily extended and thousands of additional acres of raw rich river bottom being offered for lease. This development will continue until water is flowing to all of the water-guaranteed 107,000 acres.

In April 1965, the tribe received authority to grant 40-year development leases for citrus farming. There are 7,000 acres on the mesa near Parker ideal for such development. An 870-acre lease was given to Sunny Valley Citrus Co. of Mesa last fall.

With the major roadblocks to progress removed and the smoke of burning brush from cleared land mingling over the river with the dust kicked up by heavy land-leveling machinery, the tribe can look at recent progress and plan for future development with some satisfaction.

Agriculture Booms In Water-Rich Indian Lands

The Colorado River Indian Reservation is probably the largest area in the Southwest with an adequate guaranteed supply of water. The Indians not only have the water for development but they have it now, in contrast to so many hopeful western areas.

Superior Lettuce

Peanut Harvest

The Colorado River dams and their desalting basins have changed the muddy red waters to blue and the U. S. Supreme Court has assured the use of these waters to develop the reservation. The Court set the annual agricultural diversion of water from the river here at 717,148 acre-feet or enough water to supply consumptive use for 107,588 acres, whichever is less.

In mid-1963, at the time of the Court's decision, 34,000 reservation acres in Parker Valley were being irrigated. By mid 1965, 47,000 acres were being farmed or prepared for crops The Colorado River Tribes will develop another 60,588 acres here by 1975 or sooner. Parker Valley will then have 93,588 acres while 7,000 mesa-land acres will be farmed above the valley near Parker. The remaining 7,000 acres are across the river in California.

Agricultural water is cheaper here than in most Southwestern irrigation areas and the soil is excellent. Farmers pay $9 an acre annually for five acre-feet of water on loamy land or for eight acre-feet on sandy land. This rate has prevailed for over four years. The bottomlands here are inherently rich in minerals, requiring the addition only of nitrogen and phosphates for a sustained yield of crops. River water contains approximately sixteen parts per million of potassium, sufficient for production of various crops suited to this area. In addition, the water contains about one ton of gypsum per acre-foot of water. This is fortunate.

If it were not for the gypsum, which comes dissolved with the water, we would be in serious trouble," says Tim Dye, Land Operations Officer of the Bureau of Indian Affairs, Colorado River Agency. "This is because the land here is high in

Tall, Tall Corn

sodium due to the way the valley was formed in the old days of spring floods. The floods came in hot weather and due to algae and "microbial action, sodium was left in the clay. The gypsum is a built-in corrective agent acting on this sodium chemically to change it and allow it to be washed away in drainage waters." Lettuce men here say the quality of the water may be responsible for the top-quality lettuce raised in the valley.

Economically, the development of the valley will be one long construction job spurring the local economy. In mid-1963 the BIA and the tribe approved a plan—The Interim Report—to completely develop Parker Valley in eleven years or less. Indian Commissioner Nash and Secretary of the Interior Stewart Udall approved this blueprint for progress. The construction needed to develop the remainder of the valley for farming will include the following: 40.6 miles of main laterals (9.5 miles completed by December, 1965) 147.1 miles of sublaterals, 50 miles of drainage ditches, 5 pumping plants, and 15 miles, of dikes. These works will cost $22,127,000. The federal government will appropriate the major portion of this money, though $48,000,000 of the work will be financed by lessees. The $12,800,000 cost of clearing, leveling, and otherwise preparing the land for crops will also be borne by lessees.

The Interim Report's figures on the completed 93,588-acre Parker Valley are interesting. It estimates an annual farm operating budget of $13,950,000, a labor force of 3,360 farm workers and another 1,140 non-farm workers. (The entire valley population is now 2,000). The report notes that the reservation is strategically located "near the rapidly expanding market of yearly 10,000,000 people in the Southwestern part of the United States."

The water in the Colorado River that the tribe does not use for irrigation flows through fifty miles of reservation. This gives the tribe 100 potential miles of valuable property for leasing. Over 8,000 residential-commercial acres along ten miles of river have already been leased.

The Backbone of the Reservation Economy and the most successful development to date has been agriculture. The 13,000 newly-leased acres are being readied for crops or farmed by a number of large agricultural arms. Bruce Church, Inc., The Garin Co., Sunny Valley Citrus Co., Sax Eaton

Farms, and Wilco Produce Co., are some of the new lessees.

The Church lease is the big one—6,308 acres. Its development indicates, perhaps, Parker Valley agriculture of the future. Under the management of Fred Andrew, the progress report as of last fall was as follows: 4,500 acres brushed and cleared, another 2,000 acres leveled, 1,500 acres cropped or in crop, 300 acres on a leaching-settling program, a cattle working area and a feed lot pen for 800 head under construction, eleven new homes for management built, nineteen trailers for employees, a 9,600 sq. ft. shop in use, an ice house built, a 4,000 foot airstrip built, many miles of farm roads developed, seven miles of underground monolithic piping laid and in use, fifty men employed including twelve Indians, and many more men working for various contractors working on the farm.

The feed lot, the fourth in Parker Valley, will eventually hold 10,000 cattle and will process 20,000 yearly. The underground irrigation system, new to Arizona agriculture, will be extended until forty miles of it cover the entire lease. This is an expensive installation with many advantages. Andrew says his firm plans to have the lease completely developed in five years or less and is presently ahead of schedule. He is still sweetening the land with grasses, grains, and sorghum. Cotton is a year or two away and the first vegetables are two years away.

The major crop changes in the future would seem to be large-scale vegetable growing and the introduction of citrus and perhaps grapes. The new lessees are vegetable growers in other areas and state frankly their intentions to do likewise here. The Bruce Church lease underground piping is designed for vegetable runs as the pipelines run east and west down the middle of 40-acre fields, providing the short north-south runs preferred for vegetable crops.

Superintendent Homer Gilliland of the Bureau of Indian Affairs, Colorado River Agency, here says that local growers and shippers have told the Santa Fe Railroad they need more loading areas at Parker. The tribe expects to lease land to the railroad for a spur track. A new cotton gin (the 3rd here), several new fertilizer firms, an alfalfa buyer, a flying service, two new airstrips and many new residences and trailer homes are some of the developments evident in the last two years.

Prime Sheep

Chapter Three

Modern History

Photo by Jeffrey L. Garton

The Mohave As Nationalist, 1859-1874

by Clifton B. Kroeber

Reprinted with permission of The Proceedings of the American Philosophical Society.

AFTER defeat, few Indians were able to maintain their own relationships with whites or with other tribes. Soon after military conquest some died away, driven and murdered, blocked off from normal contact with other human beings, on reservations or alone. Of the feelings of these small doomed peoples we have known little, save from such a rare witness as Ishi.[1]

Other Indians whose names we know were crisis figures, who formidably resisted conquest or who rose up against the conqueror at a later day. So it was with Philip, Black Hawk, Joseph, Sitting Bull, Cochise, Geronimo, and many more. They are in our histories not so much because they fought, as most Indians did, but for the greater danger and fear they caused the whites.

But for most tribes the years just after defeat brought neither rebellion nor extinction. Of this life of post-conquest peace we have sparse report; but of recent years historians and anthropologists have begun to write the life histories of those tribes that fought once but no more.

Such a tribe was the Mohave of the Colorado River, and there is substantial record of their life after defeat. Of particular interest is the tribal leadership in its relations with whites and with other Indians; for the Mohave, unlike the congeries and bands of the Southwest, or yet the tribelet-groupings of California, were a true nation. A collection of several thousands of people, they lived in a well-defined territory common to them all, spoke a common language, "all mixed freely with each other,"[2] and felt a very strong sense of identity and of difference from all others within their ken. Their political organization was minimal, based on a hereditary chieftainship, with no divisive elements of regional or other special character. Their strong sense of oneness did not depend upon isolation from other Indians, for the Mohaves were great travelers who ranged far and wide in present-day Arizona and California. Long before the white man's invasion their nationalism had taken on a warlike aspect, and they had driven all enemy tribes from their vicinity along the banks of the Colorado. By the 1850's, the Mohave occasionally made war after long overland treks, to reach the Cocopa of the lower Colorado or the Pima-Maricopa on the Gila. No powerful enemy lived near them and, while they stood ready to defend Mohave Valley,[3] it does not seem that they suffered frequent attack there.

During and after the military conquest by the whites, there was a war and a peace party among them. After their submission in 1859 these differences hardened into a geographical division of the tribe. Two Mohave leaders, Homoseh quahote and Yara tav, eventually living in two different places, each acted on behalf of a part of the tribe. This continued until 1874 when the more active of the two men, Yara tav, died. By that time the U.S. Army and other white people had, in any case, succeeded in dominating western Arizona. This left no room for Mohave leadership in any large way. Chiefs still functioned locally but played no part in important affairs beyond the homeland. Thus the rise and fall of Mohave nationalist response to the coming of the white man ran its course within twenty years, from the middle 1850's to the middle 1870's.

By the late 1840's and early 1850's they were aware of the white man's near approach. U.S. government expeditions led by Lorenzo Sitgreaves (1851) and Amiel W. Whipple (1854) found them a happy and confident people. Whipple, with a respectful and observant attitude, obtained the services of two warriors as guides.[4] Remarkable to the whites for their huge stature and the ease and dignity of their address, these men, Cairook and Yara tav, would play key roles in the events to come. They were of the small company of professional war leaders called *kwanami* (fearless).

To the Mohave this status was of great moment. War, and defense of their Valley, had long been an important aspect of their lives. On the offensive against weaker tribes, usually victorious, they had so institutionalized war that the *kwanami* literally devoted their lives to defense and war. In the custom of their people, they dreamed what would occur, then suggested and led the raids, distinguishing themselves in the front of battle.[5] In the troubled times to come, the leaders of both peace and war factions would be *kwanami.*

Into this relatively secure existence, events of the 1850's brought worry and insecurity, then finally a series of disasters that ended in 1859 with the loss of tribal independence. To begin with, the Mohave had known of the fate of tribes to the east of them. They then observed the subjugation of their friends the Quechan, who occupied long stretches of the Colorado River banks including Yuma Crossing.[6] They knew that the small U. S. garrison at Fort Yuma wished them ill and had twice attempted to stage expeditions against them, in 1851 and in 1852.[7] They received unexpectedly bad treatment from the exhausted expeditionaries of Lorenzo Sitgreaves, in 1851.[8] The years brought other disturbing experiences: the large size of Whipple's expedition of 1854, and the great stir created by the whites upon discovering that the Mohave were holding Olive Oatman, the lone survivor of a family massacred by another tribe.[9] During these years, the Mohave knew of the larger and larger numbers of emigrants and government trains passing by, on the Gila Trail to the south and along the Mormon road to the west.

In the fall of 1857 the Mohave suffered a disastrous defeat in their last great raid on the Pima-Maricopa of the Gila River. Joining their friends the Quechan, they fought what may have been the last large Indian battle in North America, and certainly a terrible loss from which few of the Colorado River Indians returned.[10] Only a few months later, the tribe experienced approaches by the Anglo-Americans that seemed for the first time aimed at permanent settlement in the Valley.

Mormon missionaries appeared from the north, with overtures from the nearby white settlements among the Paiute. From the south came two steamboat expeditions, led by Alonzo Johnson and by Lieutenant Joseph C. Ives,[11] clearly not such cross-country visitors as the Mohave had known since the 1820's. Unbeknownst to them, the Mohave were now involved in the war preparations being directed against each other by the Mormons and the U. S. Army. Not understanding the conflicting desires of these two opposed groups of white men,[12] the Mohave showed their confusion in their equivocal dealings with Lieutenant Ives, early in 1858. It appears that a fear of white settlement in their Valley was now in the Mohave mind.[13] A few months later such fears were openly expressed.

The first group of settlers to attempt to reach California by Lieutenant Edward F. Beale's western wagon route appeared in Mohave Valley in August, 1858. This was the Mohaves' first sight of an emigrant party entering their territory with women and children. They repeatedly expressed the suspicion that these white people had come to settle in the tribal lands;[14] and, when the travelers outspanned, settled down to rest near the river, and began to cut the prized cottonwood trees, the warlike faction among the *kwanami* led a retaliatory attack. With eight people killed and almost all the stock in Indian hands, the emigrant party reeled back toward Albuquerque.[15] The U. S. Army reacted quickly, first sending a small party directly across the California desert to reconnoitre a fort site in Mohave Valley; then dispatching a large body of troops up the Colorado to overawe the tribe; and, after that confrontation, locating a military post in the Valley in the spring of 1859.[16] To ensure peace, nine hostages were lodged at Fort Yuma. Soon these men broke jail, seven surviving to return to their tribe, and a period of small hostilities ensued at Fort Mojave. The final crisis came when the commandant of the fort provoked the one and only Mohave battle against the whites, in the summer of 1859. Thoroughly worsted in this fighting, the Mohave came in at the end of August and agreed to fight no more.[17]

We can hardly guess at the effect of these blows to the morale of individuals and their national feeling. What is clear is that there had been a division of opinion among the war leaders, as to the wisdom of barring all whites from Mohave territory. This difference of view was apparent even before the 1858 attack on the emigrants. Some of the *kwanami* had boasted that they feared the whites not at all, and wanted to fight rather than to chance the indignities of a life dominated by the white men. Other *kwanami,* respecting the Anglo-American strength, would have done much to avoid conflict. But the whole pattern of belief concerning encroachments on the territory, and favoring a resort to war, was so strong that both groups conducted the debate in warlike language.

The would-be peace party could go only so far in advising moderation. Even where it was clear that the various clashes with white men in 1858 and 1859 had been to some degree invited by warlike *kwanami* (although basically caused by the whites), the peaceable leaders felt compelled to speak bravely, and to play their part against the invader should he come.[18] Thus, Yara tav had not been present for the attack on the wagon train, in 1858. He later spoke of it with great disapproval, and with Cairook tried to persuade the tribe to peace. But these efforts shattered against the firm stand for traditional attitudes of defiance, represented by Homoseh quahote and other *kwanami*.

Although fighting had now ceased and Fort Mojave stood in the Valley, the rivalry and disagreement among kwanami remained. In 1865 came a final break, when the Mohave divided into two distinct parties for the first time in recorded history. The larger number remained in the Valley with Homoseh quahote as chief.[19] The smaller group followed Chief Yara tav southward into other Mohave lands that presently became the Colorado River Reservation. Yara tav henceforth spoke for all southern Mohave, he spoke for peace, and in the eyes of U. S. Indian agents and other officials he was chief of the tribe on the Reservation. His right to such honor—in aboriginal times a rather empty one, but to the whites always significant—seemed the stronger because of his acquaintance with so many other tribes, and his willingness to deal with them and with the whites. So had occurred the collapse of a political balance among aboriginal leaders; and at the same time the surviving kwanami gained new importance with their own people, as intermediaries favored by the whites. Such a shift was occurring in other American Indian tribes after conquest, as their ritualistic politics gave way to or merged with a kind of leadership that would mediate between the cultures,[20] meeting problems that were new to the Indians or unaccounted for in their native institutions.

The United States government effected no reunification of the tribe, although the Department of Interior tried for a generation to bring all Mohave together on the Reservation. This policy was resisted by those tribesmen still living in the Valley, who clung to their traditional ways and their familiar farm lands. Quite as important in the frustration of the Department's policy was continuing disagreement and misunderstanding among civilian and military policy makers at Washington, D. C. Such discord produced a habit of local dealings with each Mohave group, rather than any unified control or a single direction of policy. During the 1860's and 1870's, only in times of great emergency did whites or Indians, north or south, work closely with each other.

Given the additional fact that Anglo-American settlement had not yet begun in northwestern Arizona, Yara tav found himself in much the same freedom of movement and association as before. He would use these advantages, and with no formal standing among the whites he continued as if empowered, as if the Mohave were as free as ever. Until his death in 1874 he would seek the safety and integrity of his tribe, amid dangers small at first but larger and more uncontrollable as time went on. His was a nationalistic leadership, despite his abandonment of the warlike habit that had so typified the Mohave in the eyes of others. After 1859 he used new means in a new situation, to uphold the old sense of autonomy and of identity that had lain at the religious core of national feeling among the Mohave. The extent of his success, and the depth of his final failure, trace the waning of Mohave nationalism in the years following the tribe's loss of independence.

As yet there is small trace of Yara tav's activities during the early part of our Civil War,[21] when Fort Mojave stood empty for two years and few white men came to northwestern Arizona. But early in 1863, still residing in the Valley, Yara tav was busy in peacemaking with enemies and renewed visiting with friends. A great traveler like all his people, he went on a long trip with a Paiute leader[22] whose friendship was important because his people were now a menace to the Mohave. Then, while among the southern Yavapai, Yara tav introduced them to the earliest American gold prospectors entering north-central Arizona.[23] In midyear he played a leading part in the negotiations for peace between Indians and whites that took place at Agua Caliente near the Gila River.

The initiative for this meeting probably came from two white men, John Moss and the old mountaineer Pauline Weaver, who were interested in the mining reconnaissance in northern Arizona. There may have been one, or more than one, meeting at Agua Caliente; but in any case a major attempt was made both for peace among Indians, and for a rapprochement between Indians and whites.[24] Here the Mohave and the Pima-Maricopa made their final peace after generations of hostility. Very likely, members of other tribes and bands, of the Yavapai, Yuma, Tonto Apache, and perhaps also the Walapai, exchanged pledges with the Pima-Maricopa. Weaver also tried to ensure safety for the Indians, excepting the Pima who already had an accommodation with the whites, by issuing them written statements and probably giving them verbal passwords as well.

No such agreements could long prevail, of course, when neither civilian nor military government yet had control of the country, and while the incoming settlers knew nothing of this treaty and cared not at all for peace. Weaver and Moss were speaking only for themselves. Still, the Agua Caliente meeting was remarkable enough in attempting to forestall hostilities in western Arizona, and in recognizing that the process of peace in that region must be of two kinds: one among different tribes and bands of Indians, another involving Indians and whites. As for Yara tav and the Mohave, the trip to Agua Caliente was a necessary and prudent act. The Piman enemy, long established as friends of the U. S. government, had once already made common cause with a rancher, in a firearm attack deep into Yavapai territory in northern Arizona. Now Yara tav grasped the opportunity to avoid this sort of danger, making his peace in good time.

Still in 1863, his white friends took Yara tav to San Francisco, then round by ship to New York. From there he went on to Washington, to see the man he called "Abee" Lincoln; then the Mohave chief returned to the River complete with uniform and sash.[25] By 1864, through his attractive manner and much friendly service to troops and other U.S. officials, Yara tav was well known to them all. As a go-between he did important service on all sides, and for some time he had more influence than any Mohave could have held in aboriginal society.

Finally, however, the whole country burst into war. Paiutes to the north and west made the desert trails unsafe, and the Army put military posts along the routes to California and up the Colorado on the way to Utah. The widely dispersed and autonomous' nature of Paiute settlement, and the vast size of the area in which they lived, helps to explain why their hostilities against the whites and other Indians would continue for more than five years—an unrecognized little war of isolated campaigns and tiny outbreaks all the way from the High Sierra out into Nevada, Utah, eastern California, and the northwest corner of Arizona.[26]

Meantime, to the eastward a series of small incidents grew into war between the whites and the Yavapai. In the same year of 1865, bands of Walapai attacked along the new wagon route from Prescott to Mohave Valley.[27] They were trying to avenge the murder of two of their leaders, but what followed was a general war on them by the whites. From this time until 1875 when all resistance stilled, northwestern Arizona was thoroughly unsafe for human life. Vigilantes roamed the land; murder followed murder; soldiers, rangers, and Indians of many tribes and bands marched and countermarched, sometimes seeking each other out but often colliding quite at random.[28]

Yara tav sought to adapt his policies of peace to this new situation, so full of dangers on all sides. He could only hope that the Army would defend his people against possible Paiute attack.[29] Meantime he must somehow help his friends the Yavapai, and if possible the Walapai as well.[30] What he may have tried to do to reunite the Mohave we do not know; certainly the estrangement from Homoseh quahote continued as before.

These new policies failed to re-establish peace. As for the Yavapai, welcoming them to the River Reservation proved unfeasible. This was where the U. S. government planned they should live, and where Yara tav hoped to locate them. But the food supply where farming had never been intensive before Yara tav's group arrived—was insufficient to support the Yavapai the year around. The nervous settlers in their Colorado River villages looked upon these Indian visitors as enemies. They could not understand why Yara tav was a friend to such Indians, whom they felt to be mere thieves and raiders.[31] The chief's bonds with the Yavapai thus quickly proved to be a liability in normal relations with the whites. In 1866 these tensions grew to ugly proportions, on account of two new incidents. In one, a group of hungry Yavapai were massacred by a militia force that probably misunderstood the Indians' intentions.[32] Soon after, the Yavapai retaliated by murdering an Indian agent, George Leihy. To the settlers, the question now was whether Yara tav could ever restrain these Yavapai from what seemed continuous attacks upon the whites.

In 1867 Yara tav made the last of his several attempts to restore peace in Walapai country. Here again, events outpaced his efforts. New Army forces based on Fort Mojave struck out in a major war for the Walapai homeland. In this struggle back and forth across what is now northwestern Arizona, Mohave policy came one step nearer paralysis, closer to a lockstep with the whites. Yara tav had to deny a plea from one band that sought his aid in ousting all white men from the country. He now threw his own efforts against this band of Walapai that had committed itself to a final war.[33]

Meanwhile Yavapai stragglers still appeared on the River Reservation. They would come, for fear of the Army coursing through their homeland, and in search of food. They would depart, for fear of the settlers along the Colorado, and for lack of food on the Reservation. This situation brought a final and tragic loss of Yara tav's freedom of action. From 1867 to 1872 he had to serve simply as confederate both of the Army and of the more violent among the settlers. Menaced by them with reprisals against his people, equally threatened by the hostility of an Army lieutenant acting as Indian agent, the Mohave chieftain must now scout out the Yavapai and Walapai and tempt them into ambush, or capture them and bring them in.[34] In such conditions Yara tav could no longer make policy in good faith. He could do nothing at all to reduce the raging war.

During these years just past, 1865 to 1872, Yara tav had been acting in a situation whose main conditions came to be conflict and insecurity. First of all was the disunity and confusion among the whites. They now consisted of at least four different groups, in much larger numbers and spreading over all the Territory of Arizona, acting unpredictably or at cross purposes with each other. There were settlers, first appearing on the River north of Yuma in 1862, and in the interior in 1863.[35] There were U. S. Army groups, now campaigning in all directions. There were superintendents and agents of Indian affairs; and there was the territorial government—usually but not always reflecting the feelings of the settlers.[36] For Yara tav, the changing Indian relationships were now nearly as crucial as the alignments among white men. Once these aboriginal relations had amounted to a set of "amities and enmities,"[37] in which the Mohave found more friends than enemies. Now, with some bands far from their original homes, and with many small groups of Indians facing extinction, the older patterns were fast breaking down. For the Mohave this meant first of all a great threat from their one-time friends[38] the Chemehuevi, a Paiute band living on the Colorado. The first break in relations with these neighbors came in a bitter little war in 1865;[39] and, although the Chemehuevi took refuge in the California desert, they would come back in time and probably to fight.

There was now a terrible necessity simply in getting a living from the land. Arizona was overloaded with people, in view of either the Indians' or the whites' employ of the resources they knew. This need quickly became tragedy for the Indians. In the interior of Arizona they were driven from their water supplies, and were now so harried that they could no longer make their annual rounds, to collect and to hunt food on which their lives depended. They were subjected to systematic destruction of their stored food, in a systematic campaign begun by the Army in 1867; but there was also the constant danger of death from any white man passing by their homes, at any time.[40] On the other hand, many Anglo-Americans found life in Arizona hard and dangerous. Often they were inept miners,[41] and the mineral resources were not all they had hoped. As cattlemen or farmers, many found that they could not yet work in safety.[42] For some years to come, without a surveyor's office,[43] no white man could be sure of title to his land. For almost everyone in Arizona, life was more than usually insecure.

The new threat confronting the Mohave was in the north and west, from the Paiute-Chemehuevi. A treaty had been patched up between Chemehuevi and Mohave in 1867, and the smaller tribe had filtered back into its riverside valley. But now in 1869 and 1870 they and their relatives the Paiute were preparing a new war. Tension built up on both sides, through murders of a few individuals.

By this time the Mohave were less able to face danger confidently. They would have no help from the U. S. Army, whose Reservation force dwindled to but six men early in 1870, and whose garrison at Fort Mojave showed no inclination to defend Homoseh quahote's group there. The Mohave owned few guns, whereas the Paiute were said to be heavy with firearms. Worse yet, each of the two groups of Mohave must call all available men whenever danger threatened, thus exposing the crops to almost sure destruction. This condition of constant fear had much to do with reducing Yara tav's activity on the larger stage, east of the River, during 1869 and 1870.

When attack did come in Mohave Valley, it was beaten off; but such a narrow victory[44] had its depressing effect. This was not the old, aggressive warfare of raids led by the *kwanami*. That was gone, and nothing new had entered in that might sustain the warrior chiefs.

The final episode is equally devoid of meaning for tribal leadership and for the old feeling of national pride. During the drive against the Yavapai begun by General George Crook in 1871-1872, Yara tav acted as informer against the men Crook was seeking. They had murdered passengers of a stage, near Wickenburg in November, 1871. At a meeting of Yavapai and Army leaders (September, 1872), Yara tav gave signs to indicate which were the wanted men.[45]

In this act we see the Mohave walking down a line marked by the whites. There was no more scope for national policy, nothing for the go-between but his daily bread. From the first the northern chief, Homoseh quahote, had walked this narrow line. Slowly, step by step, the more ambitious Yara tav had been forced to lay aside his policy of national initiative, even of peace itself. Now he was a simple instrument of the conquest.[46]

In Chief Yara tav's struggle of fifteen years, before, during, and after the defeat, we see the last phase of Mohave nationalism as it had been before the white man came. Although no longer independent, and no longer engaged in war, he well exploited the brief period of relative calm between 1859 and 1865, in the interest of Mohave welfare and general peace. His role as go-between was a most valuable one, the more so because no other person, Indian or white, took such a large view of the tribal conflicts, or tried so hard to pacify all the groups in conflict.

But with war to east and west from 1865 onward, this policy narrowed and finally faltered to nothing. Threatened by former friends, facing active enemies among the Paiute-Chemehuevi and the Walapai, under irresistible pressure from the whites, the southern Mohave leader felt himself forced to desert the few friends he still had in other tribes. Through the late 1860's and the early 1870's Yara tav had to give increasing account to the possibility that his southern Mohave could be dispersed, by attacks or by failures of the Reservation food supply. This urgency was not so much overlooked as simply not understood by the whites, excepting only some of the agents on the River Reservation. But such fears drove Mohave policy increasingly after 1865.

For the Mohave of the north, the fifteen years following defeat brought many of the same results; but the impact of conquest was less severe and less complete. By 1867 the chief Homoseh quahote, and the *kwanami* Asakyet, already were acting as scouts and spies for the Army against the Walapai.[47] This part of the tribe bore the brunt of Chemehuevi attack in 1870, and soon stood friendless among surrounding enemies. But the soldiers' supervision was not so close as the southern tribesmen experienced from Indian agents on the Reservation. People in the north were farming as they had before, without such constant fear of famine, thus without such marked dependence on the white man's gifts. As the years went by, the temper of life for Mohaves in the north and in the south would continue to diverge.

Yara tav was too intelligent and too well informed to seek a new war against the conqueror, as native leaders would do elsewhere in the American West in similar circumstances. Now an old man of failing influence among his own people, he chose instead to bend before the pressure from whites and Indians alike, and to abandon his role of peacemaking nationalist. So passed the last of those native leaders who, on a vast stage stretching from southern California to central Arizona and from lands north of the Colorado to those south of the Gila, had practiced Indian diplomacy whose scope "lifts one at a bound out of the peasant-like, localized and murkily dim knowledge of the true

Californians into a freer atmosphere of wild and bold horizons."[48]

In the more constricted life that lay ahead, the tribal sense of nationality would not disappear. It lived on with the people in Mohave Valley, where a stronger feeling for original values still survived. This more traditional attitude had been seen during the years after military defeat, in Homoseh quahote's policy of peaceful coexistence, differing so markedly from Yara tav's more emphatic collaboration with white men on the Reservation.[49] The Fort Mojave group lived more to itself for a time to come, whereas the Indians on the Colorado River Reservation became a mixture of tribes brought there by the U. S. government. They had closer relationships with white settlers in their locality, than did their fellow tribesmen in the north.

In the twentieth century the United States government would revive the tribe as a political entity, and the older sense of tribal values is reflected in the new. But the aboriginal nationalism of the Mohave was dead by 1874. It had outlived defeat in the vigorous policy of *kwanami* leaders. Then it died, with all those conditions that gave it life.

[1] Theodora Kroeber, *Ishi in Two Worlds. A Biography of the Last Wild Indian in North America* (Berkeley, 1961).

[2] A. L. Kroeber, *Handbook of the Indians of California* (Washington, D. C., 1925), p. 727.

[3] *Ibid.*, pp. 727-728, 753-754; Kenneth M. Stewart, "Mohave Warfare," *Southwestern Jour. of Anthro.* 3 (1947) ; George H. Fathauer, "The Structure and Causation of Mohave Warfare," *ibid.* 10 (1954) ; and Leslie Spier, *Mohave Culture Items* (Flagstaff, Arizona, 1955).

[4] Amiel W. Whipple, *Report of Explorations for a Railway Route Near the Thirty-Fifth Parallel...* (Washington, D.C., 1855), pp. 110, 119, 122, 126. For Yara tav's career, see Arthur Woodward, "Iritaba, 'Chief of the Mohave,'" *Plateau* 25 (1953) ; and for the benefit derived by the Army in 1858 from Whipple's careful approach, Joseph C. Ives, *Report Upon the Colorado River of the West* (Washington, D. C., 1861), pp. 68, 70, 80, 83, 89-91.

[5] Kroeber, *Handbook*, p. 754; Fathauer, "Mohave Warfare," pp. 114-118; but especially Spier, *Mohave Items*, pp. 11-15.

[6] Sylvester Mowry to Commissioner of Indian Affairs, Washington, D. C., Nov. 10, 1857, in U. S. National Archives, Records of the Office of Indian Affairs, Letters Received, Arizona, 1824-1881 (hereinafter cited as OIA); and the manuscript Reminiscence of Tribal Warfare, given by Jo Nelson to A. L. Kroeber through an interpreter at Needles, Calif., in 1903.

[7] *Journal of Lt. Thomas W. Sweeny, 1849-1853*, ed. Arthur Woodward (Los Angeles, 1953), and entries in Sweeny's papers in the Huntington Library, San Marino, California.

[8] Lorenzo Sitgreaves, *Report of an Expedition Down the Zuni and Colorado Rivers* (Washington, D. C., 1853), pp. 17-19.

[9] A brief account by a Mohave participant is in A. L. Kroeber, "Olive Oatman's Return," *Kroeber Anthropological Society Papers* 4 (1951).

[10] The date seems to have been Sept. 1, 1857: see J. C. Wood, *Report to A. V. Brown, Postmaster-General . . .*(Washington, D. C., 1858), p. 19; and Major E. Steen to Commissioner of Indian Affairs, Ft. Buchanan, Nov. 2, 1857, OIA. A one-paragraph account is in Kroeber, *Handbook*, p. 753.

[11] Arthur Woodward, *Feud on the Colorado* (Los Angeles, 1955), a thorough account.

[12] Ives, *op. cit.*, pp. 89-91; and Paul Bailey, *Jacob Hamblin, Buckskin Apostle* (Los Angeles, 1948). William H. Goetzmann, *Army Exploration in the American West, 1803-1863* (New Haven, 1959), pp. 382-388, explains Ives' situation; the background for the conflict itself is in Norman F. Furniss, *The Mormon Conflict, 1850-1859* (New Haven, 1960).

[13] Ives, *op. cit.*, p. 67, the earliest specific mention of which I now know.

[14] Leonard J. Rose, Jr., *L. J. Rose of Sunnyslope...* (San Marino, Calif., 1959), pp. 20-21; and the elder Rose's letter from Albuquerque, Oct. 28, 1858, copied in R. G. Cleland, *The Cattle on a Thousand Hills...* (San Marino, 1941), pp. 309-311. The Indians put this question twice, perhaps three times.

[15] John Udell, *Journal Kept During a Trip Across the Plains...* (Jefferson, Mo., 1868: reprinted, Los Angeles, 1947); Leroy R. Hafen, *The Overland Mail, 1849-1869* (Cleveland, 1926), pp. 116-117; Nelson's Reminiscence; and the Los Angeles *Star*, Nov. 13, 1858, among other accounts. E. S. Curtis, *The North American Indian* (20 v., Cambridge, 1906-1930) 2: pp. 49-50, telescopes these with much later events.

[16] Edward F. Beale, *Wagon Road, Fort Smith to the Colorado River* (Washington, D. C., 1860), pp. 44-45; Nelson's Reminiscence; Yesar's dispatches in the San Francisco *Alta California*, May 7-June 11, 1859 [for which my thanks to Prof. Henry F. Dobyns]; Samuel Bishop to Major Wm. Hoffman, March 24, 1859, in Hayes Collection, no. 84, Bancroft Library, Univ. of California, Berkeley. Many letters and reports by all military authorities concerned are in the *Report of the Secretary of War*, 1859 (Washington, D. C., 1860), pp. 387-422.

[17] Capt. Lewis A. Armistead's post returns, Fort Mojave, for July and August, 1859, in U. S. National Archives, Records of the War Dept., Office of the Adjutant General; and Nelson's Reminiscence. Twenty-three Mohaves were killed in the battle. The peace talk occurred on August 31, 1859.

[18] All this is from Nelson's Reminiscence, which brings out the bitterness of the disagreement.

[19] E. D. Tuttle, "The River Colorado," *Ariz. Hist. Rev.* 1 (1928) : pp. 57-58. This chief is seen as Sickahoot; Hamosekwahota; Homose: kohot, among many versions of his name that are in the literature. For the difficult question of Mohave chieftainship, new research by Lorraine Sherer clarifies this and other poorly understood problems, in two studies appearing in *Southern Calif. Hist.* in 1965. I am most grateful that Prof. Sherer was willing to liberate the present essay from a number of serious misunderstandings of Mohave culture.

[20] Brief indication of this phenomenon is in A. L. Kroeber, "The Nature of Land-Holding Groups in Aboriginal California," *Repts. Univ. of Calif. Archaeol. Survey* 56 (Berkeley, Calif., 1962): p. 46.

[21] Woodward, "Iritaba," p. 61, has what little is known.

[22] San Francisco *Alta California*, Aug. 2, 1863.

[23] Daniel E. Conner, *Joseph Reddeford Walker and the Arizona Adventure*, ed. D. J. Berthrong and Odessa Davenport (Norman, Okla., 1956), pp. 77-91. He was there.

[24] Pauline Weaver's petition, and letter to Chas. D. Poston, La Paz, May 6, 1864. OIA; A. H. Peeples' undated letter printed in *Arizona Weekly*, Dec. 18, 1890, and Chas. B. Genung's memoir in the Prescott *Evening Courier*, May 20, 1911 (clippings in Sharlot Hall Museum, Prescott, Ariz.); Nelson's Reminiscence; and Pima remembrance in Leslie Spier, *Yuman Tribes of the Gila River* (Chicago, 1933), p. 45, naming the mediator as Pengwitcsa, "beaver eater." Conner, *op. cit.*, pp. 98, 104, 130-131, 156, 159, does not mention the treaty but places Yara tav and Weaver in the proper vicinity at the right time.

[25] Following Woodward, "Iritaba," pp. 61-64, and sources he cites; also, Chas. D. Poston, writing from La Paz, July 24, 1864,

copied in Journals, *First Arizona Legislature* (Prescott, Ariz., 1865). In 1938 Yara tav's granddaughter Tcatc stressed that this trip impressed Yara tav with the uselessness of opposing the whites: in George Devereux, "Mohave Chieftainship in Action: a Narrative...," *Plateau* 23 (1951) : p. 33.

[26] Information on this war seems not to have been gathered together. See Woodward, "Iritaba"; G. W. and H. P. Beattie, *Heritage of the Valley...* (Pasadena, Calif., 1939), pp. 324-326; Leonard Waitman, "The History of Camp Cady," *Quarterly Pub/. Hist. Soc. of Southern Calif.* 36 (1954) : pp. 53-54; letters of Capt. J. Ives Fitch, Fort Mojave, in 1863 and 1864, U. S. National Archives, Records of the War Dept., *cit. supra*; G. W. Leihy to Commissioner of Indian Affairs, Prescott, Sept. 11, 1865, 01A; and Effie M. Mack, *Nevada, a History* (Glendale, Calif., 1936), pp. 301-332.

[27] Albert H. Schroeder, *A Study of Yavapai History* (3 pts., Santa Fe, 1959), pp. 14, 18, 84; Henry F. Dobyns, The Middle Mountain People, manuscript in Univ. of Arizona Library, p. 77; *Report of the Commissioner of Indian Affairs, 1867* (Washington, D. C., 1867: the series hereinafter cited as RCIA), p. 152; Henry Ehrenberg to Commissioner of Indian Affairs, Prescott, May 28, 1866, OIA ; and John C. Dunn to same, Prescott, May 23, 1865, in U. S. Senate, *Walapai Papers* (Washington, D. C., 1936), pp. 33-34.

[28] The campaigning is best reconstructed in Ralph H. Ogle, *Federal Control of the Western Apaches, 1848-1886* (Albuquerque, 1940), passim.

[29] Capt. Chas. Atchisson, to Col. R. C. Drum, Aug. 23, 1864, and to O. H. Lee, March 5, 1865, from Fort Mojave, OIA, reports talks with Yara tav.

[30] G. W. Leihy's report, Oct. 2, 1866, *Walapai Papers*, p. 40, refers to Yara tav's attempt to mediate between white men and Yavapai "last spring," which in context could mean either 1865 or 1866. The Walapai started to fight the whites in a large way some time in April, 1865.

[31] The earliest of many pertinent reports of this may be by John C. Dunn, Oct. 30, 1864, OIA. See also Pauline Weaver's petition during the same year (*cit. supra*). Col. Wm. R. Price's letter of Feb. 6, 1870, OIA, is a much later reference to the same thing.

[32] Lt. Oscar Hutton's letter from Skull Valley, in Prescott *Weekly Arizona Miner*, Aug. 14, 1866. Ogle, *op. cit.*, and the volumes of RCIA, follow these events closely.

[33] G. W. Leihy's report of Oct. 2, 1866, and John Feudge's letter of June 30, 1867, in *Walapai Papers*, pp. 40-41; Prescott *Weekly Arizona Miner*, June 12, 1867.

[34] The incidents (at present unidentifiable in whites' accounts) are from the Indian sources : Nelson's Reminiscence and, from the other side, the Southeastern Yavapai Michael Burns' account copied in T. E. Farish, *History of Arizona* (8 v., Phoenix, 1915-1918) 3: pp. 295-300. Burns refers to three groups of Yavapai who never returned from visits to the Colorado River. One incident is known : at La Paz, Sept. 25, 1868, 10 Yavapai were murdered by freighters, with unidentified Indian help. See Ogle, *op. cit.*, p. 72.

[35] For those on the River, see Woodward, "Iritaba"; for the interior, Conner, *op. cit.*, pp. 105, 107, 111-112, 133-134, and King Woolsey to the editor, Prescott *Weekly Arizona Miner*, June 20, 1870. Schroeder, *op. cit.*, p. 84, recounts the raid by Jack Swilling and some Maricopa into Yavapai country in Jan., 1860: but these were raiders, not settlers.

[36] In several cases of ambushes and murders of Indians, the territorial government tried to identify the criminals, and to hold such crimes up to public shame.

[37] Kroeber, *Handbook*, pp. 596, 727-728. He states that there were "in a general way these opposing alignments :" (1) Chemehuevi, Southern Paiute, Mohave, Yuma, Kamia, Yavapai, and Apache; opposed were (2) Hopi, Pima, most Papago, Havasupai, Walapai, Maricopa, Halchidhoma, Kohuana, Halyikwamai, Cocopa, Dieguefio, and some others. ". . . each had its enemies of long standing, and therefore joined hands with their foes, until an irregular but far-stretching and interlocking line-up worked itself out".

[38] Ibid., p. 728.

[39] Woodward, "Iritaba," pp. 64066; Nelson's Reminiscence ; a distorted account in Conner, *op. cit.*, pp. 276-277; brief reference by Pete Lambert (Homoseh quahote's descendant), in Stewart, "Mohave Warfare," p. 258; RCIA 1865, p. 503; and letters of Capt. Chas. Atchisson, Fort Mojave, Feb. 20 and March 5, 1865, OIA. The war ended in a "treaty" signed by Pan Coyer (Chemehuevi) and Yara tav (Mohave), March 21, 1867: see G. Dent's letter enclosing the treaty to Commissioner of Indian Affairs, La Paz, April 1, 1867, OIA ; and to the same effect, Chas. B. Genung's memoir, *cit. supra*.

[40] Dobyns, *op. cit., passim*, and Ogle, *op. cit., passim*; see also John C. Dunn to Commissioner of Indian Affairs, Prescott, Aug. 25, 1864, OIA.

[41] If we believe Conner, *op. cit.*, p. 156, and Genung, in the memoir cited above.

[42] Prescott *Weekly Arizona Miner*, Nov. 6, 1869, for a representative enunciation of a case frequently stated. As background, see Robert G. Athearn, *William Tecumseh Sherman and the Settlement of the West* (Norman, Okla., 1956), pp. 137-138, for his and for Sherman's statements of the problem at that time.

[43] *Annual Report of the Department of the Interior, 1864* (Washington, D. C., 1864), pp. 101-102, including the report of an 1863 visit by the surveyor, and his reluctance to return. A preemption office may have been open at Prescott as early as 1868.

[44] For the preliminaries, and the attack, which came Oct. 15, 1870, see Woodward, "Iritaba," pp. 66-67, and sources he uses; Nelson's Reminiscence; RCIA, 1870, pp. 115-116, 131; very brief reference in Stewart, "Mohave Warfare," pp. 258-259, by Pete Lambert ; and Agent H. Dodt to Supt. Andrews, Colorado River Reservation, Oct. 3 and Oct. 19, 1870, OIA.

[45] Ogle, *op. cit.*, pp. 90-116; Prescott *Weekly Arizona Miner*, Sept. 21, 1872; John G. Bourke, *On the Border with Crook* (New York, 1891: reprinted, Columbus, O., 1950), pp. 167-177; and Nelson's Reminiscence (which mistakes the incident, and confuses it with a similar one of November, 1866).

[46] For a broad survey of such processes, see E. H. Spicer, *Cycles of Conquest, the Impact of Spain, Mexico, and the United States on the Indians of the Southwest, 1533-1960* (Tucson, Ariz., 1962).

[47] W. H. Hardy to Chas. Dent, Hardyville, June 26, 1867, 01A; and John Feudge's letter, June 30, 1867, in *Walapai Papers*, p. 41. In one such incident, Homoseh quahote with other Mohaves and some white men had massacred twenty Walapais after tracking them thirty miles from Fort Mojave.

[48] Kroeber, *Handbook*, p. 596.

[49] "Professor Lorraine Sherer suggests this qualitative difference in attitude of the two groups.

Great Chieftains of the Mojave Indians

by Lorraine M. Sherer

Reprinted with permission of *Southern California Quarterly*.

The last great chieftain of the Mojave Indians died in 1947 in Needles, California. He was *Sukulai homar*, better known by his Americanized name, Pete Lambert—the grandson of *Homoseh quahote*, who was the great chieftain when the Mojave nation surrendered to United States troops in 1859, and the son of *Empote quatacheech*, who was the great chieftain during the last decade of the military occupation of Fort Mojave. *Sukulai homar's* death ended the ancient system of hereditary and elected great chieftains which the Mojave Indians had perpetuated through the centuries.

Chief Lambert left a brief will, dated September 3, 1947, at Needles, bequeathing his papers to the Mojave Tribal Council. Among these papers was a carefully wrapped album which contained his choicest souvenirs—faded old testimonial letters written in longhand for his grandfather and his father by post commanders at Fort Mojave and less faded typewritten letters written to him by superintendents of the Fort Mojave School which occupied the old Army post after the troops were withdrawn in 1890. These old letters provide missing links in understanding a distinctive system of democratic tribal leadership. The documents take on added significance when flanked by explanations from knowledgeable Mojave Indians and supplemented by additional documents in the National Archives in Washington, D.C.

The words "chief," "head chief," and "great chieftain" in the Mojave language are borrowed from Anglo-Americans. When Mojave Indians use these words, they carry to them meanings from two native words, *yaltanack*, leader, and *huchach*, head of a group. These correspond reasonably well with "chief." When prefaced by the name of the tribe or nation, *Aha macave* (or its anglicized corruption Mojave, Mohave), the term *Aha macave yaltanack* means "leader of the Mojave tribe or nation" and *Aha macave huchach* means "head of the Mojave tribe or nation." Both terms are political titles for position and both are fairly accurate synonyms for "head chief." Mojaves are quick to point out, however, that their words for "leader" and "head" *do not* mean a ruler or boss, a common misconception of foreigners.

Mojave concepts of tribal leadership or tribal headship are expressed in a value term, *Aha macave pipatahon*, a term for which we have no synonym in English—the closest counterpart being "great chieftain." *Aha macave pipatahon* is difficult to translate because it is freighted with Mojave ideals and meanings: *pipatahon* comes from *pipa*, a person or people, and *patahon*, valued, valuable, extraordinary, outstanding. It embodies Mojave ideals of leadership of quality, and implies the criteria for such leaders. The *Aha macave pipatahon* was a tribal leader "looked up to by the people because of the kind of person he was." Mojaves give a long list of attributes, but the following few present a fair idea of what "kind of person" they visualized as *Aha macave pipatahon*.

He was one who was concerned about the welfare of all of the people; who was wise and understanding; who possessed knowledge of tribal culture, tribal history, and tribal needs; who protected tribal lands against enemies and land-grabbers; who set a worthy example for his people; who was faithful to his trust and was honorable in his dealings; who always kept his word; who gave his time and his means in working for the good of the tribe, and who could not be tempted or swerved by personal ambitions. "He might not succeed all the time, but he kept working,"

Photograph by A. P. Miller, Needles, California

***Sukulai homar**, or Pete Lambert, the last great chieftain of the Mojave Indian Tribe as he appeared in November, 1938.*

one Mojave explained. This topmost position was hereditary, its holder coining from a family in the *Malika* clan. The hereditary candidate could not assume this post, however, until he was approved by the people, hence he was also an elected leader or head of the tribe—or as some of the documents say, "the hereditary and elected great chieftain." He maintained his tribal leadership through personal integrity and professional competency. If he lost the confidence of the people, he could "step aside," or he could be removed and another elected to "take over his contract." Mojaves called an elected head chief, *hochoch* (also spelled *huchoch*), "made" by the people. Twice during the period covered by this study (1859-1948), the Mojave tribe demonstrated how their "system worked"—once in 1860 or 1861, when *Homoseh quahote* abdicated, and once in 1905 when *Sukulai homar* was removed. Both men were restored to their high positions in due time.

The year 1859 was a traumatic year in Mojave history: it marked the date of their surrender to United States troops, the establishment of Fort Mojave, and the beginning of the end of the Mojave Indian Tribe as a free Indian nation. Since that year, they have been under the jurisdiction of the War Department or the Department of the Interior.

Homoseh quahote of the *Malika clan* was the great chieftain of the *Aha macave* nation, the *Aha macave pipatahon*, in 1859. The date and the circumstances of his accession are not known, but it was *Homoseh quahote* who faced Lieutenant Colonel William Hoffman, U.S.A., commander of the expedition of the Colorado, on the morning of April 23, 1859, to hear his terms of peace. This meeting at which the chiefs and adult males of the tribe were commanded to appear was described graphically by Hoffman in reports to his superior, but he did not mention the name of the head chief. That name and a description of the head chief were provided, however, by *Gwegwi nuor* of the *Oach* clan, an eye witness of the never-to-be-forgotten scene:

> I do not know the big white Chief who represent the California government but I know our representative—Chief Humso-qu-hoat, means Orator of stars. In those days we have orators of the devine law such as the preachers of today. These orators of law are great warriors and are not afraid to die for justice, and should one of these orators die the whole tribe hold a social gathering and have very pleasant time. There is no mourning held over their dead [orator]. Chief explains the laws: **1** do as they do unto you. **2** do as they do unto others. **3** That there shall be no jealousey. **4** Protect your properties. **5** that they shall not steal. **6** that they shall not Kill. **7** was struck over in the original. **8** to make friends settle their own grievances.
>
> Chief Humsoquahoat is over 6 ft tall and not heavy built but the scars on his breast shows that he has fought many people for justice or carry out the setup [of] our government. His hair is long. He's painted in red, white and black and Armed and [a] few feathers on his head. He stood with the white chief both hands clasped and they stood face to face. When our chief spoke the last word on No. 8 he said it is going to be very difficult as we have different ways of living and different language. And to make friends we are to suffer a great loss, our properties and ourselves.

To the best of my knowledge this is the only known description of *Homoseh quahote,* although the scene of the surrender and the taking of Mojave hostages have been described elsewhere.

The great chieftain's name, *Homoseh quahote* (spelled *Humso-qu-hoat* by *Gwegwi nuor's* recorder) meant, as *Gwegwi nuor* stated, orator of the stars or orator of the star (*homoseh*, star; *quahote*, orator). It has been spelled different ways by American writers, for example: *Sickahot* (Ives, 1861), *Sikyhut* (Bourke, 1889), *Asikahote* (Kroeber, 1903), *Hamosekwahote* (Curtis, 1908), and *Homose: kohot* (Devereux, 1951). Army officers and Indian agents have contributed such variations as *Sick-a-hoot, Sic-a-hoot, Seck-a-hott, Hum-Sik-a-holt, Hum-sik-a-hote*. The clan name *Malika* symbolized the below-earth creatures such as the desert rodents, of whom the *Aha macave* creator *Mutavilya* said, "Do not despise these for they are wise ones." Mojaves call the Malika, "the understanding people."

When Fort Mojave was established in 1859, *Homoseh quahote* was not only the great chieftain; he was also the hereditary chief of the northern Mojaves, the *Matha lyathum*, whose domains reached from the vicinity of the fort almost to Black Canyon. Late in 1860 or early 1861, he abdicated the office of head chief of the tribe, a move that did not affect his lesser chieftainship. The oldest document in the Fort Mojave Tribal Records is a worn letter written for *Homoseh quahote* by Brevet Major Granville O. Haller, post commander at Fort Mojave, on May 26, 1861, two days before the post was abandoned temporarily and its commander and troops transferred to Civil War duty. Haller wrote:

> To whom it may concern: The Bearer hereof Humi-Sick-a-hott who has recently abdicated his authority as Head Chief of the Mojave Indians, in consequence of his advanced age, is well known to the U.S. Troops, and has always shown himself to be a sincere friend of the Troops, and declares his friendship for all Americans will be the same as for the Soldiers.
>
> He and his people are desirous of helping all Americans who may pass through their Country by selling them vegetables and assisting them across the Colorado River, and they would like to receive in pay Articles of Clothing, Sugar, Tobacco, etc.

Such a testimonial letter would not be expected to state the name of the new head chief, but one wonders to whom *Homoseh quahote* abdicated and why a man of *Homoseh quahote's* vigor should abdicate, pleading old age. Haller provided the name of the new head chief in a letter to Acting Commissioner of Indian Affairs, Charles E. Mix, written at his Civil War Headquarters in York, Pennsylvania, on January 28, 1862. He stated:

> There are four bands in the valley, represented by Chief Ir-a-ta-bah, the Head Chief, Sick-a-bolt, Copetan, and Pike co nay o. Below the Needles is a larger valley, with much the greater proportion of the Indians under an old chief called Ho-marr-a-tov....

Hallers' letter shows that *Homoseh quahote's* successor was *Yara tav* (spelled *Ir-a-ta-bah*). This designation was correct from the Mojave viewpoint. *Yara tav* was the head chief, but he was not the great chieftain. In Mojave terminology, he was *Aha macave yaltanack* (or *huchach*) *hochock,* the leader or head of the Mojave nation "made" by the people. *Yara tav's* election to the head chieftainship as *"hochoch"* interrupted but did not change the line of succession away from the traditional hereditary line of great chieftains. *Yara tav* was also the chief of the *Hutto pah* who lived on the east bank of the river. His name, *Yara tav,* has been spelled in a variety of ways: *lretaba* (Whipple), *Ireteba* (Ives), *Arateve* (Kroeber), *Yiratewa* (Curtis), *Yarate:wa* (Devereux), *Irataba* (Woodward). His Indian name was an abbreviated form of two Mojave words, *eecheyara,* bird, and *tav,* something good or beautiful. In the old days, according to the aged *Atalk hear,* the Fort Mojave Tribal Orator, the Mojaves gave "the full pronunciation of our Indian word for bird, plus *tav.*" *Yara tav* was of the *Neolge* clan whose name symbolizes the sun and fire.

When *Yara tav* became the head chief during Haller's tour of duty at Fort Mojave, the Mojave people had settled down to their regular ways of life and gave every indication not only of adhering to the terms of their peace treaty with Hoffman but of actually feeling friendly to the soldiers. They were hospitable also to the few miners who came through the country prospecting for gold. Fort Mojave was closed only two years before it was regarrisonned by California Volunteers, a measure made necessary by the discovery of gold and a stampede of goldseekers into hitherto exclusive Indian country.

Mojave history took a new turn beginning in 1863. Previously peaceful, the Indians were swept into the vortex of Indian-white hostilities that eventually brought both sides into warfare, a conflict that lasted for twenty years. In 1863, the tribe was faced with the loss of their lands in the Mojave Valley and removal to a reservation. *Yara tav's* status as head chief of the tribe and the dilemma confronting him and his people are detailed in reports to the Departments of War and of Interior. The Fort Mojave post commander, Captain J. Ives Fitch, C.V., in a message to the Fort Yuma commander, September 19, 1863, wrote, "The bearer of this is Irataba, the principal Chief of the Mojaves. I believe him to be a fine prince of peace with the Whites."

Yara tav's status and whereabouts during part of 1863-64 were reported by Charles D. Poston, the first Superintendent of Indian Affairs of the new Arizona Territory, to the Commissioner of Indian Affairs, September 30, 1864:

> Upon my arrival in San Francisco, two chiefs of the most powerful tribes in Arizona were awaiting the arrival of a representative from the Great Father at Washington. Iretaba, chief of the Mojaves, and Antonio Azul, chief of the Pima tribe of Indians. These chiefs are both of high rank and great consideration in their respective neighborhoods, and were treated with liberal hospitality in San Francisco by citizens and officers of the government.
>
> Iretaba was so much pleased with the customs of civilization that he extended his visit to the Atlantic cities and Washington, under the patronage of Captain John Moss, an amateur representative of the Americans in the remote region inhabited by the people of his protégé.

Poston was then promoting the establishment of an Indian reservation for the Mojaves and other Colorado River tribes in southern Mojave territory, whereas the Mojaves were protesting this location and urging its establishment in the Mojave Valley where the planting land was better and where the majority of the tribe had always lived. In describing the proposed location of the reservation to the Commissioner of Indian Affairs, September 30, 1864, Poston reported, "I also made an examination of the proposed reservation by the sinuousities of the river accompanied by Iretaba, the principal chief, who expressed much gratification at the prospect of having a *home* set apart for his people." The post commander at Fort Mojave presented a different version of *Yara tav's* feelings but concurred as to his rank. In a message to Adjutant General Richard C. Drum, August 23, 1864, Captain Charles Atchisson, C.V., reported a conference with him in which "the Chief of the Mojave Indians (Iretabu) with four others of his principal chiefs complained of the treatment they had received from Mr. Poston (the Indian Agent)." He wrote:

> ...that Mr. Poston had marked out a reservation for the Mojave Indians in the upper part of the La Paz valley on the East side of the Colorado River.... Iratabu says this reservation is covered with sand and unfit for cultivation and the Indians are opposed to giving up their good lands in the Mojave Valley and moving to it....
>
> Iratabu says if he can have the valley below the Fort Mojave reserved for the home of the Indians, he is willing to give up all claims to lands on other parts of the river, and bring his Indians from La Paz and other points to this valley.... I will here append a proposition made by Iratabu,—he proposed to assist me if I desired to fight the Chemehauva [Chemehuevi] Indians who had been stealing from the whites between here and Camp Cardif [?]...and he says if they continued to steal from white men he will raise his warriors and drive them off the river. I have full confidence in the friendship of Iratabu towards white men, but not in his tribe, if troubles with any other Indians should occur while he has more influence over them than any other chief, his control over them is not complete and they are as likely to lead him (as he is them).

Poston's selection of the site of a reservation was opposed by the War Department. General James H. Carleton, commanding the Department of New Mexico, for example, could see no reason for a reservation, and Herman Eherenberg, an engineer and one familiar with the land and the river, spoke strongly against it. Nevertheless, the reservation, as advocated by Poston, was established by Congress at its present location in March, 1865. The choice of a reservation, as well as the idea of a reservation, created an upheavel among the Mojaves. By this time, Indian-white hostilities had reached such a pitch of atrocities that neither Indian nor white was safe.

The year 1865 was a crucial year in Mojave history. It marked the beginning of the division of the Mojaves into two factions or parties, and ultimately into separate tribes, each with its own reservation. *Yara tav*, though not approving the location, led a contingent of Mojaves—estimated to be somewhere between five and eight hundred—down to the new reservation, relying upon the federal government to help make it an Indian farming sanctuary. *Hornoseh quahote* refused to leave his old homeland, as did the majority of those Mojaves who had always lived in the Mojave Valley. *Yara tav* was head chief when he led the exodus from the valley and he continued to serve through 1866.

The Superintendent of Indian Affairs, Arizona Territory, George C. Leighy, October 18, 1865, reported that Indian tribes were becoming dangerously anti-white and that bands were joining the hostile Apaches in attacking miners, merchants, and settlers:

> Abandonment of this portion of the Territory was freely and earnestly discussed. At this stage, through the influence of Iretiba, the Mojave chief, and Cue-sue-e-mar, chief of the Yavapais, worthy chiefs of their tribes, eight hundred of the Yavapais or Apache-Mojaves came in to the river, and went peaceably to work, thereby reducing the source of obtaining recruits by the hostile tribes.... The Hualapaies have not as yet come into the river.

In his report, October 2, 1866, Superintendent Leighy gave *Yara tav's* status and described his role as an unsuccessful peace-maker between whites and the Hualapais Indians above Fort Mojave. Leighy reported:

> They [the Hualapais] have been considered as in a state of war with the whites for more than a year past. An attempt was made last spring through Triteba [an obvious misprint of the initial letter] the head chief of the Mojaves, to arrange a peace with these Indians, which promised success, but the unprovoked murder of one of their most influential chiefs by a party of whites resulted in the breaking off all negotiations and a renewal of the war.

This was Superintendent Leighy's last report. He was waylaid and murdered by Yavapais Indians while returning to the reservation on the dangerous La Paz road. A report by Special U.S. Indian Agent John Feudge, Colorado River Reservation, June 30, 1867, referred to *Yara tav* as "the head chief of the Mojaves" and to *Homoseh quahote* as "a chief named Seck-a-hoot." Feudge also described Hualapais hostilities and cited an instance of *Homoseh quahote's* role as a warrior ally of white men:

> The conduct of the Walapais this past year has been reprehensible. In September a band of their tribe killed six Americans who were engaged in mining, at the time, near Fort Mojave. A party of citizens from the vicinity of the fort, accompanied by a number of Mojaves and led by a chief named Seek-a-hoot, went in pursuit of the Walapais, whom they overtook about 30 miles from the fort. Seek-a-hoot, with his party, surprised the Walapais in their camp at daylight and killed the whole party, 21 in number. I learned from Iriteba, the head chief of the Mojaves, that while most of the Hualapais are disposed to maintain friendly relation with the other river tribes and the whites, a fierce and vindictive band of the same tribe, numbering about 100, and led by a chief named Ware-e-heech-e-heech-e, are determined to avail themselves of every favorable opportunity to make war on the friendly Mohaves and the whites. The hostile determination of the chief and his followers arises from the killing of the head chief of their tribe, Wau-ba-yumba, in the winter of 1865, by some Americans; and because the Mojaves rejected the overtures made by the disaffected or aggrieved Hualapais to unite with them in conjunction with the Chimihueves and Piutes to exterminate or drive out of the country all the whites, their hatred of the Mohaves has become as great as it is towards the whites.

Feudge's report provides a setting which illuminates a letter to *Homoseh quahote* from Governor Richard C. McCormick of the Arizona Territory, October 12, a month after the episode reported by Feudge. This old letter in the "Chief's Papers," written in the symmetrical, flowing penmanship of the Governor reads:

> To Sick o hoot
> Captain of the Mohaves
> Having heard of your brave fight against the hostile Wallapais, I wish to say that the white man consider you a good Indian, and their true friend.
> (Signed) R. McCormick
> Governor

More lies behind this letter than meets the eye. At the time it was written it could have meant the difference between life and death to its bearer. The Governor's salutation did not indicate that *Homoseh quahote* was the head chief of his tribe. The letter, coming from the Governor, however, was a testimonial not to be disregarded lightly by either citizens or the military. It also bespoke recognition of the old warrior's prestige and was an open bid for further aid from the Mohaves in the vicinity of the fort. The California Volunteers at Fort Mojave had been replaced by U.S. Army troops six months earlier, but these were only one company of infantry, too few in number for effective warfare with the Hualapais. One of *Homoseh quahote's* main roles in keeping the treaty during the worsening hostilities between Indians and Arizonians during the following years was to give Mojave support to the U.S. military in suppressing Indian hostilities against white men. In this his warrior reputation and warrior skill were assets to the Army. The Mohaves' adherence to the treaty and their alliance with white people, though appreciated by the military, estranged them from the Indian tribes against whom they took sides. Some Indians accused them of being agents or collaborators of the whites.

That *Yara tav* was the head chief of the Mojave tribe from 1861 through 1866 seems clear from the records. Beginning in 1867 and continuing through 1869. a difference of opinion relative to his status and that of *Homoseh quahote* crops up. The records for the fiscal year 1868-69 illustrate this difference. and also give a glimpse at conditions on the Colorado River Reservation and in the Mojave Valley. Agent Feudge, in his report to the Commissioner of Indian Affairs, August 1, 1869, wrote:

> To appease the Mohaves and avert an Indian war Iriteba the head chief of the Mohaves, addressed them in council for several days and nights, and succeeded finally in allaying the excitement. For these successful efforts and great service on the part of Iriteba the Americans in the vicinity of the reservation presented him with a pair of costly blankets, and the agent, believing that the government would approve his action, presented him with one of the government horses, which would replace similar articles sacrificed by this chief, in his successful efforts in averting an atrocious war.

Colonel George L. Andrews, Superintendent of Indian Affairs, Arizona Territory, transmitted Feudge's report with his own to the Commissioner of Indian Affairs, September 9, 1869. In it he provided this enlightening information:

> Respectfully referring [to] the report of Agent John Feudge, I would state that I have just returned from a short visit to the Colorado River Reservation and Fort Mojave.
>
> I found on the reserve Irataba, with about eight hundred of his band of Mojaves, and no other Indians; that the attempts at cultivation were restricted to an area of not to exceed forty acres; that no barley or wheat was planted; that the agent, Feudge, had left without waiting for the arrival of his successor, and in a word the situation of affairs was anything but encouraging.
>
> Irataba, chief of the Mojaves on the reserve, accompanied me to Fort Mojave, and while there I had quite a protracted interview with him and Sikahot, the head chief of the nation. I learned there are about two thousand of these Indians in the Mojave Valley, and from what I saw, judge that they had planted much more extensively, in proportion to their numbers, than those living on the reservation..... I also learned that the Mojave Valley Indians had shared the wheat they raised with their brethren on the reservation....
>
> Those at Fort Mojave gave as a reason for not moving on the reserve that the canal is not completed, and that they did not know how it would work, but if completed and it works well, they *think* they will move down there. Sikahat is opposed to moving there himself, saying he is an old man and the Mohave Valley has always been his home. My own impression is that it will be very difficult to induce the tribe, as a whole, to remove from the valley bearing their name, both from local attachment and that the valley, though but about one-third as long as that in which the reservation is located, appears to be the better valley of the

two. Subsequent investigations may require another report on this subject hereafter.

Meantime, in a letter dated September, 1869, Captain May H. Stacey at "Camp Mojave" had reported to Colonel Andrews:

> The Mojaves are divided into two branches. One is living on the reservation near La Paz, acknowledging as chief or head man, Irataba, of whom I know nothing. The other and it is said, the greater portion, live around Hardyville and the Needles. The principal man of this branch is Sic-a-hoot, assisted by a number of smaller captains.

By 1870, *Homoseh quahote* was referred to as the head chief of the tribe and *Yara tav;* as the chief of the Mojaves on the reservation. The following excerpt from the report of Lieutenant Helenes Dodt, Special Agent, Colorado River Reservation, August 23, 1870, summarized the situation:

> This reservation was established four years ago. The then officers of the Indian Department tried to get the whole Mohave tribe on the reservation, but failed to accomplish it, and so far only about one-third of the whole tribe, led by Iritaba, one of the principal captains or chiefs of the tribe, has located here. The tribe is divided in three principal parts, whose chiefs are Sickahut, Iritaba, and Aschuket, the former being the head chief of the whole tribe. Each one of these parts is again divided into a number of hereditary captaincies.

On August 22, 1871, Superintendent of Indian Affairs, Arizona Territory, H. Bendell, reported to the Commissioner of Indian Affairs:

> No coalition has yet taken place between the divided houses of the Mohaves. That portion under Sic-a-hoot, at Yreteba Slough, finding themselves cut off from supplies of all kinds, may think it best to waive their views and come to the reserve. Still, I am of the opinion that they are better off where they are, and, under the direction of a sub-agent, could be made comfortable and contented. I have already recommended this proposition, and find no present cause to change my views upon the subject.

The last references to *Homoseh quahote* in the records were made in the latter months of 1872. On August 31, 1872, J. A. Tonner, Agent of the Colorado River Agency, reported to the Commissioner of Indian Affairs: "The section of the Mojave tribe under Siccahoot I did not have time to visit being one hundred miles above here at Fort Mojave. They are constantly interchanging visits with those on the reservation, but they, with their chief, do not wish to come under the rule of lritaba.

Two letters written by Captain Edmund F Thompson, post commander at Fort Mojave, dated September 5, show that *Homoseh quahote* was the head chief. The first letter stated, "I have told *Sick-a-hoot* the Chief of the Mojaves that he must bring me the Indian who committed the depredation today, and he has promised to do so." The next. day Thompson wrote, "Sick-a-hoot has not yet brought me the Indian, he is much thought of by his immediate chief Clzu-va-whe who refused to surrender him I understand.

Yara tav died in 1874. Special Indian Agent, Tonner of the Colorado River Reservation wrote in his report to the Commissioner of Indian Affairs, September 25: "The death of Ireteba last spring, who was their chief for twenty years, is much deplored, as he was the most sagacious of his tribe, and a great assistance in my plans of improvement of his people." Whether *Homoseh quahote* outlived *Yara tav,* or vice versa, cannot be definitely established from these records.

The deaths of *Yara tav* and *Homoseh quahote* did not bring "the divided house of the Mojaves" together again. The records show that *Yara tav's* successor on the Colorado Reservation was *Qolho qorau* of the *Vemacka* clan, his nephew, and that *Homoseh quahote's* successor as great chieftain was his son, *Empote quatacheech. Qolho gorau* and his followers continued to hold to the policies advocated by *Yara tav.* The "Fort Mojave Indians" as they came to be called, continued the policy advocated by *Homoseh quahote.* Throughout *Empote quatacheech's* head chieftainship they stuck by the terms of the peace treaty, passively resisted all threats and enticements to get them to the reservation, cooperated with the military and had few altercations with settlers who infiltrated the valley. Their chief problem was to hold on to their land.

That *Empote quatacheech* was ever considered by the Mojaves on the Colorado River Reservation to be the head chief or great chieftain of the tribe is open to question, but the evidence is clear that the majority of the tribe (*e.g.*, those in the Mojave Valley) reverted to the hereditary line. Like his father, *Empote quatacheech* was also the hereditary chief of the *Matha lyathum* although the population had shifted and declined through the years. His long vernacular name meant "obscured or hidden in a cloud of dust." To Mojaves a cloud of dust is a figure of speech which signifies war or trouble. This name, like other Mojave names, has been spelled various ways. Among the spelling by post commanders at Fort Mojave are: *Em-porte-quitu-chichua, Potachecha, Porta-chi-chi, porta-che-che, Pote-che-cha, Po-to-che-chu*. He was also called John Potachecha.

Among Chief Lambert's papers in the Fort Mojave Tribal Records are two letters written in longhand as testimonials for Em-pate quatacheech by post commanders. One letter signed by Captain J [ames] J. Van Horn, December 12, 1878, reads:

> The bearer hereof "Em-porta-quitu-chichua" is the hereditary chief of the Mojave tribe of Indians, he is friendly to the whites and deserving of kind and respectful treatment by all with whom he may come in contact.
>
> It is therefore to be earnestly requested that, by virtue of his birth and position, he will not be molested, but be kindly treated and fairly dealt with by all persons desiring peaceable relations with his tribe, and consequently through his influence with other tribes, with whom he may be on friendly terms.

The second letter was written by Captain Augustus W. Corliss, November 13, 1886:

> I have known the bearer Po-to-che-che, Head Chief of the Mojave Indians, for some time, and have found him to be an honest, friendly, intelligent, obedient and trustworthy Indian, and I do not hesitate to recommend him for the favorable consideration, and kind treatment of anyone who may have intercourse with him.

Empote quatacheech was still the great chieftain as 1887 drew to a close. The last reference to him is contained in a letter to the Assistant Adjutant General, Department of Arizona, dated December 20, 1887, and signed by Captain Alpheus H. Bowman, post commander, Fort Mojave:

> I have the honor to state that Puti-chi-cha hereditary Chief of the Mojave Indians, Askeet and other principal men of the tribe... have desired me to write, and say that they and their tribe are much pleased to learn of the arrest of the Maricopa Indian for the murder of one of the Mojave young men and wish to thank General Miles for causing the arrest to be brought about, and although only poor Indians as Askeet expresses himself they are grateful for kindness to their people.

Empote guatacheech died sometime between December 20, 1887 and late July, 1888. Captain Bowman wrote an attest dated July 31, 1888:

> The bearer hereof Ho-be-lia (known as Pole in his minority) son of Porta-che-cha deceased and grandson of Hum-sick-a-Holt has been by popular vote and choice of all the Mojave Indians, elected and declared their hereditary leader and chief of their people and such they have in formal assembly declared him.
>
> 2nd And the Mojave Indians further agree and select Askeet and Chief John (a brother of Hum-sick-a-Holt, deceased) as principal chiefs and advisors of Pota-che-cha. [Hobelia]
>
> 3rd The Mojave Indians as a people request Mr. Henry Lambert of Mojave County A. T. to befriend and act as [guardian] to Ho-be-lia in his minority and to assist in shaping the policy of the Mojave Indians to conform to the custom and laws prevailing among well organized settlements of civilized people.

The young great-chieftain-elect was about eight years old in 1888. His "boy-name" *Hobelia* is fraught with significance to Mojaves. It means "a gift to the dead," which is one part of the Mojave ceremonies for the departed. As the funeral pyre of a departed Mojave is lighted to release his spirit to the Shadow Land, Mojaves cast into the flames their gifts to him—gifts which will re-assemble from the smoke to become his possessions in after-life.

No references to *Hobelia* appear after Captain Bowman's attest in 1888. Captain Bowman was Fort Mojave's last post commander. To him fell the task of officially transferring it from the War Department to the Department of the Interior to be used for an Indian School. His reports and the evacuation of all but a small detail of "clean-up" troops on July 1, 1890, marked finis to the military era among the Mojaves.

The exodus of the troops from Fort Mojave was looked upon by the Fort Mojaves as a sign that they would have their lands again after the thirty year period of military probation. On August 22, 1890, the representative of the Department of the Interior took over the premises of the fort. He was the new superintendent of the Fort Mojave Indian Industrial School, S. M. McGowan, whose assignment by the Bureau of Indian Affairs was to administer a program of compulsory Indian education through the medium of a boarding school. By removing Indian children from their homes and placing them in boarding schools away from contacts with their own cultures, and by providing there a controlled Anglo-American environment, the Indian Bureau expected, with-in twenty-five years, to break up tribal ties, weed out old customs, substitute the English language, and, in short, produce a crop of Indian American citizens who would be given land, individually. The authority of the military, which had not included deep seated cultural change, was now invested in superintendents of schools and reservations and expanded into all aspects of Indian life. Superintendent McGowan explained the new policy of the United States to acting Chief *Asukit* and the tribe. According to the tribal records:

> He told us the White Father at the White House in Washington is in charge of the affairs of the Indians and is going to give them an education so that they might become American citizens and to be self supporting Indians. In twenty five years Education will benefit you people as it did all races. You will be given your land and water rights when the Government comes to it and you will have no trouble in securing those things belonging to you...
>
> When your children grow up and within 25 years they will be fairly well educated and get their lands and make homes for themselves and will become a worthy American Citizen.

The great chieftain-elect was about ten years old when the War Department transferred Fort Mojave to the Department of the Interior. Chief *Asukit,* acting for him, quieted the excited old Mojaves and organized his esteemed old war scouts into "educational promoters" with the titles of Captains. They aided the superintendent in enforcing the compulsory education law. Chief *Asukit* himself resided on the old Fort Mojave premises where he could keep an eye on affairs. The Mojaves, who for thirty years had remained in their ancient homelands through peaceful persistence, sought now to retain their tribal entity and lands through the same means, adapted to new circumstances, for an extended period of twenty-five years.

The young great chieftain-elect. was enrolled in the school in 1892. His name *Hobelia* had been dropped and a new name, *Sukulai homar* (*sukulai,* plant; *homar,* a child, young), meaning a young plant, had been given to him by the Mojaves. He was called by "his other name," Pete Lambert. He became officially the *Aha macave pipatahon,* or the hereditary and elected great chieftain of the Mojaves on September 14, 1896. An attest in the "Chiefs Papers" signed by Jelin J. McKoin, Superintendent of the Fort Mojave School (1896-1902), reads:

> BE IT KNOWN TO ALL MEN: That at a Great Council held at Fort Mojave, Arizona. by the Mojave Indians, upon the 14th day of Sept. 1896, Capt. Pete Lambert was unanimously elected Great Chief of that tribe.
>
> That this action of the Mojave Council was duly approved by me, and that Capt. Pete Lambert is from this day forward to be respected and obeyed as Great Chief and that this office he shall hold during good behavior.
>
> I trust that he will be a good Chief and will long continue to hold this office.

In witness whereof I have hereunto set my hand and seal and the day and year above written.

Among the "Chief's Papers," also, are two congratulatory letters. The one from Commissioner of Indian Affairs, William A, Jones, dated October 10, 1899:

Superintendent McKoin informs me that the Mojaves recently elected you to be their leader and that you are a good friend of the school.

It gives me pleasure to know that the Mojaves have selected as their chief one who wants to see his people educated and to advance in civilization. It is a credit to the Mojaves to have put such a man at their head and I trust that you and all your band will make every effort to adopt the ways of white men as they are taught at the school and to resist the evil influences which they try to throw around you in whiskey shops and other demoralizing resorts. Be sober, be industrious and give your children a chance to become wise in the white man's way.

You have my very best wishes.

The other letter, written by S. M. McGowan, superintendent of the Fort Mojave School during *Sukulai homar's* school-boy days, dated January 22, 1900, began, "My dear Pete." Wrote McGowan:

I received your letter yesterday, which notified me of your elevation to the honorable position of chief of the Mohave tribe of Indians.

I am glad because of your promotion and hope that you will be the means of leading the younger Mohaves out right into the bright light of our best civilization.

I hope you will always stand for the schools and education and enlightenment. I trust your voice will always be lifted for the elevation of your people. Stand by the schools; see that your people send their children to the Mohave school first, and then after five or six years insist upon these children going to some larger and more advanced school.

I can remember when I first took you into the Ft. Mohave school and what a time I had in cutting your hair for the first time. I can see now all the old Mohave women standing around crying, while you covered your long hair with your arms and told me that I wouldn't dare to cut that hair off, but the hair was cut in spite of all your efforts and the direful predictions of the Mohave women. I compelled you to have your hair cut off, not because of any objections to the long hair in itself, but merely because the long hair was a symbol of savagery.

I hope you will be just as firm and emphatic in your commands, when you know you are in the right, as I was in insisting upon the cutting of your hair.

When Supt. McKoin asks you to bring him 150 children or any number of children, don't rest either night or day until the Superintendent's request is obeyed.

Stand for the right and all the best people will stand by you.

During his first two years as great chief, *Sukulai homar* had as his advisors Chief *Asukit*, and a venerable scout named Chief *Spatterbone*. Both died in the latter half of 1898 or the first half of 1899. In his report for the fiscal year 1898-1899, Superintendent McKoin wrote the Commissioner of Indian Affairs, "Chiefs Samuel Spatterbone and Asakeet, who were great friends of the school and had much influence over the Indians, died, leaving no one among the tribe who could fill their places in bringing in children to fill up the school." This unpalatable task fell to the young Great Chieftain of the Mojaves.

The administration of the school changed in the spring of 1903. The new incumbent, Duncan McArthur, was made the agent for all Indians within thirty miles of the school, along with the superintendency of the school. The remaining three documents in the "Chief's Papers" were written by McArthur. They serve both as testimonials of Chief Lambert's hereditary and elected status and the manner in which this status was invoked. One was a notice addressed "To the Captains and Leading Men Among the Mohave Indians," dated August 20, 1903:

I wish to advise you, through Pete Lambert, Chief that all children of school age not attending school should report here for enrollment Tuesday, September 1st, next.

You are urgently requested to use your best efforts in accomplishing this result. Any person refusing to place children under their care in the Government School should be required to call upon the Superintendent with said children to offer their reasons, if any, fur not co-operating with the Govermnent in the matter of educating the children.

A similar, but more revealing letter addressed, "To whom it may concern," dated November 11, 1904, reads:

This is to state that the bearer, Pete Lambert, chief of the Mohave Indians, is interested in the education of the Mohave children and is a great help to the Government in the placing of Indian youth in the Fort Mojave School. He cooperates with the school authorities in securing constant regular attendance of pupils and has been authorized by the undersigned to have captured and returned to the school any runaway pupils who may be found at Needles, Cal. or elsewhere.

All good Mohave Indians are hereby requested to support their tribal chief in his laudable work for the good of his people.

The third letter, dated December 12, 1904, was a notice "To whom it may concern." In it Superintendent McArthur refers to Lambert both as the hereditary and elected chief of the Mohaves, and commends him for a voluntary act which violated an ancient *Aha macaw* tradition.

This is to state that Pete Lambert, hereditary and elected chief of the Mohaves has this date had his long hair cut off as an example for other male members of his tribe to follow in the change from tribal life and customs to the customs and modes of living of American citizens.

This voluntary action of the above mentioned Chief of the Mohaves is commended by the undersigned.

This letter concludes the "Chief's Papers" so carefully preserved by Chief Lambert in his treasured album. It is also the last document in the Fort Mojave Tribal Records in which he is referred to as the Chief of the Mojave Indians until 1930. For the next quarter of a century his name appears in the Tribal Records accompanied by the title "sub-chief" or "chief," always subsidiary to his replacement, Chief Sherman Ross, "Chief of the Mohaves."

The precise date of *Sukulai homar's* removal from the great chieftainship cannot he pinpointed from the Tribal Records, nor can the circumstances be established clearly without recourse to unsifted oral information. The available records do show that in 1905, the Fort Mojave tribe relieved him of his head position and elected Bill Ross "to carry Chief Lamberts duties for life." One entry says, "his appointment came through the failure of Chief Lambert to carry on his contract as head of the tribe handed down from many generations." This action must have taken place sometime in the latter half of the year because *Sukulai homar* was the head chief when the superintendent of the Fort Mojave School required all of the tribe to take "American" names in the spring and summer of 1905.

Chief Bill Ross, whose Indian name was *Kwalemeech* (also spelled *Qualemeech*), was a respected and prominent old Mojave who had served with War Chief *Asukit* for years in both military and civil affairs. He died shortly after his election and early in 1906 his son, Sherman Ross, "inherited the chieftainship from his father, Bill Ross!" Chief Sherman Ross was called *Avi chavar* by his tribesmen although his legal American name is consistently used in the Tribal Records and always appeared with the *X* used as a signature. *Avi charvar* was of the *Oach* clan, whose name symbolizes the clouds, rain and wind. His vernacular name meant "next to the highest mountain" (*avi*, mountain; *chavar*, almost as high, next to the highest). *Qualemeech* and *Avi chavar*, like *Yara tav*, were *hochoch* (*Aha macave yaltanach hochoch*), head chiefs made by the people. Unlike *Yara tav*, however, they did not come from a line of hereditary chiefs. By this time in Mojave history only two hereditary chiefs of the old lines were left —*Sukulai homar*, hereditary chief of the remnants of the *Matha lyathurm*, and *Anyia hear*, son of War Chief *Asukit*, and successor to his father's chieftainship. The former was disqualified by the tribe, the latter was too specialized, his interests being mainly education; hence the Mojaves broke tribal precedent and "chose the best man for the place." *Avi chavar* proved to be "the right man."

The details of the young Great Chieftain's removal are historically unimportant, but the principle invoked by the tribe is very significant. In removing the hereditary and elected Chief of the Mojaves from his position, the Mojaves invoked the criteria conveyed in their time-honored expression, *Aha macave pipatahon*. The old Mojaves who knew *Empote quatacheech* and those who venerated *Homoseh quahote* felt that *Sukulai homar* "was a disappointment," that "he was too young."

Avi chavar was a figure who commanded attention and respect anywhere by his demeanor and his height. He was reared in the *Aha macave* traditions, deeply concerned about his people, and had almost uncanny foresight. He understood English and could speak it well, but he preferred to use his native language and talk through an interpreter. He accepted the head chieftainship at one of the darkest periods in Mojave history. He and the tribe faced a backlog of unfinished problems dating from 1859, problems that time and circumstances had compounded. Always the land, the peace treaty and the land!

Among the more pressing problems were the uncertainty of their land claims, aggravated by settlement in the Mojave Valley and the eviction of Mojave landholders by newcomers who insisted that they "go to the Colorado River Reservation where they belonged;" knowledge that the government had granted the railroad every other section of land on part of their old domains, and news that the government was planning to dam the Colorado River, thus ruining much of their old lands for agriculture in the overflow of the river. The tribe also felt tyrannized by the superintendent of the Fort Mojave School and unheeded by the Agent at the Colorado River Agency. And they were outraged that their ancient family names had been bypassed for new "American" names. Thus, *Avi chavar* began his leadership. His tribal council, or Fort Mojave Executive Board, consisted of Chiefs *Sukulai homar* and *Anyia hear* (often spelled *Anniyerra*) and four prominent middle-aged or old Mojaves called "Captains." The personnel remained relatively unchanged throughout his administration. Of these men, *Sukulai homar* was the youngest, and the only one who "had gone to school." The Fort Mojave Tribal Records until 1920 are skimpy, because the chief and his council kept their records the traditional Mojave way, by memory. However, Chief *Avi chavar* prevailed upon the Council to employ an English-speaking and writing Fort Mojave School graduate, Hal *Oneyuravarya* Davidson, to work fulltime as secretary, interpreter, and special representative. Systematic tribal records thus began in 1921.

Official communications between the Fort Mojave tribe and the Commissioner of Indian Affairs, Charles H. Burke, from 1922 through 1925 show the status of *Avi chavar* (Sherman Ross) to be that of Chief of the tribe and *Sukulai homar* to be that of subchief. They also show that the major problem confronting the tribe was obtaining a title to their lands under the terms of the treaty made "with the Federal Troops." A letter, signed The Fort Mojave Indian Tribe and Chief Sherman Ross, May 16, 1922, presented their case to Commissioner Burke. It said, in part:

> Our fathers tell us it is 70 years since we made the aforesaid Treaty with the Federal Troops. As you know we have no way of keeping written records of our history, but it has been handed down from time by our ancestors from one generation to another until every Mojave child that reaches the age of understanding knows his tribe history, the working of its Council, and the existence of all treaties. We know that our government in Washington keeps the records of all treaties made with the Indians, and we know that ours still exist and can be found in the Hall of Records; we have presented the fact to every superintendent or Indian Agent that comes to the Mojave Indian Fort and school, and also every government official that we have met but without results. We have lived under the treaty for the last 70 years and complyed with all its requirements. But it seems that we must produce it before we can get a clear title to what is justly ours. We know that the water in the streams, also the land, belongs to the states unless it has been reserved by the government, and we must

have the treaty to show that the land belongs to us. Therefore, Commissioner, we ask you to make a personal matter for us, look up this treaty and all records pertaining to the Mojave Indians, and give us the details. We feel sure you will do this for you know we send you our Petition.

This letter and Commissioner Burke's reply, August 7, bear the following notation, "Copied by Hal. O. Davidson, entered the records the 26th of March, 1925. Approved by Chief Sherman Ross. Approved by sub-chief P. Lambert." The Commissioner enclosed a photostated copy of Major Haller's letter of 1862, and gave this information:

I have ascertained that the Fort Mohave Reservation was established by Executive Order Dec. 1. 1910, and Feb. 2, 1911. The Reservation contains 31,328 acres, of which 14,000 were embraced in the Original Military Reservation at Ft. Mohave which was abandoned and turned over to the control of the Interior Department by Executive Order dated Sept. 19, 1890....

Referring to the statement in the letter signed by you and other Indians that a treaty was entered into by the Ft. Mohave Indians and J. Van Horn representing the Government in the year 1861, will say that there is no record of any agreement or Treaty as stated. A careful examination has been made of the Annual reports of the Com. of Indian Affairs for the years 1861 and 1862, and there is no reference to such a Treaty. It is possible that some officer in the Army may have made some promise to the Indians in 1861 or prior thereto, but if such is the case, it would not constitute a Treaty, and would be of no value at this time.

I find in the files a letter to the Comm. of Indians, Hon. Chas. E. Mix, dated January 28, 1862, and signed by G. O. Haller, Major of the 7th Infantry, who has been a short time previously Commander of the Post at Ft. Mohave. As this letter refers to the Ft. Mohave Indians and speaks of them in complimentary terms, I will enclose a *Photostatic* copy of the same for the information of yourself and the other Indians.

You will understand that it is the policy of the Department and the Indian Bureau to assist the Indians in everything it can to become civilized and self-supporting, and to see that they are protected in their rights. If there are any Treaty Obligations that have not been fulfilled on the part of the Government, I do not know what they are. A Treaty, to be binding, would have to be executed formally by the Indians and a representative of the Government authorized to treat with the Indians, and have the ratification of Congress.

The promise of some officer in the Army or other person in the service of the Government not authorized to speak officially would not be a Treaty, or an agreement having any binding effect. If you can furnish me with any further statement with reference to any Treaty that you claim is in existence and has not been complied with, I will gladly make a research to see if it can be located. It would appear that the Reservation occupied by the Ft.. Mohave Indians was created by Executive Order and not by a Treaty.

A series of letters and petitions between 1926 and 1928 were directed by the Tribal Council to Governor George W. P Hunt of Arizona asking his help in obtaining riparian rights. These were signed in rank order by Chief Sherman Ross, Mojave Tribe, Chief Pete Lambert, Chief *Anyai hear* Goodman, and other members. One petition thus signed urged the Governor to intercede with Commissioner Burke in their behalf, which he did.

The names and titles of the Chief of the Mojaves and his Tribal Council are contained in a letter written by Governor Hunt to his successor, Governor-elect John C. Phillips, December 17, 1928. A copy of this letter, on Executive Office stationery, and bearing the Governor's signature, was given to the tribal secretary for the Mojave records. Governor Hunt wrote:

I am writing you this letter at the request of a committee of leading Indians of the Mohave and Walapai tribes.

I am glad to recommend these Indians as peaceful, lawabiding residents of our State. During my term of office as Chief Executive of Arizona, these Indian tribes have frequently been represented in natters by the following members:

H. O. Davidson, Secretary, Mohave and Walapai Indians, Needles, California.

Chief Sherman Ross, Mohave Tribe, Ft. Mohave Indian Reservation.

Chief Aniyarre Askit or Joseph Goodman, Ft. Mohave Indian Reservation.

Chief Pete Lambert, Ft. Mohave Indian Reservation.

Capt. Homirpook Hamilton, Ft. Mohave Indian Reservation.

Capt. Ha chur Courtwright, Ft. Mohave Indian Reservation. (Acting for Geo. [Jack] Harrison).

Chief Philip Quasula, Seligman, Arizona.

Chief Bob Schrum, Peach Springs. Arizona.

Capt. Jim Fielding, Valentine, Arizona.

I have found the word of these Indians to be good and that their statements can be relied upon for tenth. I recommend them to you with pleasure."

Avi chavar died suddenly in the summer of 1929. He left no male heir. The date and circumstances of *Sukulai homar's* restoration to the status of Chief of the Mojaves have not been found thus far in the Tribal Records, but the fact that he succeeded *Avi chavar* is clear from correspondence, reports and minutes of meetings. From 1930 until 1940, the names of the two last chiefs of the Mojave Indian Tribe appear together, that of Chief Lambert first; that of Chief *Anyia hear,* second. *Anyia hear* continued to serve on the Council with responsibilities for education, which changed after the Fort Mojave School was closed and Mojave children entered local public schools in 1931. He was bedridden from 1941 until his death on January 19, 1947. He left no children to carry on his heritage. *Sukulai homar's* long experiences as a member of Chief *Avi chavar's* Council made him conversant with tribal affairs and a head chieftain's responsibilities. He also had the benefit of a Tribal Secretary who had grown up under *Avi chavar's* firm tutelage.

One record exists that both establishes *Sukulai homar's* restoration to the great chieftainship and reaffirms his lineage. It also contains the only clue in the Tribal Records of "what happened in 1905."

A long account of a Mojave Tribal meeting in Chief Lambert's place on February 2, 1946, with Hal O. Davidson presiding, says in part:

> Our Chief, Pete Lambert feels it is necessary to call all who may be able to come to this gathering and he will not be able to carry on his duty as head representative of the Mohave tribe any longer, due to the fact that he is now sick in bed with paralytic stroke [suffered] a few days ago. His desire is, he has kept some papers or records pertaining to Chief of Mohave Tribe, his grandfather, and members, when the white people just came here, about 100 years ago.

The documents in the "Chief's Papers," quoted earlier in this study were read to those assembled, accompanied by Chief Lambert's recollections of Mojave history after the coming of white men. This record contains his sketchy chronology including the following cryptic notes:

> 1905. Chief Sherman Ross inherited chieftainship from his father who died. His father, Chief Bill, was elected to carry Chief Lambert's duties.
>
> A felony was committed. The Chief [was] involved and his interpreter, Lyn Jim was killed, 1905. Ross approved [proved] to be an able man until his death.

Chief Lambert's announcement of his inability to serve longer as the tribe's "head representative" was not accepted as a resignation. His Tribal Council "acted for him" during his physical helplessness. "He could not get around, but his mind was clear." A letter from C. H. Gensler, Superintendent of the Colorado River Reservation, whose jurisdiction included the Fort Mojave Indians, March 22, 1946, was directed to "Mr. Pete Lambert, Chief of Mojave Indians." Its contents dealt with pending negotiations to purchase land and building materials for a housing project for Mojaves whose homes were destroyed by Colorado flood waters. This seems to be the last letter directed to the chief. Subsequent correspondence in the Tribal Records were addressed to H. O. Davidson, Chairman of the Business Committee. The Business Committee or re-named Council "acted for" Chief Lambert until his death. Chief

Lambert died at his home in Needles, California, September 19, 1947. He was cremated with the "long ceremonies" accorded important men. This includes the Feather Ceremony which is given to men who have lost their lives or devoted their lives for the benefit of the people, or whose ancestors for over one hundred years had earned this greatest of all Mojave tributes. In 1948, the Fort Mojaves memorialized his name in a street in the newly built Mojave Village, along with the names of their most important men during the last half century.

The Great Chieftain left no heir of the hereditary *Malika* line. Thus came to an end the great chieftainship of the Mojave Indians. After a lengthy period of trial and error, the Fort Mojaves finally reorganized their local government in 1957 under a constitution approved by the Secretary of the Interior. They elected a Tribal Council of seven members, the "one with the most votes to be chairman or head man." Interestingly enough, the Chairman of the Fort Mojave Tribal Council was Mrs. Frances Malika Stillman, of the *Malika* clan, the clan of the hereditary great chieftains.

Photo by Jeffrey L. Garton

Chapter Four

Pottery, Beading and Other Art Forms

Wilene Fisher with examples of her pottery and beading.

Beading to Delight In

by Wilene Fisher

For as long as I've been beading, people have asked me, "Where did you learn how to bead? Who taught you how? It looks difficult." My response is always the same. "No one actually sat down to teach me. I've been blessed with a gift," and "no I don't find it difficult." I thank God and my ancestors for this gift to create. Not only do I bead, but I also paint, sew and make Mojave Effigy pottery from either clay found along the river or commercial clay.

It was a simple life growing up in Parker along the Colorado River. I recall my maternal grandmother, Lena Bryan, from Fort Mojave in Needles, CA., always sitting and beading. She would take her wares to the non-natives and sell her beadwork, and sometimes we, children, were privileged to tag along. I didn't know her but I was told that my paternal grandmother, Kate Fisher, was also a beader, a seamstress and was well known for making beautiful Chemehuevi baskets.

My fondest memories of beading are when I temporarily lived with my great-uncle, Sam Brockman (Gee-Chee), also from Fort Mojave, Needles, CA. My Gee-Chee and I lived in a very humble two bedroom house. Day after day he would sit on the edge of his bed with a small TV tray in front of him covered with assorted colors of beads, needles, thread and beadwork. I recall the wooden beading looms with beautiful beadwork sewn on the threads, leaning against the wall of the bedroom. At night he would take out his gourd and sing his family Mojave songs. Little did I know at that time that I was being taught how to bead. On occasion elderly Indian women would stop in to visit and bring beads, talk about beadwork and what was going on in the community. This was always a treat because my Gee-Chee would bring out his finished beadwork and display all the work that he had completed.

My very first piece of beadwork was a daisy chain. Before that I would just sit with my Gee-Chee and he would give me beads to string and make simple bracelets and necklaces. Years passed and I would see beadwork and think to myself, "I can bead that." I pulled out the old beads of my grandmother and Gee-Chee and would try to bead. It worked because all those memories that were instilled as a child came back to me. I would just create beadwork like the works of art of my ancestors. Although there are many techniques when it comes to beadwork, I use the techniques I visualize in my mind from my childhood. My passion is in creating Mojave/Chemehuevi designs, but I also enjoy producing contemporary as well as other tribal designs upon request.

I come from a lineage of very talented family members and I understand that I have been blessed with a gift to create and work with my hands just as they did. I want to hand this gift on to my family members. My nieces and nephews enjoy beading when they visit. So far I have one niece, Paulene, who is a natural and I hope to see many more of our younger generation continue to have an interest and carry on and preserve this important part of our heritage and culture.

Above: pottery and beading by Wilene Fisher

Above: examples of beading by Wilene Fisher

Manufacture of Pottery by Mojave Indian Women

by Dr. Edward Palmer

Reprinted with permission of proceedings of the *Davenport Academy of Natural Sciences.*

At the landing of Europeans on the American continent, they found the native Indians in possession of pottery, the excellence of which was praised by the strangers. The manufacture of pottery seems to have been carried on all over the American continent, that of Chili and Peru being of superior quality to that of any other section. The pottery gradually assumes an inferior quality northward, and becomes especially so in the northern and eastern mounds.

There seems to be two divisions of the American Indians, the Toltecs and Aztecs, both of whom are found to be makers of pottery, but of very different qualities. The Toltecs are makers of the superior pottery, and are represented by the Pimo Indians of Arizona, the Moqui and Rio Grande Indians of New Mexico. This division is distinguished from the other, not only by their pottery, but also by their superior dwellings and the manner of disposing of the dead, by burying instead of burning, as is practised by the Aztecs. The pottery of the Aztecs is very inferior to that of the Toltecs in quality, decoration and glazing; in fact, it is of a rudeness that would almost warrant the conclusion that they had borrowed the art from their neighbors, and had just completed their first lesson—that of making a plain, rough pot.

Both these divisions of Indians existed at the discovery of America. The women have always been superior to the men in their knowledge and successful prosecution of the domestic arts and manufactures, and have always been the sole pottery makers. If a man or his children depended upon him to make a pot to cook or eat from, they would starve before they would have one. As the female artists of both divisions use the same means of constructing pottery, it may be interesting to many to know how pottery is made by the native women of our continent.

Last summer I visited the Mojave Indian reservation on the Colorado River, Arizona, for the purpose of making a collection of their native foods, manufactures, etc. Wishing a set of dishes of their make, I engaged the services of a native woman. She was instructed to bring whatever was necessary to make the pottery to the agency so that I could see the process.

The next day she appeared, as desired, accompanied by an assistant. They were somewhat aged, approaching to four score years, and possessed of many wrinkles. Their hair was cut off straight in front, just above the eyes, the remainder reaching down to the shoulders, where it too was evenly trimmed all round. On the head was a round, rather conical hat, made of split twigs, and water tight. Around the waist was suspended the only article of dress, a skirt reaching to the knees, made of strips of willow bark, intermingled with strips of old blankets, pants, and various colored calicos obtained from the whites. This mixture of various colored strips was fastened to a belt of the same materials. The jewelry worn by one consisted of a number of white pearl buttons, strung and hung around her neck. The other wore a string of small sea shells with a larger one in the center. Thus attired they were ready for work.

One of the women laid down a quantity of clay, some paint, several round flat stones of different sizes, and two wooden paddles. The other took her hat from her head, went to the well and filled it with water. They both squatted down on the bare ground, and commenced by sprinkling water from the hat on the clay, using their hands to work the clay to a consistency like that used in manufacturing bricks. After being told the kinds and sizes of pots required, each selected one of the round flat stones upon which to form the bottom of the contemplated pot, using the stones according to the size of the article to be made. Pieces of clay were taken and laid upon the stones. A wooden paddle was used by the right hand to form the mud on the stones into the bottom of the future pot. The ground near by was smoothed off, and these bottoms carefully placed on it. The next thing was to build upon these bottoms. As much clay was taken as was considered necessary, and rolled out in the hand until it was of the same thickness, and long enough to go round the bottom. This was then applied to the bottom and pinched together by the thumb and fingers of the right hand as white ladies do pie crust. The flat stone was now removed from the bottom, and held in the left hand on the inside of the embryo pot, close against the attachment of the addition to the bottom, while the paddle in the right hand patted the outside, nearly obliterating all traces of the joint, while the stone served the same purpose to the inside.

As piece by piece the pots were built up, and the seams nearly obliterated by the stone and paddle, the hands were dipped in water and rubbed over the vessels, inside and out, until a smooth and even surface was produced, thus making the union perfect, and hiding all appearance of the pots having been built up. When the pots had been completed to the desired height, the rim was formed by holding the round stone under the last piece built on, and gently tapping as the stone was moved around the edge. If it was to be ornamented by indentations, a stick was suitably pointed, and the designs executed therewith. In the course of a few hours seven pieces of pottery of various sizes, and designed for different purposes, all even in thickness and smoothness of surface, were produced. The great difficulty was in regulating the quantity of clay for each addition, as the circumference increased or diminished, but they successfully accomplished the task, so that they are justly entitled to the reputation of skilled workers in clay.

All the pottery completed, a smooth piece of ground was selected, exposed to the direct rays of the sun, to which the vessels were removed to dry. As the drying proceeded any crack that appeared was filled up by dipping the fingers in thick, muddy water. The pottery was repeatedly turned so as to dry evenly. All defects that showed themselves were corrected before the burning. Some of the vessels were to be ornamented with paint. This was done during the process of drying, so that it might dry evenly with the clay. The artist mixed her paint with water on a flat stone, and made a brush by twisting a piece of cloth from one of the strips of her skirt. The decorations were now applied, consisting of parallel lines and dots, neatly and regularly made. The painting and drying completed, the next thing was the burning.

A quantity of wood of even sizes was selected, and laid in two piles and ignited. They arranged the pottery tops downward, so that fire could be put all around and on the tops, causing the heat to be uniform all over. A sharp watch was kept over the burning, so that an even degree of heat was applied to all parts of the same vessel at the same time. The potters repeatedly examined the vessels by removing the fire with long sticks in order to see that an even burning was being effected. As soon as the pottery was sufficiently burned, the fire was removed and the pots allowed to remain and cool. Vessels made for cooking and for holding water were not glazed, but those to be used for other purposes were. The glazing was done by rubbing salt water over the vessels while warm, and reburning them to set the glazing.

These artists, though homely and plainly clad and besmeared with dirt, had performed their work well. Judging them by their works, it must be acknowledged they had done as well as most men and women of the paler and better-to-do race could have done with like materials. Dire necessity and compulsion would be necessary to compel most of us to attempt the task. Considering the beauty of the pottery, its symmetry of form, quality of workmanship, the rude tools, the kind of materials used, and also that necessity had been their only teacher, these female artists, though Indians, had, by their works, proven themselves heroines in domestic art, challenging competition by either sex of Americans under like conditions. Credit must be given to the female for her good works, let her be of whatsoever race or color.

Mojave Pottery, Mojave People

by Jill Leslie Furst

The early tourist patrons of Mojave figurines did not record the names of the potters, and we do not know the name of a single nineteenth-century craftswoman. Nevertheless, some figurines from that time were clearly made by the same hand.

More recent Mojave ceramic artists are not all anonymous, however. By the middle of the twentieth century, the tourist trade from the trains had largely died out, but a few elderly potters were still alive, and some of them taught their craft to younger family members.

Ceramicist Annie Fields was a member of me Colorado River Indian Tribes, the southern group of Mojaves, who lived near Parker, Arizona. She was born in 1884, lived in Needles, and died there on May 2, 1971, at the age of 87. She created figurines, human and animal effigy vessels, and bowls with fantastic handles. Fields made the majority of her work in the 1950s and worked intensively for only a decade or so. Still, considering her age, she may well have been one of the young women offering figurines to tourists at the Needles railroad station, and perhaps even to Alfred Kroeber, who was so disdainful of this nontraditional art.

Fields developed a distinctive figural style. Because her sculptures are relatively new, many of them are in good condition and have retained their full complement of hair. She paid close attention to the delicate details of clothing and jewelry, and the females wear beautifully crafted miniature beaded collars and earrings. The faces are particularly engaging. They have large eyes, with black dots for pupils, and they sometimes seem a bit baffled or startled. Females wear the common tattooing on their chins, usually consisting of lines extending from the lower lip down the chin.

Fields gave her men and women face paint in geometric blocks placed horizontally across the face. At first glance, the painted pattern seems to be in the lighter, yellowish color, but actually Fields used the technique of negative painting, applying blocks and lines of darker red over the light yellow base color to create the marking. As noted above, Mojave women often tinted much of their faces, arms, and bodies red, for both beauty and protection against sunburn.

Fields frequently made seated figures with their legs stretched straight out in front, but she also crafted standing images. The bodies are usually slender, and torsos and arms show little modeling. The coiffures suggest Quechan as well as Mojave prototypes. Quechan images often had a deep hole in the head to receive swatches of hair, which were bound with a band to form a roll around the crown. Fields sometimes inserted the hair into a depression on the top of the head. She may have seen examples of her southern neighbors' work and incorporated elements of their techniques that appealed to her.

Elmer Gates was born in 1929 and lived in Poston, Arizona, on the Fort Mohave Reservation. He learned to make pottery from his aunt, although Mojave men were not usually potters. In turn, he taught pottery making to a number of young Mojave, Maricopa, and other Native American and Euro-American artists, including Rick Dillingham. He was well acquainted with Southwestern ceramic styles and experimented freely with shapes, techniques, and motifs. He worked intensively but intermittently in ceramics and in the 1970s made pottery for the Colorado River Indian Tribal Museum. He also sold his work through the Tribal Museum. Gates died in 1990, at the age of sixty-one."

Gates developed a distinctive figural style. He simplified and stylized his bodies, giving them a smooth and nonmuscled appearance. Their oval faces have bulging eyes and prominent noses that often begin at the hairline. He painted the faces, bodies, and upper legs buff yellow, added fine red lines for face painting, and tinted torsos, feet, and lower legs dark red. The females have prominent breasts, but some flat-chested figures with large, round beaded collars covering their upper torsos may also be female. Gates used black yarn for hair, which began just above the bulging eyes, and often stitched a center part into it. He used strongly contrasting colors for skirts and belts.

Betty Barrackman often signed her work with her clan name, Norge. She has lived in Needles for a number of years and is a self-taught pottery maker, creating human and animal effigies, bowls, spoons, and some remarkable smoking tubes during the 1960s and 1970s. Unlike traditional Mojave potters, she often fired her pieces in a kiln. Rick Dillingham, who appreciated Norge's style, noted that her husband was active in tribal government and that she took care of an extended family. These activities prevented her from producing a large body of work.

In his unpublished manuscript, Dillingham also listed Amelia Aspa, the curator of the Mojave Tribal Museum, who made pottery for a short time, and several other Native Americans who were not Mojaves but who worked in a Mojave idiom. These artists included Estelle Fisher, a Hopi married to a Mojave, and Edna Polacca, perhaps Havasupai, who studied with Elmer Gates. Barbara Johnson, a Maricopa, also worked for a time in Mojave style as well as with Maricopa traditional forms. She signs her work with her initials, "B.J."

Further Issues

Much remains to be learned about Mojave ceramics. What, for example, is the relationship of nineteenth- and twentieth-century Mojave pottery to ancient forms? The Southwestern and California peoples produced a great variety of figures, vessels, and implements, both in the precontact period and after the arrival of the Spanish. Did Mojave forms emerge from an older tradition, and if so, which one or ones?

Still to be determined is the relationship of nineteenth-century Mojave forms to the work of other people. Did Mojave images evolve from their own local, precontact traditions? Did Quechan figures predate them, and if so, did the Mojaves adopt Quechan forms? Or did the Quechans learn from the Mojaves? The significance of individual motifs, and even of figurines themselves, has yet to be discovered. Certainly some of the elderly Mojaves remember the names and meanings of the old patterns, and a patient listener might learn a great deal more about this important subject.

Then, too, how many Mojave women made ceramics in the nineteenth and early twentieth centuries? Each image is distinctive, and it may soon be possible to establish a body of work for a dozen artists, even if we do not know their names. Perhaps, too, the elderly Mojaves might recognize and remember the work of now-deceased mothers, aunts, and sisters. It would be wonderful to attach names to the figures.

Differences in technique and form are detectable in the figurines, and perhaps the utilitarian ceramics also share characteristics that enable us to determine if vessels were made by the same hand. These questions are basic to our understanding of Mojave pottery and remind us of how little is actually known about this craft.

In the 1920s, Rogers noted that only two or three Mojave women still made pottery. Today, Annie Fields and Elmer Gates have passed on, and few potters have stepped forward to carry on this lively tradition. Perhaps the examples in the Dillingham Collection will stimulate young scholars to begin the vital research necessary to understand the arts of the Mojaves. More important, perhaps young Mojave artists will explore their heritage in ceramics so that it may continue into the next century, and even into the next millennium.

EFFIGY VESSEL WITH HUMAN HEAD, ONE HANDLE, AND FOUR SPOUTS

ELMER GATES

MID-TWENTIETH CENTURY

POSTON, ARIZONA

HEIGHT CA. 8″ (21.5 CM)

SAR 1994-4-238

Photograph by Peter T. Furst

Elmer Gates's distinctive effigy vessels typically have large ear flanges and long necks. They are well formed and painted with fine, precise details.

Rick Dillingham, who studied with Gates in the early 1970s, left a brief record of his formal instruction and informal comments about ceramics. Dillingham wrote that Gates had dreams of a serpent emerging from a vessel, or more strikingly, of a snake wearing a vessel as a helmet. Gates took these as omens that his pottery would develop cracks during firing. He expected the snakes to "show up" as the fissures. His cure was to fast, and he advised other potters who had trouble with firing cracks to do the same. According to Dillingham, Gates "said nothing about the details of the fasting other than no sugar and cream in his coffee."

Gates apparently counted dreams as an important element in conducting his life and in making ceramic wares. Dillingham noted wistfully, "I know there is much more interaction between dreaming and pottery making," but he was unable to obtain further information from Gates.

OWL EFFIGY

ELMER GATES

MID-TWENTIETH CENTURY

POSTON, ARIZONA

HEIGHT CA. 6″ (16.5 CM)

SAR 1994-4-105

Photograph by Peter T. Furst

The fine craftsmanship here is typical of Elmer Gates's work. The figure is symmetrical, the painting well executed and carefully distributed over the images surface. The owl effigy vessel represents an innovation by Gates. Traditionally, the owl was not an animal that the Mojaves depicted or even discussed at any length because of its associations with death and the underworld.

Some people believed that after death a person first became a spirit, which then died again and transmuted into a species of owl. When the bird died, it turned into a different type of owl, and again into yet another owl, and then into a water beetle. Finally the life force dissipated into air. If any body parts remained after cremation, the charcoal also transformed into owls: the arms and the muscles of the upper arms changed into 'one kind of owl, the heart into another.'

When the living heard an owl at night, some believed it was the returning spirit of a dead Mojave. Others said that owls were not the dead but evil omens of death if they entered a house, perched on a human being, or called out near a house at twilight.

LIFE AND DEATH DIVINATORY OBJECTS

ELMER GATES

EARLY 1970s

POSTON, ARIZONA

HEIGHT, BOTH 5″ (14.7 CM)

SAR 1994-4-85A AND -85B

Elmer Gates was both a traditionalist and an experimenter. Traditional Mojaves were enthusiastic gamblers, and they believed that their games and contests predicted future events. This pair of objects lies within general Mojave ideological traditions; at the same time, Gates here introduced a new form.

These amulets are life and death charms. They are flat clay slabs with modeled human faces at the top, richly decorated with geometrcs and polished on the lower part. Their bodies are painted red, and the back of each carries an incised symbol. On one, a half-sun rising over a horizon line stands for life; on the other, a hill with a cross above it represents death. Or the rising sun may signify day and positive results, while the cross may be a star above a hill, symbolizing the evening and waning possibilities. Gates intended them to be tossed into the air like dice and read where and how they fell.

MALE FIGURE

NORGE (BETTY BARKACKMAN)

MID-TWENTIETH CENTURY

HEIGHT CA. 10″ (25.5 CM)

SAR 1994-4-68

In this image, Norge caught the robust nature of Mojave men, whose size and vigor were frequently remarked upon by travelers. Lieutenant A. G. Tassin, who was stationed at Fort Mohave in the 1870s, extravagantly described the Mojaves as robust men and women "nearly eight feet in height." A decade later, Captain John Bourke wrote that both men and women were "famed for beauty of form; many of the gentler sex are lovely to look upon, in spite of tattooing."

Like most Mojave artists, Norge emphasizes the head and upper torso. This figure's long hair is parted in the center. Bulging eyes, outlined in black and containing pupils, dominate the face. Some motifs, particularly those on the chin, may represent tattoos, while those on cheeks and forehead are more likely to be temporary painted designs. Mojave men generally did not tattoo their faces above the chin.

The figure wears elaborate dark body paint. His torso and arms are marked with the horizontal stripes worn by Mojave men but not women. On his legs, the artist painted a series of circles. The significance of both motifs is unknown.

SPOON

NORGE
(BETTY BARRACKMAN)

MID-TWENTIETH CENTURY

LENGTH CA. 9″ (24 CM)

SAR 1994-4-130

The handle of this elaborate spoon by Norge is decorated with a small human head, complete with beaded earrings and necklace. The bowl may be painted with the yellowhammer's belly pattern, based on the bird's ventral side. It consists of bent triangular shapes, speckled inside and tipped with black. Rows of diamonds adorn the handle, which contains a rattle. The designs are well organized, fit the form, and differentiate one part of the implement from the other.

Several artists began to use small faces on their works in the twentieth century. Norge attached faces to her traditional smoking tubes, in addition to the one on this spoon. Annie Fields often placed faces on the rims of bowls.

Spoons and knives were the only serving and eating instruments known to the Colorado River people. In the ancient First Times, Mastamho decreed that the Mojaves would use spoons, and he gave the implements a name in the special ritual language denoting that they were his gifts to humanity. Potters formerly made them by shaping clay over a rock base.

FEMALE FIGURE

ANNIE FIELDS

MID-TWENTIETH CENTURY

HEIGHT CA. 7″ (18.2 CM)

SAR 1994-4-67

This winsome female figure is typical of Annie Fields's style. Her figures tend to be large. Even seated, this one is more than seven inches high, and many Mojave standing figures are not much more than an inch or two taller. The head is large in proportion to the body. The rather small nose separates two large eyes, outlined in black, containing black pupils. Her face is painted in rectangular blocks, and two tattooed lines and a row of triangles extend down from the corners of her mouth. The expression, typical of Fields's figures, is charming and faintly surprised.

Because Fields created most of her figures in the 1950s, they remain in good condition. Nearly all still have their hair, large and small beaded collars, clothing, and unabraded body paint. Like Gates, Fields tucks the arms of her figures under long beaded collars.

Fields was a member of the southern Colorado River Indian Tribe, although she worked in Needles, California, for many years. The seated position and the indentation in the top of the head to receive the hair connect her work to that of the Quechans, who lived to the south of the Mojaves.

INFANT IN CRADLEBOARD

ANNIE FIELDS

MID-TWENTIETH CENTURY

NEEDLES, CALIFORNIA

LENGTH 17" (44.5 CM)

SAR 1994-4-261

Photograph by Peter T. Furst

This cradleboard by Annie Fields is as wide at the base as at the top, suggesting that it was a girl's cradle and that the finely made and well-painted image bound inside it was female. The face paint is typical of Fields's work, with rectangular blocks in a dark color over a light body. Like her other figures, this one has a large head and upper body.

Prior to the 1880s, Mojave infants were bound in cradleboards for much of the day and night. Usually they stayed in cradleboards until about nine months of age, when they began to take their first hesitant steps. After that they returned to the boards only at night to sleep. A child left the cradle permanently after being weaned and receiving a personal name. Then it became a true "inhabitant of the house." If the child subsequently died, his or her property—including the family's house—would be burned. But if a child still in its cradleboard died, the house did not have to be destroyed, because the youngster was not yet one of its true inhabitants.

The Mojaves were extremely careful to observe many taboos when a child died. Otherwise, the parents would become permanently sterile. The cradles of deceased children were broken and thrown into the Colorado River. However, if the parents did not want additional offspring, they burned the cradles.

EFFIGY VESSEL WITH HUMAN HEAD, ONE HANDLE, AND FOUR SPOUTS

ANNIE FIELDS

MID-TWENTIETH CENTURY

NEEDLES, CALIFORNIA

HEIGHT CA. 6″ (15 CM)

SAR 1994-4-222

Photograph by Peter T. Furst

This effigy vessel by Annie Fields wears face paint and chin tattoos that are nearly identical to the patterns on her female figures, suggesting that rounded vessels with liquid-dispensing spouts were classified as feminine. The faces on Fields's vessels have the same pleasant, slightly puzzled expressions as her human figures and the large eyes with big black pupils that the Mojave defined as beautiful.

Many potters made effigy vessels, and the form was already relatively stereotyped when they were sold at Needles. Usually each had a round handle, long beaded earrings, a beaded necklace, geometric red face painting, black tattoos on the chin, and from two to four spouts. The heads lacked both hair and the painted black patch marking where the hair was glued on human figures. The purpose and meaning of the faces remain a mystery.

Effigy vessels with human heads were not utilitarian. They are too small to store much liquid, and their handles are too fragile to be used for transport. This example is only six inches high, and it is average size. Most likely, they were made for sale to tourists, who put them into curio cabinets.

BIRD EFFIGY

ANNIE FIELDS

MID-TWENTIETH CENTURY

NEEDLES, CALIFORNIA
HEIGHT CA. 4″ (12 CM)

SAR 1994-4-129

Photograph by Peter T. Furst

It is difficult to tell exactly what kind of bird Annie Flelds's effigy represents. Its slightly curved beak resembles that of a raptor. The little creature may be flying or about to land.

The Mojaves had a rich lore describing the origin and behavior of birds and their relationship to human beings. Mastamho, the creator and organizer of the universe, transformed into a bald eagle after setting the world in order. Chicken hawks, also predators, were symbolically related to warriors. The Mojaves said that the actions of the birds established the patterns for later human behavior. Sparrowhawk, for example, was a prototype for a handsome man who could not attract the women he desired. In the ancient First Times, he stood apart at a dance with the dreaded Quail, the first curing shaman, who was not permitted to perform at a festive occasion. A shaman's dance was too dangerous for a social event. Ever after, Sparrowhawk stood apart at festivities and did not approach women. Thus, some men behaved in this way.

Despite the importance of birds and the number of bird effigies made for sale at the turn of the twentieth century, relatively few clay images have survived. Annie Fields made several, and Kroeber published a simplified bird without a base. The feathers of birds frequently appeared as painted motifi on ceramics.

The Desert Southwest: Four Thousand Years of Life and Art

by Allan Hayes and Carol Hayes • Photography by John Blom

The Mojave

About 150 miles north of Yuma on the Colorado, the army built Fort Mojave in 1859. Back then, it was spelled "Mohave," and Arizona still has a Mohave County, but California has the Mojave Desert. In the 1970s, the Tribal Council at the Fort Mojave Reservation decided to go with California's spelling.

Fort Mojave happened because the government decided that a transcontinental railroad should cross the Colorado at what is now Needles, and this went through Mojave Indian country. Although the Mojaves were interested in commerce and the potential income, they didn't suffer interlopers lightly, and a wagon train massacre or two was enough to convince the army to build a fort.

The expected shootout with the Mojave never happened, but there was enough conflict with the neighboring Paiutes to keep the fort running until 1870, after which the government set up the Fort Mojave Reservation.

Official attitudes toward the Mojaves were pretty much like official attitudes everywhere else. In The Mojaves, Gerald A. Smith writes that in 1877, Lt. A. G. Tassin, who was stationed at nearby Camp Mohave, wrote that they were the finest Indians to be found on the American continent, docile and powerful, and that the women were chaste. On the other hand, the 1879 BIA report placed "Colorado River Indians among the lowest in scale of civilization. The reservation since its establishment has done little for the elevation of the Indians. No real efforts at Christianization or education."

Progress came to Needles in 1883 when the railroad arrived, and jobs for the Mojave men followed. A contemporary account praised the physical capacity of the Mojave men, offering the startling statistic that they were capable of lifting "200 or 300 pounds." (We should also report that Lt. Tassin wrote that early Spanish explorers encountering the Mojave saw "men and women of splendid physique, being nearly eight feet in height.")

The Fort Mojave School opened in 1890, and by all accounts, it seems little different from all the other BIA schools—children taken arbitrarily from their families, given Anglo names, punished for speaking their native language and Christianized whether they liked it or not.

However, if Smith has it right in his book, the school met its goals far better at Fort Mojave

left: A typical anatomically explicit nineteenth-century Mojave doll. He lost his legs long ago, along with his clothing, bead necklace and earrings. What's left of him is 6.75″ tall.

Right: Where Plains Indians carried infants on a cradle board, California Indians wove cradle baskets. This 4.75″ long baby was made ca. 1880. He not only has a high-end basket, he already has tattoos and face paint, and sports the blue and white beads that adorned Colorado River pottery dolls for more than a century.

BACK ROW:
Red-on-buff four-spouted jar, 6″ high, ca. 1910; Red-on-buff pitcher, 10″ high, ca. 1900;
Red-on-buff pitcher, 5″ high, ca. 1930; Red-on-buff pitcher, 4.375″ high, ca. 1920.

MIDDLE ROW:
Red-on-buff teapot, 4.75″ high, ca. 1900; Red-on-buff dish fragment, 8.75″ wide, ca. 1900;
Red-on-buff pitcher, 4.75″ high, ca. 1890; Red-on-buff cup, 4.125″ diameter, ca. 1920.

FRONT ROW:
Red-on-buff jar, 3″ diameter, ca. 1920; Red-on-buff wedding vase, 5.5″ wide, ca. 1920;
Red-on-buff four-spouted effigy jar, 5.5″ high, ca. 1880; Red-on-buff cup, 3.25″ diameter, ca. 1910.

The railroad came to Needles in 1883, and Mojave tourist pottery followed right away. It's easy to picture traders showing potters the china of the day, saying, "Make things like these." Below, you see creamers, teacups, a water pitcher and a teapot. But you also see Mojave originals: jars with four spouts usually made with elaborate loop handles, sometimes made with an effigy head, sometimes without. Mojave pottery designs were mostly consistent and traditional. The checkerboard pitcher is something of a surprise, but the dish in the second row tells the real story. It has a design that shows up on several other pieces in the picture. When we bought it, it came with a card that reads, "Found south east of Needles, California, in the bank of the Colorado River. The design on the piece is known to living Mojave Indians as 'Rain on the Cottonwood Tree Leaves.'"

than it did on other reservations. He says, "By the early 1900s, most of the younger members of the once-great Mojave nation could read, write and converse in English. The boys were particularly expert in writing, and the girls could run the sewing machine and make their own clothing."

Apparently, despite their historic reputation for ferocity, the Mojaves learned to coexist in the Anglo world earlier and more comfortably than most other tribes in the desert. They also managed to keep their art reasonably intact through most of the twentieth century. Unlike their Quechan neighbors to the south, the Mojave held tight to their ancient pottery tradition, with its Patayan and Hohokam overtones. Here, you don't see any pieces that might be from the O'odham or from anyone else. Even teacups and cream pitchers made to please Anglo tastes remain pure, instantly recognizable Mojave.

Annie, Elmer and Betty

Mojave pottery remained vital for most of the twentieth century, kept alive by a steady flow of tourists through Needles, first by train and later by Route 66 and 1-40. In the second half of the century, three potters produced most of it.

Not that there were ever a lot of artists before then, either. In her book *Mojave Pottery, Mojave People*, Jill Leslie Furst points out that Malcom Rogers wrote that in the 1920s, only two or three Mojave women still made pottery.

One of them would have been Annie Fields, who lived in Needles and died in 1971 at the age of 87. It wouldn't be much of a stretch to attribute some of the pieces on the previous page to her.

However, the work that made her famous came in the 1960s. When an interested Anglo talked her into returning to pottery-making in the 1950s, she started making the pieces that brought Mojave pottery to the attention of the outside world.

Elmer Gates died in 1990 at 61. He lived 60 miles south of Needles on the multi-tribe Colorado River Indian Reservation, somewhat removed from the center of tribal life at Fort Mojave. Most of his best work dates from the 1970s and 1980s.

After taking a few years off while she raised her family, Betty Barrackman is active again, making pottery and doing traditional Mojave beadwork. If you find a Mojave piece signed "B" or signed "Norge," you're seeing Betty's work, and no, she's not Norwegian. Norge is her clan name.

Today, Betty is the only active traditional Mojave potter, and she and her husband Lew have a strong voice in maintaining traditions. Lew is a tribal historian and has served terms as Tribal Chairman. We got some measure of their importance when we passed Barrackman Court on the way to their home. We asked Lew if it was named after him, and he said, no, it was named after a relative, but Barrackman Road on the other side of the Colorado River was.

When we met with the Barrackmans in 1998, Betty made it clear how much she admired Annie Fields and also let us know that, for her tastes, Elmer Gates wasn't anywhere near traditional enough. Her appreciation of Annie Fields shows in her work. In fact, if you're not attuned to some subtle differences, you could easily confuse one of Betty's pieces for one of Annie's.

Elmer Gates's work, on the other hand, doesn't look like any other Mojave pottery. His clay is finer, more like Quechan ware, and his pieces are more carefully finished. Most are painted more accurately than any but the finest pieces from a hundred years earlier.

Untraditional though his work may appear, he made all the traditional forms. All three potters, Annie, Elmer and Betty, made four-spouted jars, either with effigy heads like the one by Elmer Gates on the page opposite, or with loop handles, like the one at top left on the previous page. They made dolls, standing or seated, dressed them in traditional clothing and adorned them with blue and white beads. And

Annie Fields made countless frogs, all around 6″ long, in the 1960s. Betty Barrackman told us how, according to Mojave legend, the frog carried a firebrand in its mouth and brought them the gift of fire. Annie Fields's cigarlike firebrands started a new tradition.

they made pipes and cloud blowers, smoking tubes like the Mojave had used for centuries.

With Betty, there's still a link to the Mojave pottery past. A few young potters experiment with not-quite-traditional forms, but as Betty told us, making pottery is hard and digging and working the clay is even harder. These days, young Mojaves would rather work in the casinos than go to all that trouble.

BACK ROW:
Red-on-buff olla, Elmer Gates, 10.5″ high, ca. 1980; Red-on-buff water jar, Elmer Gates, 8.5″ high, ca. 1980.

MIDDLE ROW:
Polychrome standing doll, probably Elmer Gates, 7″ high, ca. 1985; Red-an-buff frog figurine, Elmer Gates, 6.5″ long, ca. 1980; Polychrome doll, Betty Barrackman, 9″ high, 1998; Polychrome effigy bowl, Betty Barrackman, 7.25″ diameter, ca. 1970; Polychrome doll, Betty Barrackman, 8″ high, ca. 1995; Red-an-buff four-spouted effigy jar, Elmer Gates, 7.25″ high, ca. 1985.

FRONT ROW:
Red-on-buff jar, Elmer Gates, 4.25″ diameter, ca. 1975; Polychrome fish effigy bowl, Annie Fields, 6.375″ long, ca. 1965; Red-on-buff cloud blower, Annie Fields, 7″ long, ca. 1960; Red-on-buff seated doll, Elmer Gates, 4.375″ long, ca. 1970; Red-on-buff pipe, Annie Fields, 4.25″ long, ca. 1960; Red-on-buff frog figurine, Betty Barrackman, 4.75″ long, ca. 1995; Red-on-buff seated doll, Elmer Gates, 5.875″' high, ca. 1980.

Here they all are, with firebrand-bearing frogs, four-spouted effigies and dolls. We have our fingers crossed on one of them, however. The smaller standing doll in the middle row might be by Matt Brenner, who worked in Elmer Gates's studio. Otherwise, it's all Annie, Elmer and Betty in the second half of the twentieth century.

The Mojave Beading Tradition

by Jan Knight

Reprinted with permission of Interweave Press and the author. Photographs by Joe Coca.

Traditional loomworked necklace.

Betty Barrackman's home sits near Needles, California, the first stop on Interstate 40's westward trek to Barstow, Bakersfield, Los Angeles, and the Pacific Coast. Here in the eastern Mojave Desert, where blooms finally come in early May to the ocotillo and the creosote, the Mojave yucca and the screwbean mesquite, Betty's home provides an oasis for visitors from more humid climates. A bougainvillea wraps around her chain-link fence; another is just coming to maturity in the middle of the front yard.

Inside, deep, cool colors abound in the carpet and furnishings; comfort calls from her husband's easy chair and the soft seats of the sofa, next to which sits a tray filled with turquoise- and silver-colored beads and the makings of a necklace. Betty offers water or root beer, then instructs her visitors to make themselves comfortable and ask questions, anything at all.

It is tempting to stay and ask questions all day. Betty, 74, and her husband of more than fifty years, Llewellyn Barrackman, 81, make up a substantial portion of the twenty elders of the Fort Mojave Indian Tribe, a people that now number 1,040, according to Llewellyn, tribal council vice chairman. Their home is on the reservation that spans about 45,000 acres along the lower Colorado River. On this land are homes and crops, as well as a casino, a golf course, and much history. The Mojave are the Pipa Aha Macave—"People who live along the river"—and they believe that their tribe has inhabited this land since time began.

Llewellyn and Betty may be elders, but they face the future in modern terms. Llewellyn, who was instrumental in bringing the casino to the reservation in hopes that it would create jobs, has served on the tribal council for forty-one years, twice as chairman. He and Betty have raised twelve foster children. In recent years, they have actively opposed plans for a nuclear waste dump on sacred Mojave ground near their home and only await the signature of California's Gov. Gray Davis to put that chore behind them.

These are contemporary endeavors, but the Barrackmans haven't forgotten that they hold a vital thread to the past, and they strive to share their wealth of knowledge about Mojave tradition. This wealth shows in the beauty of her hands, now troubled by rheumatoid arthritis but nonetheless agile, despite beadworking for more than forty years-smooth fingers adorned by rings and thumbnails kept long to separate and hold rows of beads, sometimes more than thirty across, while she works the loom.

Llewellyn and Betty Barrackman

"I did it because my mother did it, and I wanted to be like her," says Betty, whose long hair flows neatly behind her shoulders. "We beaded together. Her way of beading wasn't secret, but yet it was secret, because I learned it from her."

This beadwork included necklaces, chokers, earrings, and belts, items that sold well at the Needles train depot before World War II and before passenger trains gave way to interstates and planes. Betty remembers that she and twenty to thirty other sellers took their beadwork to the depot every day. Travelers on their way to and from the coast selected beadwork with patterns that depicted Mojave life: a warrior with a bow; a thunderbird; a piece of pottery representing in beads the color of Mojave Desert sand.

Perhaps the most coveted of beaded patterns was the "tortoise back" that Betty wove into ceremonial capes for the Mojave women. The desert tortoise, now on a federal endangered species list, is sacred to the Mojave. Their spiritual mentor, Mutavilya, told the tortoise, or Kah-pet, to teach the Mojave about using plants as medicine. Other Mojave reptilian messengers include the frog and snake. Mutavilya gave these animals to the Mojave as sacred instructors, Betty says; they are channels to the meaning behind the natural world and teachers of skills needed to survive in the desert. Each reptile works its way into Betty's handiwork, which includes not only beadwear, but pottery and clay dolls.

Betty is most proud of her capes, which she works without a form. In the past, other Mojave women used the rounded bowls of Mojave pottery to hold their weaving in place, Llewellyn says, but Betty holds a cape in her lap while she works.

"Sometimes I'm up late and I bead when I can't sleep," Betty says. "The capes with their open weave are priceless. When you own a cape, you're very, very wealthy. Not in money, but, well, how? Yes, spiritually wealthy.

"We're all buried in our capes." Betty explains. "But no one makes them any more and they are very hard to come by."

Llewellyn remembers that the capes were once adorned with tassels made of dimes, a practice that the U.S. government put a stop to during the 1930s. He suggests that seekers of antique Mojave beadwork use the dimes as a guide to genuine pieces.

The Mojave began beading centuries ago, when European explorers made their way West. Spaniards, Betty says, brought beads of blue and white and traded them for water, shade, and

Betty with her beadwork.

Display of Betty's work at the Avi Casino

directions out of the valley. As more explorers arrived, the color selection expanded.

Traditionally, beading was woman's work. Today, however, Mojave men are taking part. Betty's 46-year-old son, Joe, beads; she has an example of one of his necklaces on her table of samples. But while making beadwear was a woman's craft, wearing it was shared by both genders—primarily as adornment, Llewellyn says, although some beading patterns may have identified the wearer's family clan and served as reminders of ancestry. Betty notes that unlike the Mojave, other Native American tribes use appliqué in their beadwork. She can do that and offers it for sale, but prefers the Mojave approach.

"You see," she says, pointing to a loom-worked necklace of white and river-blue beads, "no threads are seen. And each side of the chain matches the other side to close the pattern."

Betty sells necklaces that are about eighteen inches long and offers many patterns to choose from; she also sells chokers and other beadwear. Cases in the Mojave Room at the reservation's Avi Casino display her most precious beadwork, as well as her pottery and clay dolls. Included in the display are ropes that run forty-eight inches or longer, six or more strands thick, and wrap several times around the neck.

Betty's beadwork has won acclaim from "the outside." In 1995, the state of Arizona named her "A Living Treasure" for her beadwork and pottery. That same year she was named Needles's "Woman of the Year" for her community contributions.

Llewellyn makes Betty's looms with wood and nails. Their simple but solid construction allows her to be aggressive with her beadwork, Betty says, a trait which ensures that no threads show once the work is complete. She uses No. 8 cotton thread for the warp and nylon beading thread for the weft. She splices the threads to make sure that no ends show through. She finds many of her beads in Los Angeles shops, and the closure bead for the necklace on the tray near her sofa is pre-World War II from the region how known as Czechoslovakia.

Sometimes, she runs her beads 34 across.

"I have to compliment myself on that because it was a chore," she says, pointing to one of her wider designs.

Currently, Betty is in charge of a $50,000 cultural arts grant whose aim is to help her instruct younger members of the Fort Mojave Indian Tribe in beadwork, pottery, and other traditions. She hopes to find a space near her home where junior and senior high school students can come to learn.

Betty's handiwork

Display of Betty's work at the Avi Casino

"Time is of the essence," she says. "I say, 'Elders, sit up and take time and sit and teach.' I think that's a wonderful thing."

Time is very much on Betty's mind. She worries about the arthritis that sometimes plagues her hands: "I've prayed and prayed to Mutavilya not to take the feeling away in my fingers," she says. "But I go with the feeling and ask Mutavilya to keep me well so that I can continue to teach my people. I say it is like this—you can take computers away, you can take telephones away." She points to her beadwork. "You can't take this away."

Beading is a new interest for Jan Knight, former editor of Herbs for Health magazine. She lives in Fort Collins, Colorado.

To see the display of Betty Barrackman's, work or for more information about her beading patterns and beadwork, contact her at (760) 629-4159.

The MOJAVE

According to Llewellyn Barrackman, tribal elder and vice chairman of the tribal board, the Fort Mojave Indian Tribe's earthly origin is Spirit Mountain, which sits northwest of the reservation in southeast Nevada. The tribe's spirit mentor, Mutavilya, created the Colorado River and its plants and animals, and instructed the tribe in the "arts of civilization," which included skilled farming, trade networks with tribes as far away as the Pacific Ocean, and construction of villages.

The Mojave's resistance to intrusions by the U.S. military and non-Indian settlers led to the establishment of the Fort Mojave military outpost in 1859. That same year, the U.S. government divided the tribe into two groups, moving the "Mohave," to Parker, Arizona, and keeping the other, the "Mojave," on the land along the Colorado River near Needles.

Llewellyn left the river for a short time during the 1950s. When he returned in 1958, the tribe numbered less than 500 people. Today, the population stands at more than 1,000.

Once train travel declined after World War II, the opportunity for the Mojave to sell beadwork at the Needles depot dwindled-and, in turn, the craft of Mojave beadwork was practiced by very few, he says.

Today, only Betty Barrackman, Llewellyn's wife, holds the secret to the Mojave beading way.

"She is the last for the beading," he says softly.

Historic Mohave Bead Collars

by Michael Philip Tsosie

Reprinted with permission of *American Indian Art Magazine.* (Winter, 1992).

The historic beadwork of the Mohave and Quechan (Yuma) tribes of the Colorado River region has been a source of both tribal artistic achievement and scholarly frustration for many years. While the large netted bead neck ornament or collar has been admired for its beauty and complexity, almost no information on its history, use or construction has been published since the collar first appeared more than one hundred years ago.

This article provides a concise history of the Mohave bead collar, a description of its netted construction, and a brief diagnostic analysis in order to distinguish Mohave collars from those made by other tribes. The data derive from original research based on a comprehensive survey of published and unpublished sources, observations made in nineteen museum and private collections, and interviews with contemporary Mohave beadworkers on the Colorado River and Fort Mohave Indian reservations in 1991 and 1992.

One of the earliest accurately dated photographs of a Mohave woman wearing a collar, taken by J.C. Burge in 1884 at Needles, California. This and other photos demonstrate that Mohave women were wearing fully developed bead collars by 1884. These Burge studio portrait photographs are often mistakenly attributed as having been taken by Ben Wittick during his visit to the Mohave in August 1883. The confusion resulted from the brief partnership formed by Wittick and Burge in 1886 during a joint exhibition of their work. Thereafter, for various reasons, Wittick was given credit for Burge's Mohave photographs. Courtesy of the Museum of New Mexico. Neg.No. 15955.

The classic Mohave bead collar is a large circular ornament made of a mesh of vertically netted glass beads. The bead technique employed in the manufacture of the collar is usually referred to as netting. The collar is attached to the neck of a female and spreads fully across her back and chest, hanging off the ends of her shoulders and upper arms. This item has been referred to as a cape, collar, necklace and apron by Anglo-Americans. The Mohave, however, refer to it as "*vethamam,*" which translates in English as "the lengthy one," "where it ends, fits" or as "*hulap,*" which is the generic term for necklace (Harrington 1991; Tsosie 1991). For purposes of this study, the term collar is used rather than cape because a collar is an ornament worn over clothing whereas a cape is a garment to cover the upper body.

HISTORY

Mohave bead collars are not well documented in the standard published literature. The information that we do have has been gleaned from many sources including written records, photographs and objects in museum collections. Unfortunately Mohave sources of information—including collars—are becoming increasingly scarce. The paucity of bead collars in Mohave possession is due to the mortuary practice of destroying the property of a deceased person. Since a deceased person's bead ornaments were often thrown into the funeral pyre, and mourners sometimes contributed their own bead ornaments as well, few bead collars more than fifty years old have survived to the present day in Mohave ownership.

The Mohave bead collar as a symbol of indigenous wealth, artistry and fashion has been produced since the early 1880s. In the years that followed, the collar became an integral component of the "American" style of dress; and it is still worn today by Mohave women as an essential part of what is now considered the "traditional" mode of dress.

The netted bead collar first appeared among the Mohave in studio portraits of women in 1884. Prior to this time there is no mention of the bead collar in the known historical accounts given by Americans between the time of the first recorded American contact in 1854 to the first reference to the collar in 1883 (Sitgreaves 1853; Whipple 1855; Möllhausen 1858; Gordon 1988; Ives 1860; Domenech 1860; Palmer n.d.; Palmer 1877; Wheeler 1889; Loew 1876; Hoffman 1876; Campion 1878; Conklin 1878; Summerhayes 1908; Stratton 1983; Brennan 1980; Tassin 1877; U.S. 1865-1880). Most Americans did not specifically refer to a bead collar in their description of Mohave dress styles but instead commented in a general manner on the Mohave's fondness for glass beads and their manufacture of bead necklaces (U.S. 1879:4).

Photographs and drawings of Mohave people during this period do not show either men or women wearing bead collars (Whipple 1855:33; Ives 1860:Pl. 6; Möllhausen 1858:250-251; Conklin 1878:78-81; Campion 1878:266-267; Tassin 1877; D'Heureuse collection 1863; Gardner collection 1868; BAE:O'Sullivan collection 1871; Gentile collection 1871). There are no examples of Mohave bead collars in the collections of early American ethnographic collectors who visited the Mohave, such as Amiel Weeks Whipple in 1854, and Edward Palmer in 1869, 1870 and 1876,

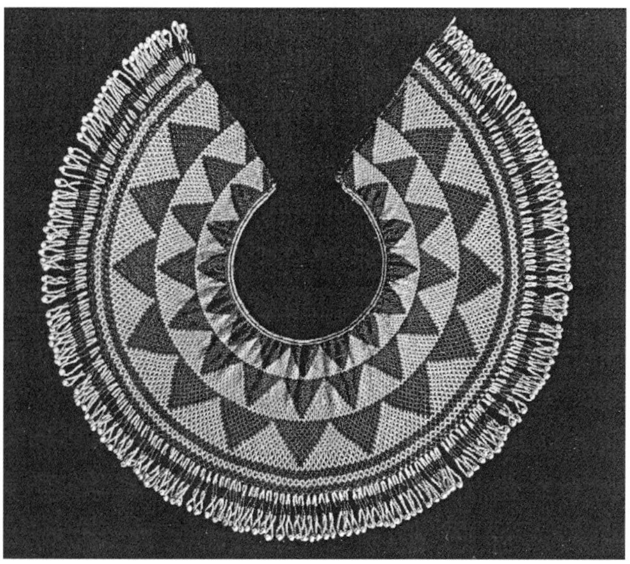

Mohave bead collar collected about 1890. 22" diameter (55 cm). This collar is done in size 11 navy blue and white beads in a geometric design using a forty-five-degree angle pattern. Note the double horizontal base cord neckline and the fact that the ends of the collar are not netted together, which is typical for nineteenth-century Mohave collars. Courtesy of the Peabody Museum of Archaeology and Ethnology, Harvard University. Cat. No. T1238.

Mohave couple circa 1884 photographed by J.C. Burge at Needles, California. Both the man and woman are wearing American clothes selected and arranged to please their sense of contemporary indigenous fashion. The woman's outfit of bead collar, cloth skirt and trimmed cape quickly evolved into a distinct style that was particular to Mohave women. Courtesy of the Smithsonian Institution, National Anthropological Archives. Neg. No. 2801-b-5.

nor did these collectors mention the collars in the written accounts of their journeys (Palmer n.d.; Tsosie n.d.; Whipple 1855). Knowledgeable members of the Mohave tribe have no memory of exactly when the Mohave began to make bead collars; contemporary Mohave beadworkers commented only that they had no idea when the first Mohave collar was made or who made it, but they believed that the Mohave have always made bead collars (Tsosie 1991). Since the existing written documents, photographs, museum collections and oral tribal history record no information on the bead collar prior to 1883, it is highly unlikely that they were produced before that date.

The first known example of an accurately dated bead collar from the Southwest is one that the Dutch ethnographer, Herman ten Kate, collected in the spring of 1883, while traveling and conducting physiological and ethnographic research among the tribes of the Colorado River region (Blackburn & Hudson 1990:141-142; Kate 1885:110). Ten Kate collected a large number of both Mohave and Quechan objects, including bead ornaments, which are now preserved in the Rijksmuseum in Leiden, Netherlands. One of these bead ornaments has been positively identified as a collar (Cat. No. 362.69) but its definitive tribal identification as either Mohave or Quechan has not yet been established (Hovens 1992).

The bead collar next appears in 1884, in studio portraits of Mohaves taken by the photographer J.C. Burge at Needles, California (Smithsonian, NAA, BAE: SPC collection; Museum of New Mexico, Photo Archives: 15955, 15961; Palmquist 1992). In these portraits, young Mohave women wearing modified American clothes have adorned themselves with netted bead collars in the style and form now identified as Mohave.

These Mohave portraits also demonstrate that use of the collar coincides with a noticeable change in the dress style of younger women. By the late 1860s, the earlier willow bark bustle skirts described by the U.S. military personnel and other Anglo- adventurers of the 1840s, 50s and 60s had been replaced by bustle skirts made of a combination of both willow and cloth cords (Emory 1857:109-110; Ives 1860:66, Pl.6; Palmern.d.:24, 32, 61; Palmer 1877:32-33; Whipple 1855:33).3 During the same period, Mohave women began to cover their breasts with pieces of calico cloth, handkerchiefs or plaid blankets that were draped across the chest and pinned (Conklin 1878:78, 80; Palmer n.d.:32; U.S. 1879:4; American Museum of New Mexico, Photo Archives:15955, 15957, 15961). Among older women, it appears that only by 1883 was the bark and cord skirt replaced with an equivalent made of cloth strips (Broder 1990:31, 83, 87, 92-93; Kate 1885:110-111). At the same time, younger Mohave women appear to have adopted yet another style of dress that varied greatly from the above described indigenous style. This "American" style consisted of a sewn cloth skirt, sometimes full length, and a blouse or at least a cloth cape that completely covered the upper body. By the late 1890s and early 1900s these skirts were full length, and matching or complementary geometric designs were sewn on the bottom third of the skirt and the edge of the cape, creating a complete outfit that complied with American standards yet suited Mohave tastes and sense of fashion (Kroeber 1913:332; Smithsonian, NAA, LOC collection:03522800; Smithsonian, NAA, SPC collection:Box 4877)

The bead collar became an integral part of the dress style adopted by Mohave women in the late-nineteenth century. In the Wittick/Burge photographs dated at 1883-1884, collars were always worn with this style of dress but never with the indigenous style of bare chest and short skirt. Later photographs document that the Mohave women continued to wear collars with their Americanized dress, especially when they were dressing for special occasions (Southwest Museum, Photo Archives:P.3073, P.37730; Smithsonian, NAA, LOC:Mohave collection). The collar does not appear to have been a part of everyday dress (Tsosie 1991, 1992).

The next specific reference to a collar is found in the published memoirs of a schoolteacher on the Colorado River Indian reservation in 1887. Referring to his observation of the conditions of the Mohave at the time, George Nock stated: "The Mohaves manufacture very little, only beaded capes, pottery, and hair rope" (Walker 1967:265). This information is further substantiated by a bead collar in the possession of the museum of the Colorado River Indian tribes, which was purchased from the Mohave by the Indian agent, George Busey, in 1887-1888 (Colorado River Indian Tribes Collection, Tribal Museum, Cat.

No. 73-24-13).

Two additional published references from this time period tend to support the above references about bead collars. Captain John G. Bourke wrote the following about Mohave women during his visit to Fort Mohave in 1886. "Several of the squaws [women] wore beautiful necklaces of glass beads and in their fabrication of these necklaces show themselves not a whit behind their sisters of the tribes in the Missouri drainage" (Bourke 1889:170). He must have intended a comparison only in terms of general technical skill in beadwork, since netted bead collars or necklaces are unknown on the Northern Plains. In addition, the Indian agent at the Colorado River Agency wrote of the Mohave in 1890 that "Some of the women do very artistic work in beads and pottery" (Allen 1891:616).

Mohave girls, Gertrude Athequatha (Laffoon) and Elizabeth, dressed up to visit the school matron, Colorado River Indian Reservation circa 1905. Both girls wear the Americanized dress style that included bead collars. The bead strand necklaces worn with the collars here gradually went out of style in the twentieth century. Courtesy of the Southwest Museum, George Wharton James collection. Neg. No. N.37730.

Alfred Kroeber, who published the definitive ethnography of the Mohave in 1925, also wrote about beads and bead ornaments among the Mohave in those early years: "They took to imported glass beads more eagerly than most Californians [Indian tribes]. . . . Men as well as women coiled strands of blue and white venetian beads in thick masses around their necks; women wound them around their wrists; and donned showy shoulder capes of a network of beads. A definite style seems to have evolved early, which made use almost wholly of the two colors mentioned" (Kroeber 1925:739-740).

After 1890, Mohave bead collars began to be collected and accessioned into museum collections around the world (Blackburn and Hudson 1990:103, 141-142, 171; Isaac 1990:76; Bronitsky 1992; Tsosie n.d.).

The available information indicates that netted bead collars were first made by either the Mohave or Quechan between the years 1879 and 1883 (U.S. 1879:4; Conklin 1878:80; Kate 1885; Blackburn and Hudson 1990:141-142). Although a similar review of the published literature on the Quechan for the same time period failed to iden-

Mohave bead collar collected with an Americanized Mohave dress at the turn of the century from the Colorado River Indian reservation. 9.5" diameter (23.6 cm). This collar is done in size 11 navy blue and white beads in a geometric design using a right-angle pattern. Note the smooth transition of the design from the netted body to looped fringe. Courtesy of the Smithsonian Institution, National Museum of Natural History. Cat. No. 210954.

tify that tribe positively as the original source of the bead netting technique and/or collars in the Colorado River region (Emory 1857; Forde 1931; Spier 1936; Trippel 1889; U.S. Census 1894:217), it is a distinct possibility that the Quechan developed bead netting and then transferred the technology to their close friends the Mohave. However, unless additional research determines the exact origin of bead netting and production of collars among the Colorado River tribes, the people who first developed and used the netting technique to make collars in the Southwest must be said to be the Mohave and Quechan.

At present, the photographic record specifically documents that bead collars were a fully developed form of ornamentation among the Mohave by 1884. Unfortunately, no records located at this time indicate developmental stages for the netting technique employed in the manufacture of the collar. This lack of a developmental stage could be considered evidence of external intervention or Anglo-American introduction of this technique and/or type of ornamentation. However, there is currently no documentation to support this hypothesis. European scholar Christian Feest considers the netting technique to be an indigenous development in ornamentation in native North America:

> Among the various kinds of interlacing in North America, only wood fibre and sinew netting is pre-European.... Netted fabrics with a potential for design can be made with the help of dyed porcupine quills or glass beads.... Similarly netted fabrics can be produced with glass beads instead of wrapped quills. However, netted beadwork has a different distribution from netted quillwork and in the southwest and in the Arctic has evolved independently. The similarity which nevertheless exists between the netted beadwork collars of the Greenland Eskimo and those of the Mohave, Mono, or Washo attests to the limitations imposed by the technique (Feest 1980:116).

Although other tribes in the region, such as the Cocopa, Walapai, Yavapai, Maricopa, Pima, Cahuilla and Paiute have also produced and/or worn netted bead collars within the last one hundred years, documented bead collars from these tribes made prior to 1883 have not been located. Based on the available information, it appears that all of these tribes began to produce or wear collars at a much later date than the Mohave, usually at the turn of the century or in the early-twentieth century. For example, Pardue writes that the netted western Apache collar or shawl necklace dates to only the early 1900s (Pardue 1989:117); Anita Alvarez de Williams dates Cocopa bead collars only to the early 1900s as well, and provides no evidence that the Cocopa were the

A contemporary Mohave, Florence Wilson, dressed in her best, which includes a satin ribbon dress and bead collar. In the late twentieth century, the ribbon dress gradually replaced the distinctive cotton Americanized dress popular in the late nineteenth and early twentieth centuries among Mohave women. Note how Mrs. Wilson's collar is worn at the edge of her shoulder and upper part of her arm. The placement of the collar is distinctively Mohave. Colorado Rover Indian Reservation, 1977. Photograph by Jerry Jacks.

originators of either the bead netting technique or collars (Alvarez de Williams 1991:41-43).

In addition, the ethnographic work of Phillip Drucker indicates that the netted collar developed among the Mohave and that this technique and style of ornament were diffused outward along the established indigenous trade routes to other tribes in the Southwest. In his study of Yuman-Piman culture trait distribution, Drucker observed that in the nineteenth century the Mohave produced collars and then exported them to neighboring tribes such as the Walapai, Yavapai and Maricopa (Drucker 1941:117). Military correspondence from Fort Mohave in 1879 also describes the trade in glass beads and bead ornaments that the Mohave carried on with other tribes (Brennan 1980:105; Kroeber et al. 1935:164-165).

Thus, the available evidence indicates that bead netting and the collar as a neck ornament originated in the Colorado River region in the early 1880s. The identification of the exact tribal source for the netting technique and collars has been narrowed down to the Mohave or possibly the Quechan. The exact date for the introduction of the collar as an ornament is not known but certainly Mohave women were wearing them at least by 1884 and not earlier than 1879. The process of the dispersion of the bead netting technique and the collar to other tribes is being investigated but little is known at present. One hopes that additional research will enhance our knowledge of the history of these beautiful beaded objects.

COLLAR CONSTRUCTION

The use of the collar as ornamentation among Mohave women has remained constant for more than one hundred years. The tradition of wearing the collar is still associated with the fashion that evolved at the end of the nineteenth century. Despite the recent overall decline in the manufacture of these elaborate collars, they continue to be an integral part of what is considered by modern Mohaves to be ìtraditionalî female dress. Today this mode of dress is seen on Mohave women of all ages on special occasions; the definition of "special occasion" varies from one individual to another, but an important consideration in the decision to wear traditional dress is the use of the outfit as an ethnic identifier at a public event both within and outside the community. On the Colorado River Indian reservation, younger Mohave women often wear the traditional dress and collar when competing in American Indian beauty pageants to identify and distinguish themselves not only as Mohave, but also as a traditional Mohave. Older Mohave female beadworkers wear their dresses and collars when retailing their work to outsiders, especially tourists, because the outfit not only identifies them as Mohave and displays their skill as beadworkers, but may facilitate communication between the buyer and seller when inquiries are made about the collar (Tsosie 1991).

In addition to its cultural value, one of the most intriguing aspects of the collar is its use of bead netting, which is a rare technique in North American Indian ornamentation (Feest 1980). Orchard identified and described this technique in his classic 1929 book, *Beads and Beadwork of the American Indians*:

> Examples of a net-like weave of beads, including several variations, have been collected from many parts of the North American continent, the same fundamental principal being applied throughout; that a bead is made to function as a knot in netting. Most of the specimens are neck ornaments.... In this instance (Mohave) the supporting strings for the beads are vertical, doubled over a foundation cord with two beads between the crossings. . . . A band about an inch and a quarter wide is made of meshes with one bead between the points; the remaining width has the meshes extended by the use of two beads. A fringe along the lower edge is made by beading about an inch of the vertical strings and tying the ends together in pairs, with a large globular bead over the knots (Orchard 1975:139,145).

Although the historic Mohave collar may vary in length from three to sixteen inches, the classic, vertically netted Mohave collar is made to cover and ornament the upper body fully. The shorter collars, which are less than four inches and not under discussion here, often use a modified vertical netting technique that is a recent development—produced since about 1960. The large collars, longer than four inches, have been made by

Mohave women with vertical netting since the early 1880s and are still being produced on both the Fort Mohave and Colorado River reservations in Arizona and California (Tsosie 1991).

The collar continues to be an item of prestige and adornment for Mohave women, and is valued on the basis of length, bead size and design (Tsosie 1991). The full fitting vertical netted bead collar is considered more valuable than the modern short collar, because the latter involves less work and time to make and often has little or no design. Collars comprised of smaller beads are more highly valued than those made of larger beads, again because of the greater labor involved in construction. Executing some designs requires more work in terms of counting beads and cords, and some designs are more popular. All of these factors can result in a higher cost. When collars are commissioned from a modern beadworker or are made for personal use, the above standards establish a value.

The foundation for these vertical netted collars consists of a horizontal base cord (thread), from which vertical cords are attached to form a neckline, body and fringe using the bead netting technique. The base cord is usually single, although a double cord is used occasionally. This horizontal base cord is almost always strung with beads, which often contrast with the primary color being used in the body of the collar; in some cases red is used to make the foundation distinct from the rest of the collar (Tsosie 1991, 1992).

The ends of the foundation cord are both knotted and a length of cord at least six inches long is left to serve as a tie to connect both ends of the foundation around the neck. In collars made after the 1930s, the cord tie was sometimes replaced with a metal hook and eye fastener or lengths of narrow silk ribbon (Tsosie 1991).

The vertical cords for netting are secured to the base cord by either a half-hitch knot or a joining bead. In either case the vertical cords are free and can be used independently.

Two methods of spacing these vertical netting cords along the horizontal primary base cord predominate in Mohave collars. In the more common of the two patterns the vertical cords are secured between two beads. In the other pattern the vertical cords are secured between every bead, although this approach sometimes results in a bunched neckline. A recent variation mixes cords spaced between one bead, then two beads, then one bead. According to one beadworker, this spacing pattern allows a collar to be made for a larger woman (Tsosie 1992).

The neckline of the Mohave collar begins with the first attachment of beads on the vertical netting cords. On many collars the vertical netting process begins immediately next to the primary horizontal base cord. However, there are several variations or styles that make a distinct neckline. In one style two beads instead of one are attached to a pair of vertical cords prior to the commencement of the netting. In another style one or two beads are attached to a pair of vertical cords and then a half-hitch knot is made on a secondary beaded horizontal cord. These variations in the neckline may have structural functions since the additional horizontal cord or beads may distribute the weight of the collar better and relieve stress on the primary horizontal base cord.

After the construction of the neckline has

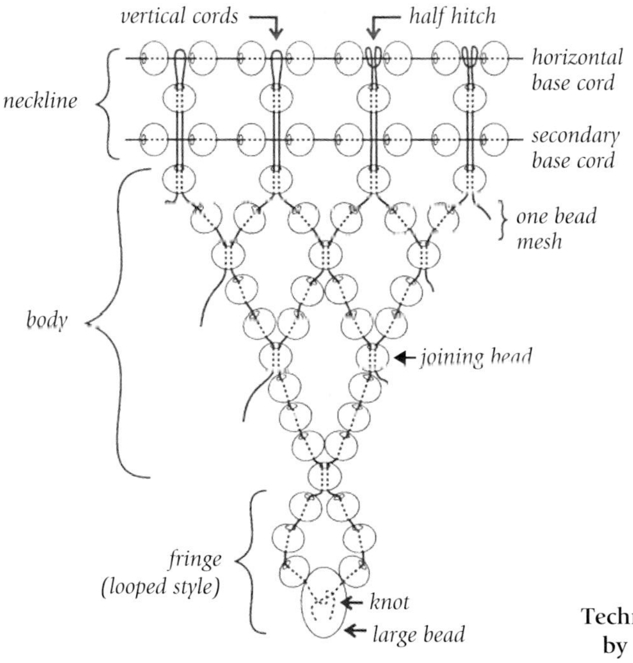

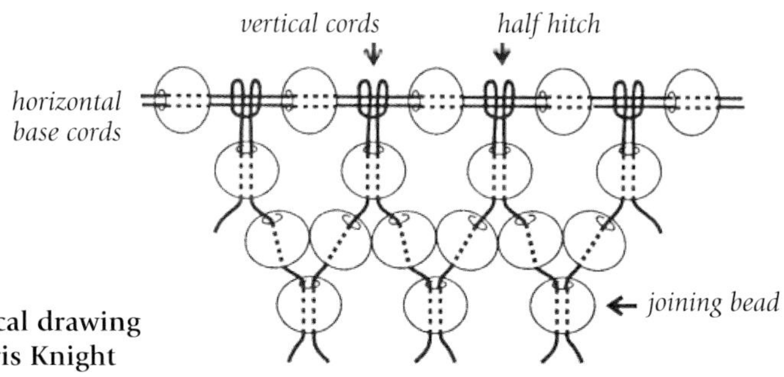

Technical drawing by Kris Knight

been completed, the beadworker begins the netted body of the collar. Depending on the design to be executed, all of the pairs of vertical cords will be counted and divided into equal bunches of some number. The vertical netting cords are then cut with a knife or scissors and the sharpened end is moistened with saliva and formed into a sharp point that can then be passed through the opening of the bead.

While modern Cocopa collars and some short Mohave collars have horizontal netting, the netting of the large Mohave collar is done vertically. The netting technique for applying beads to the vertical netting cords on the body of the collar is as follows: A pair of vertical cords are passed together through a bead and then separated. Each vertical cord of this primary pair is then threaded with one bead. At this point, the nearest single cord of the adjoining pair of beaded vertical cords is brought over to join the single cord from this primary pair. The vertical cords are then secured together with one joining bead. After passing through this joining bead, both single cords are then separated and threaded with one bead. The cords forming the original primary pair of vertical cords are then secured and held together with a single joining bead. The process is repeated and a series of diamond-shaped meshes is completed.

Mohave schoolgirl Ruby Buckles Patch, known as the "best beadworker in school," is finishing the ends or fringe of her collar on a lap pillow at the Colorado River Agency. C.1907. Courtesy of the Southwest Museum, George Wharton James collection. Neg. No N37685.

The repetition of the vertical netting technique only would add length to the collar but would not expand the width, the gradual expansion of which is necessary for a well-fitted collar to drape evenly across the shoulders. Both the width and length are expanded by adding additional beads to the vertical cord before it is joined with another vertical cord by a joining bead. The size of the mesh is gradually increased by the addition of a second, third and finally a fourth bead at certain stages in the netting process.

In executing the pattern, it is important to keep counting the cords and beads to ensure the evenness and consistency of design, particularly for right-angle patterns, where additional beads are used to anticipate and incorporate color and design changes.

The collar's fringe finish is not marked by any particular change in pattern but is usually complementary in both color and design. The fringe is started after the vertical netting cords have passed through the joining bead. The finish is accomplished by stringing beads on a single vertical cord and then either tying the end in a firm knot, or joining that cord with another and tying them together for a looped effect. The two techniques result in two distinct types of decorative fringe: straight fringe and a looped fringe. The looped fringe also has two styles, straight looped and twisted. The fringe is usually at least one to three inches in length. The end is sometimes undecorated but is more often decorated with a dime, faux pearl or large bead.

The two vertical ends of the collar are not always netted together to form a continuous circle. However, if the two ends of the collar are going to be netted together, the netting usually takes place at the end of the two-bead or the beginning of the three-bead stage in the netting process. It is rare to see a turn-of-the-century collar netted together to form a solid circle and rare to see one made within the last sixty years with the ends not netted together.

All designs and patterns in historic Mohave bead collars are geometric. Usually one design is repeated to form a pattern; and it is unusual to have more than two designs. There are two types of distinct geometric elements that are the basis for a design in a collar pattern: a triangle element and a right-angle linear geometric element. A design with a triangle element is easier to execute because the forty-five-degree angle is conducive to the accurate counting and development of a design, since the collar proportionally expands or spreads diagonally as beads are added vertically. The right-angle linear design is more difficult to achieve because the netting does not occur vertically at a ninety-degree angle. Therefore, maintaining a straight vertical line is more complex in terms of counting and applying the beads to maintain the continuity of the design in the overall pattern.

The tools for the manufacture of bead collars are few. Historically, the only identified tools were two types of looms. As reported by Kroeber, one type was a square U-shaped loom made out of boards. The foundation of the collar ran across the open side of the U, and was attached to the loom by nails at either end of the U (Kroeber 1925: Pl. 54). The second type of loom was the neck and shoulder of a pottery olla with the foundation cord tied around the neck (Kroeber and Heizer 1968:17). Kroeber also reported that he observed the rounded bottom of an inverted olla being used by a woman to make a collar in 1904 (Mohave Notes: Ethnology, Book 60, 6034, Alfred Louis Kroeber Correspondence and Papers, 71/83-c, carton 4. The Bancroft Library, University of California, Berkeley). A historic photograph shows a lap pillow being used by a young woman on the Colorado River reservation in finishing the fringe on a cape in 1907 (Southwest Museum, Photo Archives.P.37685) The use of metal beading needles in netting capes had not been recorded until very recently.

Contemporary Mohave beadworkers use whatever tools are available and convenient. Beadworkers have been observed using the U-shaped loom, the back of a chair, and the snap locks of a footlocker trunk to secure the horizontal base cord. Scissors are now used instead of a knife for cutting and sharpening the thread. Glass food jars are used to store beads, and small shallow bowls are used for holding the beads used in netting.

Likewise, the materials used for the manufacture of the collars are few. Cotton sewing thread is used for both the horizontal and vertical cords. In the past, the #8 cotton coat thread was popular because it was stiff and strong, but in recent years many types of thread have been used in bead collars, depending on personal preference and availability.

Historically, the beads used in collars were primarily Czechoslovakian seed beads ranging from size 10 to 13. The seed bead size most often found in older collars was similar to a 12. In more modern collars it is common to see a 10. Large beads, known popularly as pony or crow beads, were used exclusively as a decorative element in the fringe finish of the collars.

TRIBAL IDENTIFICATION OF COLLARS

The tribal identification of bead collars and other bead objects from the Colorado River region has been problematic because of the scarcity of written information and well-documented examples. Previous attempts at specific tribal identification of bead collars were unsatisfactory because of the inherent limitations imposed by the study of only one or two collections, undocumented collars and the absence of information from living bead-workers.

After a review of the available information from nineteen public and private collections, which included a total of sixty-eight bead collars covering a time span from the year 1883 to the present, it is apparent that there has been a great deal of experimentation and ingenuity; Mohave beadworkers did not and do not practice their art in a static manner. This is evidenced in the varieties of necklines, designs, patterns and fringe finishes that are found in the collars throughout this period.

This creativity often adds to the confusion of both scholars and museum personnel who are trying to identify specific features diagnostic of tribal attribution. However, seven key attributes have been identified which are diagnostic of Mohave bead collars, and which may assist museum professionals and collectors in narrowing the field and eliminating certain possibilities in the process of arriving at tribal identification. When attributing tribal origin to bead collars the following features should be considered: the size of the mesh in the body of the collar, the length of the cape on the woman, the direction of the netting, the design in the cape pattern, the color(s) used, the fringe and the horizontal foundation cord.

In the Mohave bead collars studied, the size of the mesh rarely exceeds four beads. The progression of the netting is consistent in that it increases from one to four. Near the foundation cord and for no longer than three inches, the mesh will be one bead. Following the one-bead mesh, a mesh of two and then three beads will continue for three to four inches. Finally, a four-bead mesh may continue for three to six inches. Modern Western Apache, Yavapai, Cahuilla, Cocopa and Paiute collars all have a much larger mesh, and the number of beads between the joining beads can range from one to eleven.

One way that modern Mohave beadworkers tell the difference between Quechan and Mohave collars is the length. A properly fitted Mohave collar should reach the end of the shoulder but not hang below the upper arm, and should lay on the upper part of the breast. Mohave beadworkers described their preference in collar length as looking "right," saying that the collars "won't get in the way, and tear" (Tsosie 1991). By contrast, Quechan collars were described as ending at the upper arm or the elbow, and completely covering the breast.

The direction of the netting in large Mohave bead collars is always vertical. Modern Cocopa and western Apache collars, however, use a horizontal netting technique. The only time the horizontal technique is used by Mohaves is in making small purses, large flat yoke necklaces and, as previously mentioned, some small netted collars.

In both the nineteenth and twentieth centuries, diamond, hexagon and hourglass shapes were very popular designs in Mohave bead collars; and the use of more than two designs in a pattern was rare.

Although twentieth-century Mohave and Quechan collars are similar, there are marked differences in regard to their color schemes. In the late-nineteenth century the Mohave preferred navy blue on a white background and used patterns similar to those found on Mohave pottery. The Quechan also favored the navy blue and white combination, but since the 1930s use it very infrequently, in contrast to the Mohave. Purple, yellow, orange, gray and green background colors, used occasionally by the Quechans, have not been observed at all in nineteenth-century Mohave collars. In the twentieth century, Mohaves still use white as the preferred background and employ minimally two colors. The two-color combination is arranged to accentuate a light/dark contrast both to enhance and to promote the overall pattern.

Two Quechan collars, collected about 1890. Both collars use the popular navy blue and white color combination but notice that the horizontal base cord has no beads attached. This last feature will often distinguish a Quechan collar from a Mohave one. Courtesy of the Arizona State Museum, The University of Arizona, Cat. Nos. 562,553

In the twentieth century, since about the 1950s, the color combinations used in Quechan collars are both bold and vivid. The high contrast offers a striking difference in color that emboldens the designs. In comparison, with the exception of the navy blue and white combination, the color combinations used by Mohaves are complementary. The objective for most Mohave beadworkers is for the colors to work together to complement the overall pattern of a piece.

The Quechan and the Mohave use color in the fringe finish distinctively as well. The Quechan often use bead colors in the fringe that sharply contrast with the back-ground color in the body of the collar. The Mohaves prefer fringe colors that affect a smooth transition with the overall design and complement the overall color scheme.

Typically, a foundation cord with no beads, especially in a collar made after about 1915, signals a Quechan rather than Mohave collar (Bee 1989:68-69). One exception is the work of a beadworker on the Colorado River Indian reservation who is a Walapai married to a Mohave, and who makes her collars with a beadless foundation cord (Coe 1986: 247). This style she learned from her teacher, who was a Quechan (Tsosie 1992). A collar with a stand-up loomed neck band attached to the foundation cord is more likely to be of Western Apache or Paiute manufacture rather than Mohave, especially if the collar has a large mesh (greater than four beads) and was made after 1900.

Mohave woman using the neck of a pottery jar as a frame for netting her collar on the Colorado River Indian Reservation circa 1905. The vertical cords are divided in bunches to keep count in executing the design. Courtesy of the Southwest Museum, George Wharton James collection. Neg. No. P.2977.

No single feature will positively attribute an undocumented collar as being from a particular tribe. However, observation of the seven features listed above and their conformity to the characteristics found in Mohave collars generally should identify a collar as Mohave or at least eliminate some other possibilities.

CONCLUSION

One of the most significant problems in working with Mohave beadwork, particularly nineteenth century examples, is that most property was destroyed at the death of the owner and/or maker. This custom is still very much a part of contemporary Mohave culture. Consequently there are limited examples of historic beadwork to be found among Mohave people, especially collars, except those collected prior to the death of the owners/makers and deposited in museum collections.

There are now, in 1992, seventeen active Mohave beadworkers on the Colorado River and Fort Mohave reservations. Among those, there are at least four bead-workers who have the technical knowledge to produce a bead collar, but only two of those are making them. Although the demand for the collars as part of the traditional dress has remained high, there are few Mohave women or men willing to commit their energy and capital into this most time-consuming process. The combination of high demand and low production has rapidly increased the price of collars purchased by Mohaves during the last ten years from an estimated $250 to $400 in 1981 to $800 to $1,200 in 1991, approximately a three hundred percent increase.

In recent years, some younger Mohaves have expressed an interest in learning the bead netting technique to keep the tradition of the collar alive, but the tribal governments of both reservations have not supported or encouraged these efforts.

Although tribal leaders have often commented on the importance of Mohave culture and the maintenance of traditions, they have in most cases failed to provide any substantial support to that end despite the abundant financial resources at their disposal. On the Colorado River Indian reservation, the local museum has policies that purposely restrict access to the extensive bead collection and thus strictly control and limit the information that would otherwise assist Mohaves in learning about netting and the collars. At Fort Mohave, only through the personal efforts of individual beadworkers has the tribe been successful in passing on the technical knowledge of bead netting and collar construction to a limited number of younger tribal members. It is the observation of this author that the existing systems of brokering access to information on Mohave culture in these two communities retard the continuation of the culture in meaningful ways. Consequently, museum collections of Mohave beadwork, including collars, remain one of the most secure sources of knowledge for Mohave tribal members to consult and study if they wish to continue this tradition in the future.

Note: Research for this article was sponsored by the National Museum of Natural History's American Indian Program. I would like to thank JoAllyn Archambault for encouragement and professional guidance; William C. Sturtevant and Garrick Bailey for editorial comments; Paula Fleming and Peter Palmquist for scholarly assistance with historic photographs; and Mohave tribal leaders Llewellyn Barrackman, Russell Welsh and Dennis Patch for making access to the community and tribal museum collections possible.

Michael Tsosie, a member of the Colorado River Indian Tribes, is a 1986 graduate of Harvard University and is currently a Community Scholar at the Smithsonian Institution, National Museum of Natural History. He is in the process of researching the comprehensive Mohave collections currently in the Smithsonian.

Another of the earliest dated photographs of a Mohave woman wearing a collar, taken by J.C. Burge in 1884 at Needles, California. This particular collar is trimmed with silver dimes on the fringe. Courtesy of the Museum of New Mexico. Neg. No. 15961.

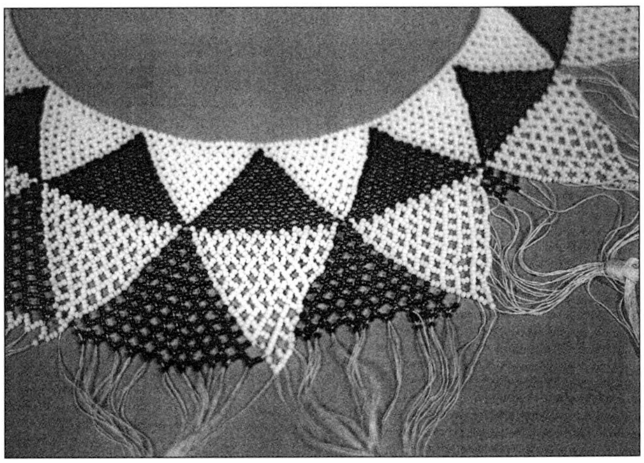

A Mohave bead collar being vertically netted using the triangle element as the basis for a design. Photograph by Christina E. Burke, 1991.

Chapter Five

Music and Dance

Rosanna Hills, Dr. Fran O'Neil, and Kelly Hills preparing to sing and dance a Bird Song. Photo by Dr. Paul Wittmer

Dancing to the Mojave Birdsongs

by Rosanna Hills

As a small child [*humad enchow*], I sat in a circle with many Mojave elders [*muuaves*]. Remembering back to the clattering of voices speaking the Yuman dialect, my Mojave language, I realized that it was foreign to me. But even then I knew from each change of a vocal chord, and small glances at me, that the conversation was private and intense. Throughout the nights with my family elders, I was fortunate enough to hear their bird songs, [*icheeyeer*]. I would listen carefully, as the men sang the cycle of songs in their deep, low voices, while the women sang in a higher register voice. It was so soothing to me, that I would eventually fall asleep.

Whenever my relatives would come over to my house [*ava*], I would wait anxiously for the singing to begin. Sometimes, the elders would tell me "stand up," and I slowly and shyly would obey. They would take my hand in theirs and show me how to take a few steps back and forth. Hearing the gourd rattle and an elder uncle singing in a deep voice, I would step to each beat of the gourd. I was happy. It was so soothing that I would get tired and sit down. Then I would fall asleep.

As a teenager I began to panic, noticing that my elders were not coming around so much. New music on the radio would be playing sometimes, but, not for long. In the evenings one or two relatives could come over to sit, talk, and sing. I would ask them to help me by showing me different dance styles and steps. I would beg them to sing my favorite bird songs [*icheeyeer*] many times, and I would dance freely. Though I was the only youth present, I was still crazy about their music. They would tell me "*keemock*!! [dance]! I would dance and dance until I was tired and then I would sit and fall asleep.

Now as an adult, as sad as it may seem, I no longer hear our elders talk, sing or dance. Many have passed away. They are on a different journey. I still hear the songs with the few birdsingers that live nearby. When I do listen to the "*icheeyeer*," I hear all the voices as I did as a child. My heartbeat gets faster and faster. As the gourd gets louder, I hear my elders' voices whisper to me, "*keemock*!" So when I dance, I dance for my people.

Today, I dance to the sound of Mojave voices and I sing alongside them now. I encourage others to learn. I was really fortunate to have heard the people, when singing was at the core of their lives. I love my people and our song and dance. Now when I fall asleep, I harmonize to the bird songs, and eventually fall off into another world, the world of my good dreams [*sumach-ahot*]. That is my Mojave way.

Photo by Dr. Paul Wittmer

The Song of the Land

by Philip M. Klasky

Betty Barrackman
Traditional Mojave Singer

The Bird Songs began at sunset. At the center of the gathering the sacred fire burned as it had night and day since the first day of the occupation. Three staffs adorned with red yarn and eagle feathers stood next to the burning logs of mesquite. The elders sat around the fire in folding chairs—old women with bronze faces etched by years in the desert sun and the labors of family life. A semi-circle of men singing to the accompaniment of gourd rattles surrounded the elders. The singers faced a group of women dressed in full regalia shifting from side to side—to the cadence of the rattle. A group of young warriors from the five lower Colorado River Indian tribes and members of the American Indian Movement in camo pants and berets encircled the singers and dancers. Around them, hundreds of Indian and non-Indian activists formed a protective shield. Earlier that day, sheriff's deputies had parked three large yellow buses along the highway to take the protesters off to jail. Across the Interstate, the Bureau of Land Management had set up a command post with dozens of rangers on guard. For days, federal officers had been watching the gathering with high-powered binoculars, taking photographs of everyone who entered the protest compound. The singing continued through the night in defiance of a federal order to evacuate the site of a proposed radioactive waste dump on land considered sacred aboriginal territory for the Fort Mojave, Chemehuevi, Cocopah, Quechan and Colorado River Indian tribes. The singing created a sense of comfort, solidarity and antiquity. The songs tell ancient tales of travels through the natural and supernatural world—the songscapes of a desert people. At the protest camp, the songs became prayers in defense of the land.

Ward Valley is a wide tilting valley located twenty-two miles west of Needles, California, in the East Mojave Desert. This part of the southern California desert provides sweeping vistas that make you feel as though you are witnessing the very curvature of the earth. The alluvial valley is an ocean of creosote, bursage, and various kinds of cacti. Occasional clumps of Mojave yucca stand like statues in the landscape. In the washes, catsclaw acacia and screwbean mesquite send out their roots over a hundred feet in search of water. After plentiful rains, splendid displays of annual wildflowers line the washes and carpet the gound. Ward Valley is surrounded by eight federally designated wilderness areas including a dense garden of bristling cholla cactus covering acres of dark volcanic foothills and the golden canyons of the Old Woman Mountains.

In the late afternoon, red-tailed hawks climb heated columns of air as a lone coyote makes its daily rounds. Notable among Ward Valley's animal dwellers is the federally-listed threatened desert tortoise; a creature of special significance to the Mohave. In 1994, as a result of legal action by a coalition of environmentalists and Native American tribes, Ward Valley was designated critical habitat for the beleaguered reptile.

From the drab brown government issue bungalows of the Fort Mojave Indian Reservation near Needles, California, the residents can see the towering granitic spires of Avi Kwa Me, or Spirit Mountain (Mt. Newberry, Nevada), the locus of origin for the Mohave people. Spirit Mountain is the residence of the spirit-mentors, Mutavilya and Mastahmo, who instructed the Mohave people to be the caretakers of the river and the land. The Mohave believe that they have lived along the lower Colorado River in the shadow of Avi Kwa Me "since time immemorial."

Grapevine Canyon is a steep desert ravine covered in wild grape vines, cottonwood trees and tall grasses. The canyon is the spiritual gateway to Spirit Mountain. The steep walls are covered in a striking abundance of petroglyphs depicting mountain sheep, spirals, stars and intricate geometric designs carved into the desert varnish. The carvings are as old as a thousand years and their meaning has been the subject of much speculation. Some researchers interpret the symbols as directional signs leading the way to food and water, others theorize that the markings establish territory or dominion.

Dennis Casebier, a Mojave Desert historian, has suggested that early travelers would have had little difficulty interpreting the rock writings since they were likely to have been accompanied by such graphic clues as a lance sporting a bloody scalp or baskets overflowing with grapes and seed. With these ephemeral signs vanished through time, the petroglyphs remain open to interpretation. A Chemehuevi friend once told me that to understand the ancient carvings he sits quietly in the canyon and simply invites their meaning to wash over him.

Mohave Indians are considered a part of the Yuman language group along with the Cocopah, Quechan, Maricopa, Walapai, Havasupai, Yavapai and Paipai. Aboriginal Yuman territory covered extensive sections of Arizona, California and Nevada. "Mohave" comes from the name the desert dwellers call themselves, the Pipa Aha Macav, translated as the "People Who Live Along the River."

The Mohaves farmed along the banks of the lower Colorado River, using the seasonal inundation of the riverine lowlands to irrigate and fertilize fields of beans, corn, melons, pumpkins and a variety of wild seeds—an agricultural technique similar to that used by the ancient Egyptians. Before forced to assemble on reservations, the Mohaves lived in scattered settlements or rancherias throughout their territory. They traveled extensively through the Mojave Region and traded with other Indian tribes as far as the Gulf of Mexico and the Pacific coast. To find their way along these routes, they used songs as their guides.

Mohave Creation and Traveling Songs describe the paths their ancestors took as they surveyed the physical world and learned how to use the resources their creator had given to them. Geographic features described in the narratives of the songs are associated with historical events and legendary figures. The songs were used as oral maps guiding travelers using physical features on the land, the seasons, stars and celestial cycles. Only fragments of these ancient songs are practiced today.

Mohave Bird Songs are ceremonial songs adapted from the oral heritage of other past inhabitants of the Mojave Desert Region. The Cahuilla Indians lived in the inland basin between the Colorado Plateau and the Pacific Coast. According to Mohave elder Llewellyn Barrackman, tribal members brought Cahuilla Indian Bird Songs back to his people sometime in the early twentieth century. Some researchers believe that the transfer may have actually occurred earlier.

Cahuilla Bird Songs speak of a mythic journey that happens in mythic time and in abstract space. Opinions about the true meaning of the songs differ among Cahuilla singers and range from global travel to journeys that take place on a regional scale. According to Paul Apodaca, Professor of Social Science at Chapman University and an expert on Cahuilla Bird Songs, the songs describe a three time revolution around the world. The songs are composed of short, cryptic statements open to interpretation and include, among other things, elaborate descriptions of birds. This range of interpretation reflect the different ways in which the Cahuilla perceive their world

In an intriguing display of cultural synchronicity, both the Cahuilla Bird Songs and traditional Mohave Creation and Traveling songs shared certain features that may have facilitated the process by which the Mohave adopted them. Apodaca explains that there was a good probability that the Mohave were attracted by the performance similarities between their songs and those of the Cahuilla. The use of the rattle, the melody structure and presentation style made the Cahuilla Birds Songs familiar and attractive.

Initially, the Mohave used the adopted Bird Songs at recreational events, then through time, as the Mohave Traveling and Creation songs passed on with those who sang them, the Bird Songs took over many of the ceremonial roles of the Mohave's original songs. Mr. Barrackman explains that the Bird Songs were used as geographic guides for aboriginal desert travel. Elaborate descriptions of migrating birds aided the traveler in the timing of the journey. Travel from one source of food and water to the next would be dependent on the appearance of the birds described in the songs. In this way the traveler would be assured of sustenance at the next stage of the journey. These multi-dimensional oral maps of story, place and seasonality assisted the traveler through an unforgiving terrain while weaving stories into the cultural tapestry. The features of the land, historic events and mythic travels described in song are all part of the Mohave's songscape.

Another view of the origin of the songs is explained by Wally Antone, a Quechan Bird Singer. "The Creator gave these songs to the Mojave Desert people, the Mohave, the Quechan and the Cahuilla—we all tell the same kinds of stories." Since the words in many of the songs are in an ancient dialect, Antone learned the meaning of the songs from his teachers. "To learn to sing is to be given a gift, to be fortunate, to be appointed by the Creator." Antone explains that there are over 300 Bird Songs that are sung in sequence. At funerals, the songs are performed to eulogize the deceased and describe some of the major events in their lives.

The Chemehuevi migrated from the Colorado Plateau to their present location along the Colorado River. Their language is designated as a branch of the Uto-Aztecan family which is distinctly different from the linguistic stock of the Mohave. The name "Chemehuevi" is derived from the Mohave name for their traditional neighbors but the Chemehuevis refer to themselves as the Nuwuvi, or "The People." The Chemehuevis hunted and gathered in a demanding environment and farmed occasionally on the flood plains of the Colorado River.

Ancestral Chemehuevi songs describe origination myths, travels, migrations and hunting rights. The land described by the songs are the collective territory of the Chemehuevi people. The geographic areas described in the songs were hunting ranges inherited by groups and individuals. The songs have been used in mourning, hunting rituals and at social gatherings. Songs were passed down along family and clan lines. Men and women were forbidden to mate with anyone from their immediate song group and, in this way, exogamy, or reproductive diversity, was maintained. This marriage of custom and survival was mediated through the song of the land.

Llewellyn Barrackman is the current vice-chairman of the Fort Mojave Indian Tribe and has served as their chairman twice over the last forty years. Betty Barrackman is a master craftswoman who is well known for her elaborately beaded capes, pottery and clay dolls sought after by museums. Their home is filled with Indian artifacts gathered through years of travel throughout the Southwest. On the wall of their living room is a photograph of Mr. Barrackman with the feathered headdress of a chief. While visiting the Barrackmans in their home on the reservation, Mrs. Barrackman spoke of the Mohave Creation and Traveling songs that were lost with those who had sung them. With an air of secrecy and reverence, she opened the bottom drawer of a cabinet and showed me a collection of reel to reel tapes of the ancient Mohave songs by one of the last Creation Song performers.

In 1972, an amateur ethnographer and professional sound technician recorded the songs of Mohave elder Emmett Van Fleet at the 82 year old singer's home in Parker, Arizona. The tapes had never been heard by members of the tribe and the Barrackmans were not even sure if they were still viable. I opened the boxes and inspected the wheels of magnetic tape. They appeared to be intact and I offered to take them to a sound laboratory to see if they could be transferred to cassettes. With a mixture of purpose and apprehension, the Barrackmans placed the songs in my safe keeping. As I placed the precious cargo in the back of my truck, Mrs. Barrackman called out to me, "Drive safely and guard those songs with your life!"

The University of California Language Center was able to restore the tapes and Emmett Van Fleet's slow, textured voice accompanied by the abiding rhythm of a gourd rattle is again part of the Mohave treasury. When I returned to the reservation with the cassettes, I watched the Barrackmans listen to the old songs drifting out from a portable player. With broad smiles of recognition, they sung along with their old friend, excitedly picking out words and phrases as they rocked back and forth with the rhythm. After singing with one of the Creation songs, Betty exclaimed to her husband, "Now I can sing at the funerals!"

Along with the songs, another traditional practice is reemerging with a new purpose. The Mohave and Chemehuevi possess a long tradition of running as a means of hunting, meditation, warfare, trade and communication. Mohave and Chemehuevi runners are known for their extraordinary ability to travel great distances. Systems of communication involving a relay of runners over long distances ranged across the Mojave Desert and throughout Yuman territory. Running traditions continue with Runner Clans of men and women who perform the ritual for special events. According to Steve Lopez of the Fort Mojave Indian Tribe, runners experience a "calling" to run and develop their skills from knowledge revealed to them through dreams. Ancient running paths traverse Ward Valley, known to the Mohave people as Silyaye Ahease, (The Place of Screwbean Mesquite and Sand), where the Mohave set up camps and collected mesquite seeds and medicinal herbs. In the last ten years, Lopez has organized a number of "Spirit Runs" with members of the Indian nations along the River practiced as part of political and spiritual events at Ward Valley.

For the last two years, Native Americans and environmentalists set up a protest camp at the proposed nuclear waste site. As part of a federal environmental review of the dump project, the government decided to conduct a testing program that would build roads and clear the land to make way for drilling operations. The tests were designed to determine the rate at which radioactive wastes would migrate through the soil toward area aquifers which are linked to the Colorado River. In February, the government issued an eviction notice to the protesters to make way for the tests. In anticipation of the forced eviction, the tribes and their allies mobilized for an occupation of the site announcing that they would engage in non-violent direct action to defend Ward Valley from the destruction of habitat for the revered desert tortoise and desecration of their sacred lands. On February 18, the federal government announced that they would enforce the notice and begin removing the protesters the next day. On the eve of the order to vacate, over 400 people had congregated at Ward Valley. Through the night, Bird Singers and Gourd Dancers performed at the entrance to the protest camp.

At sunrise the songs were performed with a renewed vigor. Federal officials advanced toward the line of defense. The voices of the singers and the sound of the rattle filled the air.

The federal police waited for the command to move in on the protesters. The head of security made a call on his cell phone. A moment later, with a sign from their commander, the officers retreated. A few days later the command post, surveillance equipment and rangers disappeared.

The resistance had lasted for 113 days; one of the longest Native American occupations in the history of this country. On May 29, the government suspended the testing and the federal environmental review process. A week later the eviction notice was rescinded. The coalition celebrated a great victory, but the Ward Valley story is not over. Secretary of the Interior Bruce Babbitt has yet to cancel the project and is waiting for the outcome of a federal court case in which Governor Wilson is demanding possession of the land leading to the construction of the nuclear dump.

A landscape that is viewed as an object or extractive resource is reduced to its material value, but when the natural environment is integrated into a people's identity, preservation of the land becomes a matter of survival. This kind of relationship can foster stewardship of the land and lead to the protection of places of ecological importance and cultural significance by those who will not and cannot move from their homeland. Mohave and Chemehuevi songscapes are landscapes of cultural essence. Elder Barrackman explains that, "the Mojave have no place to go. This is our home. We are the Pipa Aha Macav, the people along the river, instructed by the creator to protect it."

During the decade-long contest to protect Ward Valley, the ancient songs have brought a certain guidance and power to the struggle. Perhaps someday, in the telling of a great mythical battle, the defense of Ward Valley will be sung in lavish detail.

Note on the spelling of Mohave/Mojave: In 1859, when the United States military subjugated the tribe, the Mohave people were divided into two groups. A portion of the population was relocated to the Colorado River Indian Reservation at Parker, Arizona. This group spelled their name with an "h." The Mojaves who remained near Needles spelled their name with a "j" after Fort Mojave which was established on the banks of the Colorado River. The two groups continue to use the difference in spelling. In this article, the tribe is referred to historically and as a whole as the Mohave. Mojave is used only when referring to members of the Needles group.

Mojave Pottery, Mojave People

by Jill Leslie Furst

Early in the twentieth century, Kroeber believed that the Mojave stories he collected could be divided into three basic types. First and most important were the Great Stories, the common heritage of all Mojave people. The Great Stories varied from place to place, but all Mojaves shared some version of these narratives, no matter where they lived. Matavilye and Mastamho were the major protagonists in the Great Stories, and in the ancient First Times, they and other supernaturals and heroes acted on the environment and called places, actions, and objects into existence. The Great Stories described the journeys of mythical beings and their transformation into birds, animals, fish, or important features in the landscape.

Great Stories were also charters for significant actions, things, and human offices, and established the proper patterns for behavior. Mastamho, especially, defined the rules for living. People burned their dead and destroyed their property, farmed with certain implements, ate only specific foods, and made pottery because Mastamho willed it so at the beginning. They lived along the Colorado River because he gave them their lands. True to his instructions, when the outside world encountered the Mojaves, the people still lived along the Colorado on their ancestral lands, paying attention to their dreams and repeating the Great Stories in songs.

The second category of stories were histories of how Mojave clans originated and how their ancient ancestors migrated to their lands. These stories properly belonged to specific families, but because the men of a clan told them publicly, people from other clans learned the outlines and general information that the stories contained. In clan tales, supernaturals other than Mastamho appeared, usually with more limited powers and functions in creating and ordering the world. People sometimes told of encounters between men and dangerous, fantastic beasts that were conquered by a strong warrior. One group said, for example, that their ancestors were much harassed by a huge monster named Mahual, who ate children. A hero, Apatchkarawi whose epithet described him as a slayer of Apaches, that is, of enemies, killed the monster and freed humanity from its predations.

Finally, the Mojaves also shared a large body of briefer Coyote stories and various tales with animal protagonists." These were often of a humorous nature.

The three types of stories were not completely separate, however. All might include information about the first appearance of landmarks, beings, and physical objects in the First Times, and serve to establish the antiquity and validity of Mojave land divisions, customs, and practices. Great Stories and animal tales sometimes preserved knowledge of historical events. Clan legends were also charters for beliefs and customs, and even stories about the trickster Coyote occasionally explained how commonly shared objects, ideas, or practices came to be.

The Mojaves told all three types of stories in a wide variety of contexts, including at planting and harvest rituals, informal family reunions, marriages, and funerals. When they told the Great Stories of the First Times, they called the events "Great Tellings" or "Great Sings."

In addition to narratives about Matavilye and Mastamho, the Great Stories (in common with clan origin tales) often described the travels of a lone person, or two brothers or companions, who made a difficult trek in ancient days. The protagonists in a Great Sing were brave or determined, but the Great Story was not character driven. Rather, the hero, or heroes, often represented all the ancestral men in a clan who migrated from one place to another. Such journeys entailed very little overt action, and often the story introduced episodes that seemed to have little to do with the main plot. The hero stopped to look at the landscape, saw a type of animal, or remembered that he did not bring a necessary item with him. Then he anticipated a future episode. At the end, the hero and his companion sometimes transformed into some feature of the landscape. Anthropologist

Alfred Kroeber described the plot as a "framework on which episodes of ornamental significance can be hung," so that each Sing consisted of "songs strung on a thread of myth." In other words, almost nothing happened, and Western listeners expecting dramatic events, colorful protagonists, and a strong moral at the end were sorely disappointed.

The Salt Sing is a good example. One version collected by Kroeber begins with the travels in the First Times of four of the First People, who were brothers in the form of mountain sheep, and ends by identifying places where the Mojaves and Chemehuevis could find salt. The four set off after Matavilye's death from Spirit Mountain, first to the east and then north into Walapai territory, where the two elder brothers went into the ground. From below, they blew their breath back at their younger brothers to block their entrance into the earth. The remaining two headed north, then west, and crossed the place where the Ukaliho River would later flow. During their journey, they debated their powers and future events, saw birds, rats, and insects, and pointed out tobacco plants, celestial phenomena, and a lake they mistook for the salty sea; they also discussed their tears. They trekked southward through the desert, and a day's walk west from Parker, their tears became salt. Then the brothers transformed into stone. The Chemehuevis gathered salt at these rocks, and their narratives about salt began there, where the Mojave songs ended.

Although plot and character development were almost nonexistent, Mojave Sings described the geography carefully and provided exact information about where natural resources occurred in the physical world. They conveyed detailed information about landmarks, historical and mythical events that occurred at specific places, and the plants, animals, and birds that the travelers saw during their peregrinations. They were sufficiently specific that a subsequent traveler could retrace the hero's steps and see what he saw.

The Mojaves performed Sings indoors, but their songs were useful for travels, particularly if someone left the security of the Colorado River and moved into the unpopulated, inhospitable dry uplands. The Sings originally may have served, at least in part, as verbal maps of Mojave lands that encoded valuable information about the seasonal location of life-sustaining natural resources.

The Chemehuevis, neighbors and sometime allies of the Mojaves, also used songs as guides for crossing the desert. These chants described trails and directed travelers to sources of food and water, presenting the information in the context of mythic journeys undertaken by ancestors and ancient heroes. The two peoples lived closely, if not always peaceably, and their proximity suggests that the Mojaves probably used their songs in much the same way. Farther afield, Native Australians developed "song-lines" to convey this kind of information. These Australian narratives also belonged to clans and told of original ancestors discovering sources of water and food in an inhospitable environment. People who wander through difficult or barren terrain remember their paths more easily if they chant their trails rather than memorize them as a series of facts, however crucial they might be to survival.

MOJAVE SINGS

The Mojaves had some thirty song cycles, or Sings, often named for natural objects, like Salt and the Pleiades, or for animals, such as Goose, Raven, Deer, and Turtle. A Sing usually comprised from fifty to two hundred songs and required at least a night for a complete recitation. Kroeber reports that in the early 1920s one man recited for more than twenty-four hours and still did not exhaust his story. Individual songs were relatively uniform, and the words varied little from chant to chant. Nevertheless, no two in any Sing were identical. The northern and southern groups of Mojaves developed their own variations of the thirty Sings, and often performers within a region sang different variations of the stories. Most singers never recited their Sings from beginning to end. Some knew all the songs, but only part of the myth.

A singer learned his songs from older people, but for the chants to be effective, he had to dream of performing the Sing. In the absence of a dream, the songs were simply words with no force or power behind them. With a dream, they became auspicious. A man dreamed about the object naming the song cycle. Salt, for example, was personified as a man and came to a future singer in dreams to teach him the ceremony's chants.

A few individuals knew three or four Sings, and often several men could recite the same Sing. No matter how many men in an area performed a Sing, they never formed a society. During a recitation, the singer sometimes stopped, repeated songs, or allowed another singer to continue. This gave him new insights into the meanings of the stories, which he often incorporated into his next performance.

Sings were not rituals or religious events but occurred in the context of other ceremonial or significant settings. The Mojaves sang songs during rites to mourn their dead, or when people related their dreams or announced upcoming events such as the birth of a child. A singer did not wear a mask or special clothing. At most, he might wear a cap of owl feathers, and he often painted his face and body, as did most adult Mojave men.

The Mojaves classified a Sing by the type of instrument that accompanied the chanting, by whether it required or prohibited performances by dancers, and by whether the story it related described warfare. One Sing might be accompanied by small gourd rattles, drums made of inverted baskets or resonating pots, or even slaps against the thighs. Another Sing might require no instrumental accompaniment. A Sing might call for dancers of specific numbers, ages, and genders. Sometimes men and women performed together. For other Sings, only young women, old men, or seasoned warriors participated. Sometimes no dances and dancers were allowed. In some cases, an accompanying chorus of a specific age or gender joined the singer. Some Sings could take place only at certain times of the year.

The Salt Sing is a good example of the specific nature of Mojave performance. It was sung inside during the winter months and only at night. The singer used a rattle, and dancers could also be included, provided they did not exert themselves. Three men faced four women, and the two lines danced only four steps forward and back.

The object of most Sings was to bring good health and general benefits to the participants.. It was auspicious simply to attend, and listeners could learn where to find resources, even—and perhaps especially if they strayed outside their own territory.

SHAMANIC SINGS

About a third of the Sings were specifically associated with shamans, and each of these shamanic Sings cured particular ailments. Narrators did not perform these stories except to heal, even though their underlying legends and chants were similar to other cycles and were based upon similar stories of travel. The Mojave people were not eager to hear shamanic songs, because shamanism inevitably brought up thoughts of witchcraft. Thus, such songs were not performed during festive events, nor were they suitable for the auspicious act of dancing. They were far too charged with the power to effect changes in human health and well-being to be associated with joy and pleasure or to be performed on social occasions.

Mojave Sings generally, and curing Sings especially, resembled Navajo curing chants. Navajo Sings were also narratives of the deeds of heroes, usually Twins, in the ancient First Times that provided detailed maps of the topography in their territory, described how features of the landscape came to be, and justified significant objects, practices, and rituals. They comprised hundreds of individual verses, and the shortest ones required at least one day or night for a complete performance. Unlike Mojave curing Sings, however, Navajo performances were auspicious, and people attended them even if they were not ill because they were beneficial to all present. Then, too, the Navajos added to their chants beautiful and intricate sand or, more properly, ground paintings illustrating the landscape and the Holy People who lived in it. The Navajos do not live far from the Mojaves, and perhaps the two forms of Sings were organically connected.

The Yuman Musical Style

by George Herzog

Reprinted with permission of the *Journal of American Folklore.*

In the summer of 1927 I recorded in the field phonographic song material upon which this study is based. At that time, in connection with an investigation of Pueblo Indian music, the Mohave, Yuma and Southern Diegueno were visited incidentally, and the material used in the present analysis secured. The music of these tribes is so remarkably uniform, that musically the area represents one stylistic unit. One Maricopa song recorded among the Pima is included, since it obviously conforms to this style, which, throughout this paper, I have for convenience designated "Yuman."

Yuman music represents a very specialized type, set off rather sharply of the music of Southwestern peoples like the Apache, Navaho and Pueblo. The presence of certain clear-cut features in almost all of the songs renders the style more consistent within itself and easier to describe than in most other cases. Since the main characteristics of the style are clear, influences from without are easily discernible. In some of the Mohave songs faint traces of eastern influence appear. A few other songs undoubtedly originated to the northeast of the Yuman area. One group of songs recorded among the Mohave is obviously of Apache origin and has been transmitted to them through the Yavapai. Finally, among the Southern Diegueno, some of the songs connected with the mourning ceremony may have been influenced by Luiseno singing.

The results of this study are based upon the transcription and analysis of 85 songs, 39 of which are given here as sufficiently representative.

The others will be published in another collection. The conclusions here arrived at can also be verified by means of the extensive collection of Mohave and Diegueno songs in the Museum of Anthropology in San Francisco.

The music of the Yuman tribes presents some quite unique features. The songs, frequently more than 100, form large, coherent series, with a set order. Such a song-series follows the outlines of a long myth and is sung when the myth is told. Some of the series can also be danced to; others are used only by shamans. Any song-series can be sung at the ceremony of burning the dead. The connection of the recitation of myth and song-series with ceremonial performances is rather loose, ceremonialism itself being rather rudimentary. This is especially true of the Mohave and Yuma, less pronounced among the Diegueno where ceremonialism is more complex and requires dancing to a greater extent. Song-series and myth are dreamt, according to the native theory. Abundant material on these questions will be found in Kroeber's *Handbook of the Indians of California*, and in the numerous papers dealing with the Diegueno.

In connection with the song-series a number of interesting problems have come to my attention which, however, require more material than is available as yet. First, there is the question of the stylistic unity of each particular song-series. The natives recognize each song-series as a distinct unit; any song can be placed in its series when heard. Even non-Yuman listeners are often able to tell to which series a song belongs. Accompaniment and text may help to identify the song, but probably more material would reveal that each particular series is characterised by certain distinctive musical features. Since only a limited number of songs could be recorded from each series, a musical characterization of each series cannot at present be complete. Another question involves the remarkable homogeneity in style which appears within the area. No traits can be found in the present collection of songs that would distinguish the style, of any one of the three tribes from the others. Mutual influence and exchange of songs must have taken place, probably for a considerable time.

Kroeber gives a comparative list of song-series of Yuman tribes, and Spier has published a list of those of the Southern Diegueno, both with extensive remarks on the use of the songs. In the following I add from my notes only what seems to supplement published information, or is necessary to accompany the music.

One of the best-known and commonest song-series among the Mohave and Yuma is "Birds" (Tciyere; Mohave, Nos. 1-4, Yuma, Nos. 11-13), sung for the dance at the annual fiesta on the Fourth of July. The songs are accompanied by the gourd rattle, and the singer ends each song by shouting repeatedly ha, ha. The Mohave learned these songs from the Yuma. However, in the material so far recorded from the two tribes, there is not much agreement. Of the first 11 songs of a Mohave version and the first 5 of a Yuma version only two songs show a significant similarity: the song given as fifth by the Mohave informant (No. 1) is certainly a variant, although not a very close one, of the song given as fourth by the Yuma informant (No. 12). This displacement in the series is of no significance in this connection, since different individuals sing a different number of songs for the same series, and even the same individual may on different occasions sing a different number of songs for the Same Series. The songs of this series are simpler in rhythm and melody than those of most of the others.

The singing of the Tumanp Vanyume series (Mohave, Nos. 5-7) must begin before sunset, "when the sun is three inches above the horizon." The songs are accompanied with the gourd rattle, and conform to the general types of Yuman style. This agrees with Kroeber's conjecture that the series is not of Serrano ("Vanyume") origin.

MOHAVE

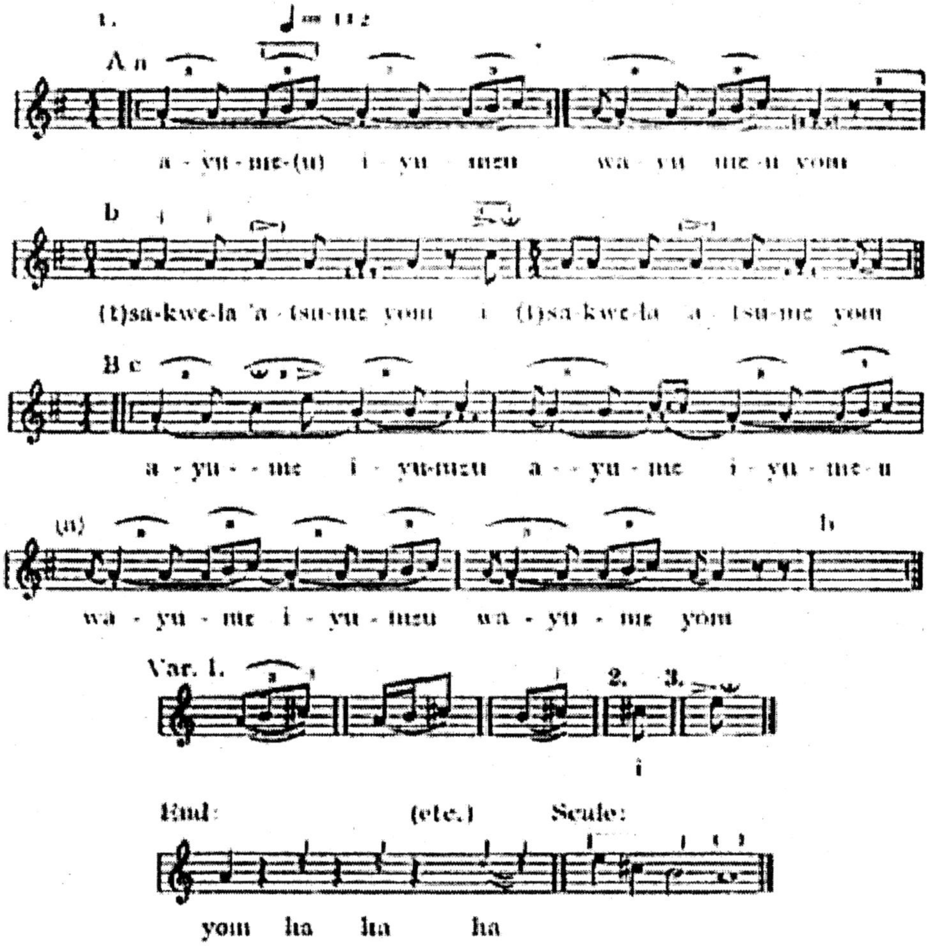

Birds (tciyére) dance-song series, fifth song. Rattle-beats on every quarter-beat: . The record contains: 4A 2B 2A 2B 2A B.

Birds (tciyére) dance-song series, sixth song. Rattle indistinct. End as before. The record contains: x (introduction) 4a b 2a 2b 7a 2b.

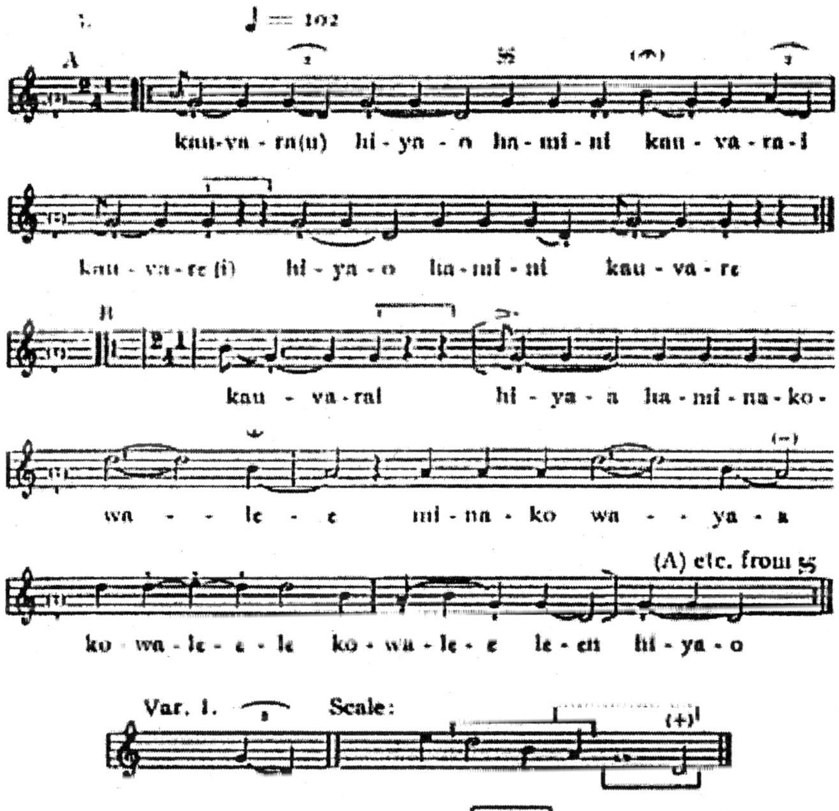

Birds song-series, ninth song. Rattling: [rhythm] etc. The record contains: 4A 2B 3A 2B 3A B. The first rendition of A begins at the sign. Ending as in No. 1.

4.

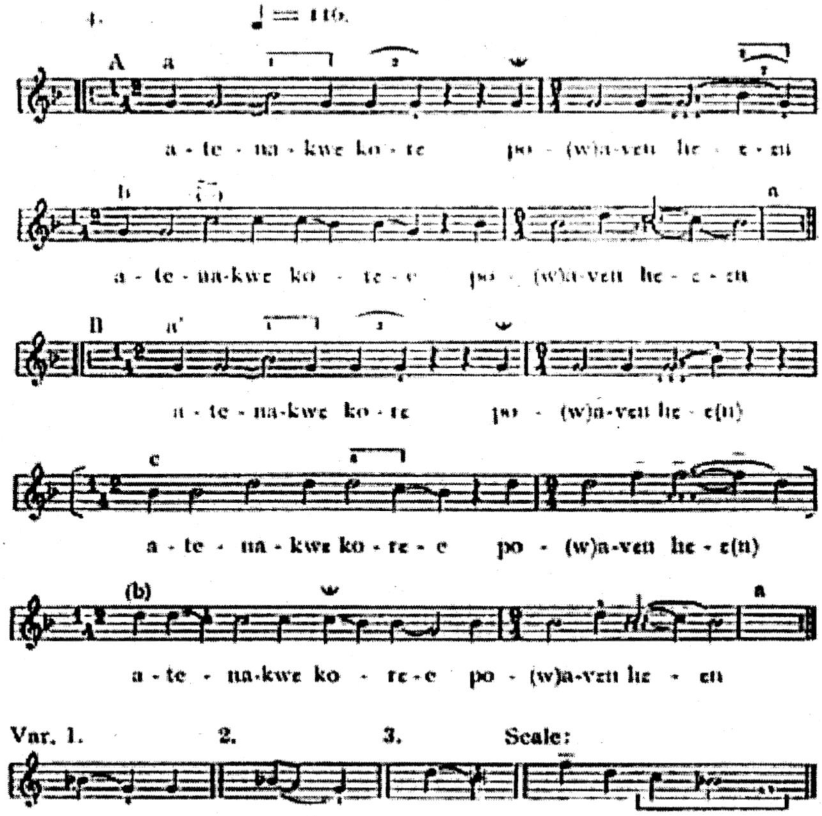

Birds song-series, eleventh song. Rattle indistinct. The record contains: 2A 2B 2A 2B 3A. The "f" is very low, almost "e".

5.

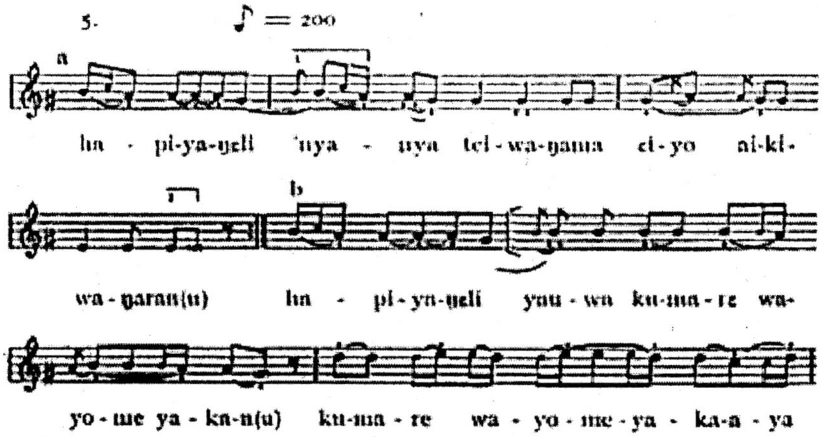

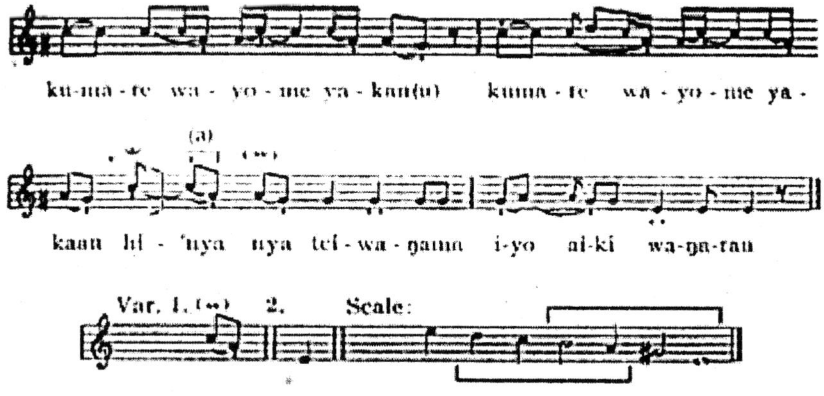

Tumáup Vanyúme song-series, first song. Rattling: ♫ ♫ etc., with eighth rests along with the rests in singing. The record contains: 4a b 3a b 2a b.

6. ♪ = 208

Tumáup Vanyúme, song from the middle. Rattling: ♫ ♫ etc. with eighth rests along with the rests in singing. The record contains: 5a 2b 2a 2b 3a 2b 2a b.

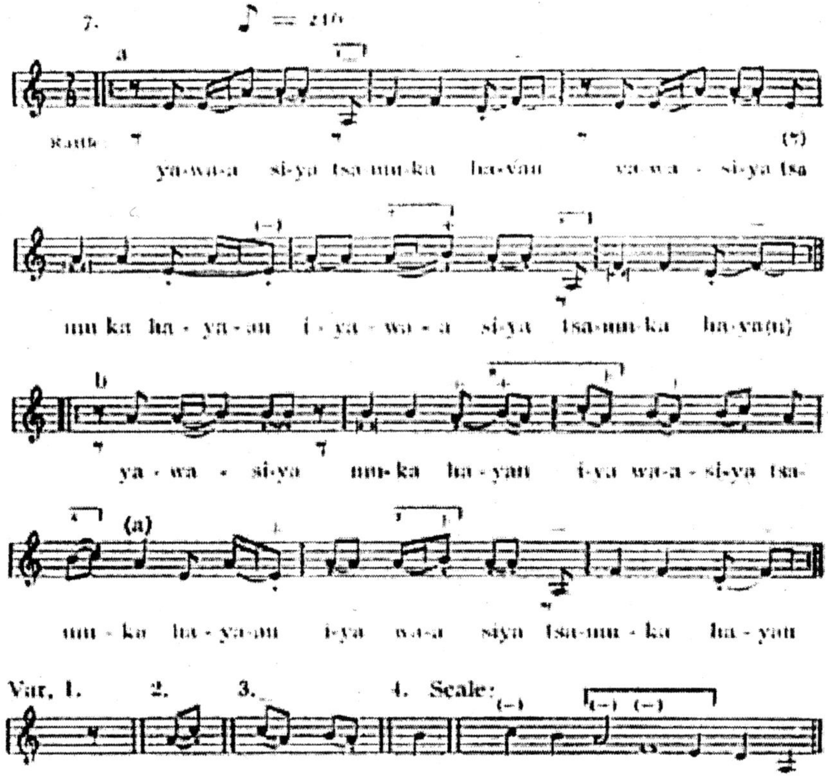

Tumánp Vanyúmc, last song. Rattling: ♫ ♫ etc., except for rests as marked below the staff. The record contains: 3a 2b 2a 2b 2a b. An alternative structural interpretation would be a division into 5 + 5 + 4 eighths, rather than the above (7 + 7). The first bar-line would then be placed after the second eighth.

Vinyemulye pa'tes song-series, second song. The first tremolo of the rattle stops at 3., the second at 5. The record contains: 7A B' 3A B'' 3A B'' A.

9. ♪ = 192

Vinyemulye pa'tes, last song. The record contains: 4a b' 2a b'' 3a b'' 3a b' 2a.

Pleiades (hatcá) song-series, first song. The y stands for bilabial v.

Tradition, Myth, and Performance of Cahuilla Bird Songs

by Paul Apodaca

A discussion as to the source of the Cahuilla Bird Song cycle is necessary due to conflicting information in existing texts as well as conflicts between those texts and the impressions of the Bird Singers themselves. We are reminded of the notes that accompany Richard Lando's field recordings of Cahuilla Bird songs available at the Hearst museum in Berkeley: "This is a song cycle of the Cahuillas; probably some are derived from the Mojave, if not all" (Keeling 1985:30).

An interpretation of how Lando came to such a conclusion is found in the statements of Alvino Siva who was present at the time of Lando's recording and was an assistant to the last hauinik, Joe Patencio. Alvino recalls singing with Joe and other Cahuilla men in a pre-arranged performance that Lando had requested. Alvino does not recall Lando speaking with Joe Patencio or the other singers regarding the songs. Alvino's sister, Katharine Siva Sauvel, had been instrumental in helping Richard Lando secure a performance of the songs at the Morongo reservation. When presented with Lando's notes describing the songs as probably originating among the Mojave, Alvino replied,

> I know, I read that. And he even said some songs were wake songs. Not true. Those are Bird Songs. In that one tape, that he taped right down here [Morongo] with Joe Patencio singing, we're singing these songs down there, palo my kwa tamalay, why then he [Lando] says that's a wake song, a Mojave [man] is standing there telling him, "That's a wake song." Because they [the Mojave] sing those songs [Cahuilla Bird Songs] in their wakes. Instead of him [Lando] saying, "Oh, is it?" and asking Joe Patencio, the elder, no, he didn't, so it's on the tape that it's a wake song. [Siva II 1995]

Tony Andreas is a Bird Singer of great renown whose approaches to song styling are documented in *Variations of Performances of Cahuilla Bird Songs* (Apodaca 1995). Tony networks with singers along the Colorado River and is familiar with the song styles and singers found there. Here he remarks on the similarity of Mojave and Cahuilla Bird Songs:

> Sometimes when I sing, I hear their songs, [it's] the same song [as used by the Cahuilla], but I get mixed up in the tune sometimes, it happens, I like their songs, their style of singing, and they like ours. In 1975, I started going over to Needles, Yuma, Parker, started going over to Sommerton, now, we [his singers] go over to Peach Springs [Arizona]. [Andreas 11995]

Though Tony enjoys the Colorado River style of Bird Song performance, he is convinced the songs originate with the Cahuilla. Tony sang for many years with Thurlow Stanley, Jr., a very influential Mojave singer who has recently passed away. When asked about the notes written by Lando regarding his identification of the songs as Mojave wake songs, Tony reacts in a manner that is remarkably similar to how Alvino presented his opinion:

> Those are Bird Songs. According to what I understand, the Mojaves learned the Bird Songs from the Cahuillas from Palm Springs or Banning. They've told me such. Thurlow [Stanley] used to tell me that and other people from Needles have told me, "These are your songs that we are singing?" Joe Patencio told me that the Mojaves used to travel from the river to the Pacific Coast to trade with the Indians there, before the Spanish. On the way back they would make a little detour and set up camp and we would all go over there and trade, and that's where they learned these songs, and they took them back with them. [Andreas 1995]

In the summer of 1992, *News From Native California* magazine published an article entitled "Mojave Bird Dance and Song" authored by Steve Lopez (1992) who is also known as Ech Kwach Nyorr. This article presents an anecdotal history of the diffusion of Cahuilla Bird Songs to the Mojave tribe by an individual. The story is based on the recollection of three Mojave elders: Nelson Barrackman, age 72; Basil Armstrong Fass, age 67; and Dorothy McCord Kormes, age 75. Their collective testimony in the article centers on a Mojave man named "Job" who is described as living among the Palm Springs Cahuilla at the turn of the century and learning the Bird Songs. He is said to have traveled back to the Colorado River and then taught the songs to his own tribe.

The article states that Job came to "like and learn the bird singing techniques of throwing gourd (as we say in the Mojave vernacular)" (Lopez 1992:20). Barrackman, Fass, and Kormes inform Lopez that Job taught the songs and dances to the Quechan at Fort Yuma, Arizona. These Mojave elders give further information concerning interpretation of the song lyrics: "Being that the Quechans could understand the Mojave language, Job taught them the songs in his own language. Thus, the introduction of 'Mojave Bird' dance" (1992:20) It is further stated that Job traveled up and down the river spreading the songs to the Maricopa, Chemehuevi, and Cocopah tribes. Lopez states that job reached the Mojave Valley in 1904 and "The Mojaves adopted this style because they could use the Mojave language that they knew to sing the songs that Job told them about" (1992:21).

In 1998, Philip Klasky presented a paper at the California Indian Studies Conference at the University of San Francisco. Klasky's research concerned Mojave funerary songs. Klasky uncovered a cache of tapes of the Ft. Mojave Indian Tribe's Creation and Migration songs, thought to be lost by many, that are in the control of the Barrackman family. The songs are sung by Emmet Van Fleet. Klasky stabilized the recordings and returned a working set of 16 cassette tapes to the tribe along with the original reel-to-reel tapes. Klasky's efforts are extremely valuable to a renewal of Mojave song culture.

A commercial recording of 27 "Bird Songs" was released in 1996 by Canyon Records as CR-6280 *Keith Mahone Bird Songs of the Hualapai*. This recording is available on both cassette tape and CD. An interesting comment appears in the liner notes of the CD recording. The note states, "Originally learned from the Mohave people around 1910, bird songs have become an important part of the Hualapai culture and are sung at both funerals (which last all night) and in social settings." The time of transference in Mahone's notes is consistent with the period of Job's travels as described independently in the article by Lopez. Inference from the description of the songs being used at funerals of the Hualapai could be seen as the importation of songs due to loss of traditional funerary songs as with the Mojave.

Leanne Hinton, in *Havasupai Songs: A Linguistic Perspective*, states, "Until about 1910, there was no singing or dancing at a [Havasupai] funeral. . . Around 1910, Mojaves began to come to Hualapai and Havasupai funerals and began to sing their funeral song cycles, such as the bird songs and *Tumanap* (Havasupais call it *tomant*). Members of Pai tribes began to learn the songs as well as the other cycles from the Chemeheuves, Mojaves, and some Paiutes at funerals" (Hinton 1984:19). Hinton furthers this view in her conclusion, "In the past 100 years or so, the Havasupai have added to their repertoire many songs that were inspired by other tribes or even directly adopted from them. Some of these have died out but others are in active use" (1984:17).

Anecdotes from Alvino Siva, Tony Andreas, Nelson Barrackman, Basil Armstrong Fass, and Dorothy McCord Kormes; liner notes on Keith Mahone's CD recording; and ethnographic research by Leanne Hinton and Philip Klasky are not definitive proof as to the diffusion of the Bird Song Cycle from the Cahuilla to the Mojave. However, rather than a vague ethnocentric statement by a Cahuilla individual, we have complementary statements from a variety of sources that support the Cahuilla contention that their Bird Songs were imported by the Mojave to be used in substitute for lost funerary songs. There is a remarkable consistency between all these sources as to not only the direction of the diffusion, but also to the period of when it happened.

The testimony indicates that the Mojave spread these songs to other tribes along the Colorado River. It is most impressive that this story is held in common as to the time of the diffusion and that the individual who may have made such a transference is even named.

Another example of differing understandings of possible diffusion can be seen in the interpretation of specific words or vocable word sounds used in the Bird Songs. The question of uninterpretable lyrics is also addressed by Hinton with Havasupai singing: "Vocables can be inserted at any time? Few songs do not have vocables... Vocables are inserted to fill out the line, to complete the rhythm" (1984: 50-53). Hinton maintains that vocables can still convey folkloric meaning.

Varying claims are made by tribal singers as to the intelligibility of particular song sections. One series of songs in the cycle uses the lyric "powamapoyama" extensively. This phrase is generally considered unintelligible by the Cahuilla singers. Alan Hatcher is a Cocopah singer who is a fluent speaker of Yuman/Hokan languages. Alan is the grandson of Jose Robles, a famous singer considered to have the status of kusiya among the Cocopah, comparable to that of a puul among the Cahuilla. Hatcher reports the lyrics are a reference to a gathering or party (Hatcher 1995) The Cocopah singers interpret the song as an invitation to gather for a celebration. The Cahuilla singers feel the song has no meaning for them other than the intrinsic value of being part of the song cycle.

While the example of "*powamapoyama*" could indicate that the lyrics have a Yuman-Hokan, or river, ancestry, the answer may be more complex. Cahuilla Bird Singer Luke Madrigal reports that in a conversation with a Kumeyaay singer, Tony Pinto, he was told that the meaning of the "*powama*" and "*powamu*" song phrases was "they are going" (Madrigal 11995) Though these two interpretations are similar in indicating the movement of people, they differ dramatically from being an invitation to gather and a description of people receding.

Another interpretation of the song was presented at the Santa Ynez reservation at the September 24, 1998 American Indian Celebration festival held at the Chumash Casino. A group of dancers called the Crane Dancers presented ostensibly Chumash dances for an audience of Casino patrons and tribal members. The lead singer announced that the group was about to perform a "back and forth" dance called *powama powama*. The singer then apologized to any Cahuilla members who might be present for mispronunciation of the lyric, seeming to recognize the song as Cahuilla and not of his language family. The Chumash are Hokan speakers.

The singer then went on to state that the song lyrics referred to a man chasing a bird back and forth from the surf to the shoreline as ocean waves lapped the beach. He instructed the crowd to form two opposing lines and to dance toward each other and then to back away. This appeared to be a variation of a dance movement sometimes used by Colorado River tribes in song performances. Alvino Siva and I sat with Chumash singer Paul Cano and watched the scene. None of us were familiar with what was being said though we recognized the song and the dance movement. It appeared that the Crane Dancers were borrowing the song from the Cahuilla, the dance steps from the Colorado River area, and adding their own interpretation to the lyrics, relating them to their coastline setting.

There are circumstances where the Cahuilla claim to understand a lyric in an entirely different manner from other tribes. I was in attendance at the California Indian Conference held at UCLA in 1994. During the conference, I moderated a panel on California Indian music where a report was made by Steven Joel Elster. Elster had been investigating indigenous music among the Kumeyaay Indians of San Diego County. Elster identified a Bird Song used by the Kumeyaay with the lyric "*mateenyai koo koorie.*" He reported that Kumeyaay singers have differed among themselves in their understanding of the lyric, giving a variety of interpretations. The most common translation was as reference to a man approaching who is crying. Katherine Siva Sauvel was attending the session and stood up to firmly state that the song is a variation of the Cahuilla word "kukul" meaning a burrowing ground owl and was a Cahuilla Bird Song that had become corrupted into "*kukulie*" or "koo koorie" after its diffusion to the Kumeyaay.

There are interesting features to the songs recorded by Keith Mahone (1996) that warrant comment. The songs follow the common compositional style sung along the Colorado River. As such, there are portions of songs and lyrics that strongly resemble the Cahuilla Bird Songs. What is remarkable about this recording, apart from the unprecedented venture of commercializing the music, is found in the liner notes.

Mahone explains that the songs are about how the songs themselves came to the Hualapai from the Mojave along the river, harkening back to the Lopez article concerning Job's diffusing the songs. He then explains that some songs are about beavers in the Colorado River while others recount the story of an individual who travels down the Colorado River to a pinnacle near present day Bull Head City in Arizona. Still other songs are interpreted by Mahone as songs to warriors killed by Apache raiding parties.

One of the most unusual of his interpretations is that the rhythm of the songs imitates the sound of a beaver slapping its tail. Mahone is quoted in the liner notes of the CD recording: "They are sung to the creations of the rocks, plants, the water, the hills and mountains. The songs respect the 'spirit' of the areas that are being approached by praising and honoring the areas" (Mahone 1996).

Mahone claims to have authored some of the songs as the liner notes explain that songs 13 and 14 are "about a "dream" journey Keith took when he was sick and being healed, where he retraced the ancestral migration from Pai Pai (in the Baja Peninsula) to Spirit Mountain on the upper Colorado River (Mahone 1996). Mahone's perspective is purportedly made from his Yuman-Hokan language interpretation of the lyrics. As such, they represent still another set of conflicting statements from a Yuman-Hokan speaker who claims to understand the Bird Songs.

Hinton discusses the addition of songs to song cycle repertoires through dreaming: "Kroeber says that these song cycles were composed through dreaming and implied that each singer dreamed his own original cycle. This implication may be false. It is quite possible for a person to dream an old set of songs that he has heard before, and for the dream to simply validate his right to sing them [He hears the singing in his dream and then wakes up and practices the songs that he heard)" (1984:19).

What we can conclude from this brief examination of diffusion is that the statements by Kroeber, Lando, Heizer, and Whipple that the Cahuilla Bird Songs are probably of Mojave or Colorado River origin and that the song cycles diffuse into Southern California are not definitive. We are reminded of Kroeber's statement in his introduction to the *Handbook of the Indians of California* (1976) that he has not examined the music.

Concern over the possible diffusion of the Bird Songs is linked to a larger question of indigenous organization. The Bird Songs are but one of a number of song cycles used by the Cahuilla. If, as stated in the literature, these song cycles originate at the Colorado River, then the religious and social organization that they support and sometimes define might also be surmised to come from the tribes of the Colorado River. If, however, the use of song cycles is part of the indigenous pattern of the Cahuilla, independent of the Colorado River, then the possible interchanging of song cycles from the Shoshonean-Takic tribes with the Yuman-Hokan tribes may have larger and more complex implications then simple diffusion from the Colorado River to the inland deserts of Southern California.

We might posit a simultaneous use of song cycles among the Colorado River tribes and the inland tribes of Southern California rather than a diffusion of song cycles. The song cycle organization method could predate the current historic groups who learned it from an older, now dissipated indigenous structure. In this manner, groups within each of the differing language families would inherit similar structures of song cycles, ceremonial use, and performance aesthetic. In such a view, the song cycles of neighboring tribes might be familiar to each other and allow for the importation of another groups' song cycles to replace those that have become disused or lost a shared organizational use of song cycles and a familiar aesthetic form might make such importations and replacements easy.

Though this results in the diffusion of a particular song, or cycle, from one group to another, it does not imply the importation of the concept of song cycles or the possible organizational structures that employ these cycles. This is an important distinction to formulate at the beginning of an examination of the use of song cycles among the Cahuilla or other groups. Are we looking at an indigenous system of the use of songs and its influence on social organization among the Cahuilla, or are we looking at a migrating system? If the system is indigenous, then we may seek one source of the value and meaning of the system within the group and its history, whereas a migrating system would find a large part of its value and meaning in the history of the interchange between the two groups or in the origins of the migrants In either case, the song cycle, once in place, takes on a valuation by those who use it which follows folkloric patterns.

Evidence used by Kroeber et al is largely anecdotal and based upon subjective impressions. The evidence arguing against diffusion of the Bird Songs from the Colorado River area is complex and often equally anecdotal. The historic question of origin is different than the ethnographic considerations that surround diffusion and usage. Some of the discrepancies cited above can be dealt with by defining which path of inquiry is desired by the researcher. Until a large scale linguistic survey is made to provide further data, anecdotes and traditional understanding remain as persuasive for the pursuit of the historical path of the Bird Songs as that produced in the academic literature. The purpose of this chapter is to describe both historic and current functions of the Cahuilla form of the Bird Song cycle and I will root the discussion in the view that song cycles are a cultural expression indigenous to the Cahuilla.

The implication that I derive from the established literature is that, within the historic period, the use of song cycles is a common element among the tribes of Southern California. This observation implies a set of common aesthetics in the nature of performance of song cycle activity that are potentially present within the geographical area of Southern California. This is consistent with Kroeber's description of mythic areas wherein differing groups share origination and other myths. The idea of the evolution of a geographic area of common aesthetic and social organization, with similar forms of folklore that bridge large linguistic differences within Southern California, is strengthened with a brief examination of material culture of the differing tribes.

Basketry, architecture, clothing, weaponry, and musical instruments of the Indians of Southern California and Baja California are remarkably similar. Albert B. Elsasser points out in the *Handbook of North American Indians* that basketry is a consistent feature in the material culture of all California tribes (Elsasser 1978). Elsasser furthers our notion of geographic aesthetic: "Despite minute differences in basketry observable from group to group, there are several features with a comprehensive regional distribution rather than sporadic or individual tribal occurrence or random spread" (1978:626).

Elsasser elaborates this concept of regional culture in his chapter "Development of Regional Prehistoric Culture" in volume eight of the *Handbook of North American Indians.*

> Nevertheless, the main conclusion is not that new groups were constantly entering the region and either replacing or absorbing earlier populations... it is proposed that, with few exceptions, the various original groups remained essentially in their first-settled regions until protohistoric times. [1978:57}

Shoshonean-Takic people are linguistically identified as a group that migrated into Southern California but the indicated pattern is that they settled into a material lifestyle already established as a regional complex. They are a specific branch within the larger Uto-Aztecan language family and are described as entering into Southern California as recently as 2,500 years ago (Lopez and Moser 1981:1).

Though the Shoshonean-Takic people undoubtedly came from areas to the east of California, once here, they settled into a lifestyle that was materially consistent with that of already existing tribes of the region. One result can be seen in basketry made by Shoshonean-Takic groups like the Cahuilla and that made by Hokan groups like the Kumeyaay that are made of the same plants, woven in the same manner, and used for the same purposes.

Chris Moser of the Riverside Municipal Museum notes, "In general, there were three stages in basketry technique that encompass all Southern California tribes: An early stage of wickerwork, a middle one of twined forms, and a final one of coiled" (1981:1) In particular, the baskets of Shoshonean and Hokan groups in Southern California utilize the wrapping of juncus textiles or *rhus trilobata* strips around a bundle of either rods of willow or deer grass. This technique is a simple but effective technology.

One major exception to this consistency

of technology is the Hokan speaking Chumash who are located to the north of the Shoshonean groups and appears to have existed with less interaction with their southerly neighbors. The Chumash employ what is referred to as the "three rod bundle" (Lopez and Moser 1981:86). On a technical note, "unlike most of the other Mission baskets, Chumash baskets do not normally have a bound under fag stitch which is so characteristic of Southern California baskets" (1981: 86).

Compositional elements of decoration make up the major observable differences between baskets of the two language groups though specialists can differentiate other distinguishing features such as plant materials used in the construction. Kroeber describes the basketry of the Cahuilla as "that of all the 'Mission Indians' of southern California" (1976:698) and the forms as standardized.

Kroeber also notes that the Cahuilla and the Diegueno use a common basketry cap made in the coiling method, Diegueno being the designation for the Hokan-speaking Kumeyaay people. Interestingly, Kroeber refers to the cap as of "The Great Basin type" (1976:700) and used by the Kosho and Yokuts tribes which can imply distribution from outside groups to Hokan speakers.

An apt metaphor, the baskets of the differing tribes of Southern California have similar if not identical organization, use, and structural features but differ in particular elements in their symbolic decoration. This similarity in organizational structure is regarded regionally and impresses itself as a common aesthetic among tribes of the differing language families.

In a similar manner, the use of song cycles may be a common aesthetic feature that impresses a structure upon groups that depend upon their use in conducting ceremonies and social organization. Elements that make up the textual or lyrical elements of the song cycles, like the decorative elements in the baskets, may differ from group to group and help to define the particularity of tribal identity. But, just as one basket weaver could conceivably import decorative symbols from an outside group into the structure of their basket if they lost their knowledge of their original symbols, a song cycle could be imported from one group to fill in the missing gap in an organizational structure if the original song cycle was forgotten or lost due to death of a key singer or to other historical interruption.

In this manner, it appears that song cycles may be imported and used to replace lost, but similar, elements among neighboring groups as they have evolved through an often hostile history with Spanish, Mexican, and American colonialists and governments in Southern California. A convincing observation to this theory is the similarity of musical aesthetic as with the use of rattles as the primary accompanying instrument among all of the tribes of Southern California. William J. Wallace writes: "The typical aboriginal instrument was the rattle, which occurred in one form or another over the entire state" (1978:644). Wallace further observes that from the 1970's onward "The throwing together of different groups on reservations and the mobile life as farm laborers followed by many California Indians has led to mutual borrowing of songs and blending of styles" (1978:648). Alvino Siva's memories of farm labor camps in the 1930's described in Chapter 3 are consistent with this observation.

This discussion addresses the statements regarding diffusion of song codes and in particular, Bird Songs, from the Colorado River and the Mojave to the Cahuilla as found in the writings of Kroeber et al. There appears to be ample information to posit the existence of song cycles among the Cahuilla and other Southern California tribes as part of a regional pattern of common aesthetic and organizational development that is not necessarily the result of diffusion from the Colorado River. Sources that have labeled Cahuilla Bird Songs as the product of Mojave transference can be argued to be based upon faulty field method and over-generalized statements. The Cahuilla Bird Song cycle can therefore be examined as an indigenous expression that is in concert with similar emanations in tile Southern California region. This is important to this present dissertation as it could be easily stated that, based upon the existing literature, any study of the Cahuilla Bird song cycle was actually a study of a transferred Mojave folk expression.

Bibliography

Betty Barrackman and Dr. Fran L. O'Neil on the Fort Mojave Reservation.

Photo by Dr. Paul Wittmer

Bibliography

Dreamers of the Colorado: The Mojave Indians

Alcock, J. (1990). Raging arroyo. In Lawrence W. Cheek. (Ed.). *Voices in the desert.* San Diego: Harcourt Brace, 1995, pp. 31-33.

Apodaca, P. (1999). Tradition, myth, and performance of Cahuilla bird songs. Unpublished doctoral dissertation, U. of California at Los Angeles.

Brennan, B. (1966). This is river country. *Arizona Highways.* 42(2), 30-38.

Casebier, D. (2007). Precarious foothold on the wild frontier. *Tales of the Mojave Road: the military.* Essex, CA: Mojave Desert & Cultural Assoc., pp. 42-52.

Devereux, G. (1951). Mohave chieftainship in action: a narrative of the first contacts of the Mohave Indians with the United States. *Plateau.* 23(3), 33-43.

Devereux, G. (1956). Mohave dreams of omen and power. *Tomorrow.* 4(3), 17-24.

Devereux, G. (1949). Mohave voice and speech mannerisms. *Word.* 5(3), 268-272.

Fisher, W. (2008). Beading to delight in. (unpublished manuscript).

Furst, J. Leslie. (2001). Mojave pottery, Mojave people. Santa Fe: School of American Research Press. pp. 21-31, 40-44, 85-86, 94-97, 131-141, 144-147, 180-181.

Gorman, F.J.E. (1981). The persistent identity of the Mohave Indians, 1859-1965. In Castlile, G.P., & Kushner, G. (Eds.). *Persistent peoples: cultural enclaves in perspective.* Tucson: U. of Arizona Press. pp. 43-68.

Hammerschlag, C. (1988). Jolene. *The Dancing Healers.* New York: Harper & Row. pp. 88-98.

Hayes, A. & Hayes, C. (2006). The desert southwest: four thousand years of life and art. Berkeley, CA: Ten Speed Press, pp. 140-143.

Herzog, G. (1928). The Yuman musical style. *Journal of American Folklore.* 41(168), 183-231.

Hills, K. (2008). Na u knov em. (I am going to tell you something). Volume 1, Issue 1 • Sept., 28, 2007.

Hills, R. (2008). Dancing to the Mojave Birdsongs (unpublished manuscript).

Hinton, L., & Watahomigie, L.J. (Eds.) (1984). Spirit Mountain: an anthology of Yuman story and song. Tucson: U. of Arizona Press. pp. 3-7, 281, 282, 284-290.

Hunter, L.G. (1979). The Mohave expedition of 1858-9. *Arizona and the West.* 21(2), 137-156.

Japenga, Ann. (2009, June). Lost and Found. *Sierra Magazine.* pp. 42-50.

Johnson, L. (2007). A story from the stones. (unpublished manuscript).

Klasky, P. Song of the land. *The Cultural Conservancy*. Retrieved November 13, 2001, from the web site: http:/www.nativeland.org/mcs.html.

Knight, J. (1999, Summer). The Mojave beading tradition. *Beadwork*, pp. 40-43.

Kroeber, A.L. (1972). More Mohave myths. *University of California Anthropological Records*. 27(xi-xii) 1-161. (Interviews conducted In 1902).

Kroeber, C.B. (1965). The Mohave as nationalist, 1859-1874. *Proceedings of the American Philosophical Society*. 109(3), 173-180.

Palmer, E. (1867). Manufacture of pottery by Mohave Indian women. *Proceedings of the Davenport Academy of Natural Sciences*. 2(1), 32-34.

Sherer, L.M. (1966). Great chieftains of the Mojave Indians. *Southern California Quarterly*. 48(1), 1-35.

Sherer, L.M. (1965, Spring). The clan system of the Fort Mojave Indians. *Southern California Quarterly*. 47(1), 1-72.

Steinbeck, J. (1988). Travels with Charley. New York: Viking Penguin, a division of Penguin Group. pp. 211-218.

Stegner, P. (1995). The teatime moon and the setting sun. In Lawrence W. Cheek. (Ed.). *Voices in the desert*. San Diego: Harcourt Brace. pp. 9-17.

Stewart, K.M. (1947). An account of the Mojave mourning ceremony. *American Anthropologist*. 49(1), 146-148.

Stewart, K.M. (1956, November). Life on the desert: dreamers of the Mojave. *Desert Magazine*. pp. 11-12.

Stewart, K.M. (1956). Mohave. In A. Ortiz. (Ed.). *Handbook of the North American Indians*. Washington, D.C.: Smithsonian Institution Press. Vol. 10, pp. 55-70.

Stewart, K.M. (1970). Mojave Indian shamanism. *The Masterkey*. 48(1), 4-13.

Stewart, K.M. (1947). Mohave warfare. *Southwestern Journal of Anthropology*. 3(3), 257-278.

Thomas, C.F., Jr. (1945). Ah-Ve-Koov-o-Tut, ancient home of the Mojave. *Desert Magazine*. 9(1), 13-17.

Tsosie, M. (1992, Winter). Historic Mojave bead collars. *American Indian Art Magazine*. 18(1), 36 49.

Waitman, L.B. (1970). Fort Mohave. *San Bernadino Museum Association Quarterly*. 18(2-3), 40-48.

Wallace, W.J. (1948). Infancy and childhood among the Mojave Indians. *Primitive Men*. 21(1-2), 19-37.